DIGITAL HERITAGE
AND CULTURE

Strategy and Implementation

DIGITAL HERITAGE AND CULTURE

Strategy and Implementation

Editors

Herminia Din
University of Alaska Anchorage, USA

Steven Wu
Innoleaders Pte Ltd, Singapore

 **World Scientific**

NEW JERSEY · LONDON · SINGAPORE · BEIJING · SHANGHAI · HONG KONG · TAIPEI · CHENNAI

Published by

World Scientific Publishing Co. Pte. Ltd.

5 Toh Tuck Link, Singapore 596224

USA office: 27 Warren Street, Suite 401-402, Hackensack, NJ 07601

UK office: 57 Shelton Street, Covent Garden, London WC2H 9HE

CD
974.4
.D54
2014

Library of Congress Cataloging-in-Publication Data
Digital heritage and culture / edited by Herminia Din (University of Alaska Anchorage, USA) and Steven Wu (Innoleaders Pte Ltd, Singapore).
    pages cm
  ISBN 978-9814522977 (hardcover) -- ISBN 981452297X (hardcover)
  1. Arhival materials--Digitization. 2. Archives--Administration--Technological innovations.
3. Library materials--Digitization. 4. Cultural property--Digitization. 5. Cultural property--
Management. 6. Library materials--Conservation and restoration. 7. Archival materials--
Conservation and restoration. 8. Electronic records--Management. I. Din, Herminia, 1968–
II. Wu, Steven, 1955– .
  CD974.4 .D54 2014
  025.17/14
                          2013049088

British Library Cataloguing-in-Publication Data
A catalogue record for this book is available from the British Library.

In-house Editor: Philly Lim

Typeset by Stallion Press
Email: enquiries@stallionpress.com

Printed in Singapore

ACKNOWLEDGEMENTS

This volume was first conceived in December 2012 with the primary goal to disseminate current practices in digital heritage covering the broad ambit of strategy, planning and implementation. To attain this objective, we have solicited contributions from institutions, companies and independent professionals from USA, Europe and Asia. We are gratified that the proposals received have helped to re-shape our initial concept. The re-defined scope will hopefully fill a gap in digital heritage publication by sharing the organization, education, technology, application and business model issues that have been successfully tackled by diverse teams around the world.

One of the pleasures in preparing this anthology is to be presented with an unparalleled opportunity to meet online with heritage professionals and administrators as well as digital culture experts. In this regard, we would like to thank the contributors for their essays that expose a swathe of challenges and solutions in heritage ecology development and technology implementation.

We would also like to express our appreciation to the publisher for their encouragement to pursue this project. In particular, we are grateful to Shu Wen Chye and Philly Lim who have been unstinting with their guidance throughout the book's preparation.

The successful completion of this undertaking is also due in no small way to many individuals who provided ongoing suggestions, advice and support as the project progressed through the stages. Specifically, we would like to mention Dr. Darrel Bailey for his unwavering confidence in this endeavor. Last but not least, we are proud to have engaged with an insightful, passionate and creative group of people with whom we would like to share the credit for this book's success.

Herminia Din and Steven Wu
November 2013

CONTENTS

EDITORS

Herminia Din is Professor of Art Education at the University of Alaska Anchorage. She was the web producer at the Children's Museum of Indianapolis and education technologist at the Indianapolis Museum of Art. In 2005, she partnered with the University of Alaska Museum of the North in Fairbanks on the LearnAlaska project, and facilitated a docent-training program using Internet2 videoconferencing for a distance-delivered program. She presented at SIGGRAPH Educator's Program on educational gaming for museums, and delivered a speech on using animation and interactive virtual technology to enhance museum learning at SIGGRAPH ASIA 2008. She collaborated with colleagues at the Metropolitan Museum of Art, American Museum of Natural History, California Academy of Sciences, and de Young Fine Art Museum to offer teacher development programs focusing on art and science integration. In 2007, she co-edited *The Digital Museum: A Think Guide* that offers an in-depth investigation into how and why museums are experimenting with new technology, and co-authored *Unbound by Place or Time: Museums and Online Learning* (2009) and *All Together Now: Museums and Online Collaborative Learning* (2011). Her research focuses on object-based learning and evaluation of the effectiveness of museum online resources. She addresses the transformation of teaching and learning by using new technologies, and aspects of emerging technology for implementing creative initiatives to enhance museum education. She holds a doctorate in art education from Ohio State University and presents regularly on museum and technology at national and international conferences.

Steven Wu has a long and varied career in the information technology industry and in government. To augment his experience in science and technology, he served at the National Heritage Board of Singapore for five years where many of his ideas on digital heritage and innovation were developed and implemented. He has also been associated with multinational corporations including Intel, Hewlett-Packard, ABB and NCR. He has published extensively in professional journals and presented at several international conferences. He graduated from Imperial College London in Computing Science and completed a Master's degree in Management of Technology at MIT Sloan School of Management.

CONTRIBUTORS

Jackie Armstrong

Jackie Armstrong is the Emily Fisher Landau Fellow in Education at The Museum of Modern Art where she works cross-departmentally on planning and conducting visitor research, as well as evaluating museum initiatives. Previously, she served as the Audience Researcher in the Education Department at the Art Gallery of Ontario. Over the years, Jackie has worked with a number of museums and cultural organizations, both large and small, growing her understanding of visitors' motivations and behaviors. In 2011, she completed an MA in Museum Studies at the University of Toronto, focusing on visitor research. Prior to that, her studies included Classical Art and Archaeology, Cultural Anthropology and Tourism Management. Jackie is interested in how museums can engage diverse publics and in using evaluation methods to help museums make informed decisions for improving the visitor experience.

Darrell Bailey

Dr. Darrell Bailey is Professor of Music in the Purdue School of Engineering and Technology at IUPUI. Prior to that, he was the founding executive associate dean of the Indiana University School of Informatics where he oversaw the process of approval for three degree programs in Media Arts and Science as well as master's and PhD programs in Informatics. Earlier, he managed the approval and implementation of the School of Music's Master of Science degree in music technology, and was director of the program from 1989–1997. Bailey's research is on the applied application of music technology in teaching and learning. He has presented at over 75 conferences, workshops, and seminars throughout the US and abroad. From 1991–1997 he chaired the International Computer Music Technology Conference and Workshop held in Indianapolis. He is the author of the Active Listening Guides for Music Listening Today (Cengage Publishing), now in its 4th edition. This is the single largest compilation of full synchronized analysis of music of western civilization, including 89 works and over 6 hours of music. His past grant activity has included a US$1.25 million grant from the Lilly Endowment to oversee the development of comprehensive media health education applications for the Ruth Lilly Health Education Center in Indianapolis. His international work has included academic exchanges and partnership development at Sun Yat-Sen University, the University of Bremen, and Tianjin University. Other international work has been with Moi University in Kenya, and orthopedic patient record management with Operation Walk in Cuba, Nicaragua, and Guatemala, and Internet2 collaborations. He holds three degrees from Oberlin College, a B.A. in music, a B.Mus. in organ performance, and an M.M.T. in music. His Ed.D. degree is from the University of Illinois.

Manus Brinkman

Manus Brinkman studied Political Science at the University of Amsterdam, the Netherlands. In 1980 he started working in the museum of the Royal Tropical Institute in Amsterdam and was the director of its Children's Museum from 1985–1990. He was director of the Museums Association of the Netherlands from 1990–1998. In 1997 and 1998 he was chair of the Network of European Museum

Organizations. From 1998–2004 he was the Secretary General of the International Council of Museums in Paris. Since 2005 he is engaged in various projects among which editing the content of the Virtual Collection of Masterpieces.

Henry Chapman

Dr. Henry Chapman is a Senior Lecturer in Archaeology and Visualization at the University of Birmingham, co-director of the IBM Visual and Spatial Technology Centre (VISTA) and co-director of the Digital Humanities Hub (do.collaboration). Henry's research interests center on the application of digital technologies within archaeology and heritage more broadly. His PhD research focused on the use of GIS technologies for interpreting and managing pre-historic landscape archaeology with a particular focus on wetlands in later prehistory. More recently, Henry's research has focused on the four-dimensional modeling of archaeological sites in raised mire landscapes using digital technologies, and the application of approaches such as laser scanning for conservation and re-presentation within virtual museums. He has authored four books and over 20 journal articles.

Eugene Ch'ng

Dr. Eugene Ch'ng is Senior Lecturer and Innovations Director at the IBM Visual and Spatial Technology Centre and Digital Humanities Hub, the University of Birmingham. He has formal education in a wide variety of fields (Fine Arts, Graphic Design, Interior Architecture, Computer Science, and Electronic, Electrical and Computer Engineering). His research has an overarching theme in Complex Systems Science research for studying and reconstructing physical, social and virtual landscapes. He specializes in Advanced Interactive Systems, enhanced Virtual Environments, Agent-based Modelling and Multi-Agent Systems requiring large computing clusters for processing of agent-interaction and computer graphics rendering. The fusion of 3D visualization and complex systems modelling is a unique strength that is applicable to a wide variety of disciplines. His research focuses on a number of complex and interactive systems related to the reconstruction of terrestrial, social, political and virtual landscapes. He also applies cutting-edge technology for facilitating user experience and learning using emerging hardware and information computation in digital heritage. Dr. Ch'ng has over 40 peer-reviewed scholarly publications and is actively involved in editorial boards, technical and program committees in international journals and conferences in his field. Dr. Ch'ng is a member of the IEEE Computer Society.

Ruly Darmawan

Dr. Ruly Darmawan is a lecturer at Faculty of Art and Design, Bandung Institute of Technology, Indonesia and member of Research Group of Design Science and Visual Culture. His research interests are technocultural studies, visual culture, and spatial design studies. With Knowledge Management Research Group — Bandung Institute of Technology (KMRG — ITB), he initiated a project entitled "Digital Library for National Heritage" or "Digital Heritage" as a part of "National Networked Digital Library" funded by International Development Research Centre (IDRC) — Canada.

Eric Deleglise

Eric Deleglise is the CTO and Co-Founder of Veldis Experience Pte. Ltd. which is an innovative provider of 3D Interactive Digital Media solutions. They create tailor-made applications in partnership with subject matter experts and use different techniques of gamification in order to create the most engaging learning and visualization experiences. Eric holds a Master degree in Computer Science specialized in technology of information and communications. In 2006 he created his first company in France and established himself as a provider of 3D applications for the national research in Paris (College De France). In 2009, he moved to Singapore where he co-founded Veldis Experience Pte. Ltd., together with two

Singaporeans. They have grown the company from two to eight employees since then.

Herminia Wei-Hsin Din

Dr. Herminia Din is professor of art education at University of Alaska Anchorage. Prior positions were as the web producer at the Indianapolis Children's Museum and education technologist at the Indianapolis Museum of Art. In 2005, she facilitated a docent-training program using Internet2 videoconferencing technologies for a traveling exhibition in Alaska. From 2007 to 2011, she collaborated with colleagues at the Metropolitan Museum of Art, American Museum of Natural History, California Academy of Sciences, and the de Young Museum to offer professional development programs for teachers focusing on art and science integration. She served on the board of the Alliance of American Museums (AAM) media and technology committee for 10 years, chaired the MUSE Awards for 3 years, and co-authored *The Digital Museum: A Think Guide (2007)*, *Unbound by Place or Time: Museums and Online Learning (2009)*, and *All Together Now: Museums and Online Collaborative Learning (2011)*, published by the AAM Press. She specializes in distance and online learning for museums, emphasizes using new media for interpretation, and presents regularly on museum and technology at national and international conferences. She holds a doctorate in art education from Ohio State University.

Vincent Gaffney

Professor Vincent Gaffney is Chair in Landscape Archaeology at the University of Birmingham. After graduating from the University of Reading he worked in contract archaeology and museums before undertaking a PhD. He then spent several years based in Ljibjana (Slovenia) whilst carrying out survey on the Croatian island of Hvar. This work developed into the major international research collaboration — "The Adriatic Islands Project." Since then he has been involved in many other studies including survey at Roman

Wroxeter and the world heritage sites of Cyrene and Diocletian's Mausoleum in Split. Other field projects have included work on the wetland landscape of the river Cetina (Croatia), fieldwork in Italy centered on the Roman town at Forum Novum and historic landscape characterization at Fort Hood (Texas). Current research projects include mapping the inundated landscapes of the Southern North Sea, agent-based model of the battle of Manzikert (1071) in Anatolia and the "Stonehenge Hidden Landscapes" Project where he leads the UK team creating 3D and virtual imaging of the landscape through an extensive program of geophysical survey of the largely unmapped landscape.

Halina Gottlieb

Dr. Halina Gottlieb is the founding director of NODEM (Nordic Digital Excellence in Museums), co-founder of the DIHA (Digital Intangible Heritage in Asia) interdisciplinary research cluster and director of the Digital Heritage Center, a spin-off from Interactive Institute Swedish ICT/Vision for Museums. She has also been a member of the Executive Committee of EPOCH (European Network of Excellence in Cultural Heritage), as well as the Swedish representative for the EPOCH Network of Expertise Centers (2004–2008), and is currently coordinating the Knowledge Triangle Network at the Nordic Council of Ministers (2011–2014). Halina earned her PhD thesis in the field of Digital Heritage entitled "Designing Engagement For Art" which explored the design and evaluation of interfaces and interpretive content of digital heritage artifacts in museum environments. Furthermore, she has organized and taught an academic course on Exhibitions and New Media at the University College of Film, Radio, Television, and Theatre in Stockholm. As an art historian, digital curator and knowledge transfer facilitator, Dr. Gottlieb has concentrated her efforts on promoting exchange of knowledge, practices and skills across fields of research related to digital heritage issues, as well as relevant cross-sectors such as the ICT and creative industries.

Deborah Seid Howes

Deborah Seid Howes is the Director of Digital Learning at the Museum of Modern Art in New York, where she oversees the development and delivery of online courses and other educational initiatives. In her 30-year museum career, she has planned, created and/or directed ground-breaking educational programs, online exhibitions and resources, print and electronic publications, websites, and study centers for world-class institutions. Exceptionally conversant with pedagogical practice and the requirements of new technologies, Howes is an effective facilitator of broad and creative thinking about the potential of digital tools to achieve educational objectives. Howes is a well-regarded public speaker for issues involving education, technology and museums, and has more than 20 years of combined experience teaching about modern and contemporary art on view in the galleries of The Art Institute of Chicago and The Metropolitan Museum of Art. She also serves as an adjunct professor for the graduate program in Museum Studies at Johns Hopkins University and advises the program committee of Museums and the Web Asia.

Christopher Jones

The co-founder of Magma Studios in Singapore, Chris is a versatile media creative who has spent the last decade creating online games, apps, animations and documentaries for museums and heritage institutions as well as global media brands. He has designed online games and mobile apps for the National Heritage Board of Singapore, The Asian Civilizations Museum, the Asian Art Museum in San Francisco, the National Geographic Channel, Science Centre Singapore, the Ministry of Education of Singapore and Dutch Public Television. Among the digital heritage projects Chris has conceptualized are a Massive Multiplayer Game entitled *World of Temasek* which recreated Singapore in the 14th Century, and an augmented reality mobile app for the traveling *Terracotta Warriors* exhibition. He has also written, directed and produced award-winning television content for the Discovery Channel, the Disney Channel, NHK Japan and the BBC.

Sarah Kenderdine

Professor Sarah Kenderdine researches at the forefront of interactive and immersive experiences for museums and galleries. In widely exhibited installation works, she has amalgamated cultural heritage with new media art practice, especially in the realms of interactive cinema, augmented reality and embodied narrative. Sarah holds the positions of Professor, Director of the Centre for Innovation in Galleries, Libraries, Archives and Museums (iGLAM), National Institute of Experimental Arts (NIEA), University of New South Wales Art and Design; Special Projects, Museum Victoria, Australia; and Director of Research at the Applied Laboratory for Interactive Visualization and Embodiment (ALiVE), City University of Hong Kong.

Anita Kocsis

Dr. Anita Kocsis is Head of Design, Society and Culture in the Faculty of Design, Swinburne University of Technology, Melbourne and visiting research fellow at the Centre for Innovation in Galleries, Libraries Archives and Museums (iGLAM); City University of Hong Kong. Anita investigates the phenomenon of the embodied and social experience in large scale interactive immersive architectures. She applies co-creative design thinking to understand, visualise and quantify the abstract, subjective and qualitative content of the visitor experience in these exhibition environments.

Christine Kuan

Christine Kuan is Chief Curator and Director of Strategic Partnerships at Artsy. Kuan was formerly the Chief Curatorial Officer and Vice President for External Affairs at ARTstor, a nonprofit image library for education and scholarship. She has also served as the Senior

Editor of *Oxford Art Online*, the largest scholarly online art encyclopedia, at Oxford University Press. She has worked in the Department of Asian Art at The Metropolitan Museum of Art. Kuan holds an MFA from the Iowa Writers' Workshop and a BA in Art History and English Literature from Rutgers University. She has taught at Rutgers University, University of Iowa, and Peking University.

Djembar Lembasono

Djembar Lembasono is CEO of Kubus Intermedia with focus on developing and distributing Open Source Software (OSS) for library. His interests are in the field Digital Library, and Library Automation. He joined KMRG in 2000 and involving in building Ganesha Digital Library and maintaining Indonesian Digital Library Network since 2012. He is a team leader of several Digital Library Project in Indonesia. Current projects are developing Digital Library for Indonesian Treasury Auditor Board, and Lontar Digital Library.

Fang-Yin Lin

Fang-Yin Lin is the president of Bright Ideas Design, a multimedia and animation production company in Taiwan. The mission of her company is to combine art and technology to represent the brightness of world civilization and to build the visual training process through pictorial way of thinking. For years, Bright Ideas has provided innovative use of animation and technology in education and exhibit context for the past 10 years including projects for the National Palace Museum, National Museum of Natural Science, and cultural institutions in China. She holds a Master Degree in art history, her company won the Grand Prix Award at F@imp 2004, and MUSE Awards in 2007 and 2013.

James Lin

Dr. James Lin is a senior researcher and chief of the education, exhibition, and information service division, National Palace

Museum, Taipei, Taiwan. He is also the vice chairman of the Chinese Association of Museums and vice president of the Museum Computer Network-Taiwan. At National Palace Museum, he is responsible for organizing and developing several national programs to introduce advanced technologies into the museum. He plays an important role in international exchange and cooperation at the Chinese Association of Museums and the Museum Computer Network, Taiwan. He received his MS degree in Computer Science and PhD in Engineering Management at the University of Missouri. He passed the national examination and had served at the Taipei National Tax Administration and had held management positions at several corporations. He worked in the Department of Information Management at Huafan University as an associate professor, department chair and director of the computer center. In teaching and research, he focuses on managing information system and other related issues.

Michael Mouw

Michael Mouw works as a creative and technical director, guiding multidisciplinary teams and vendors to design and develop experiences that powerfully engage museum visitors and users. His focus is on melding interaction design and experience design to create meaningful opportunities for free-choice exploration and inquiry. The work is often delivered through media and technology experiences linked to exhibition design using a documentary approach to storytelling, such as the *Flour Tower* elevator ride at the Mill City Museum, through visitor interactions in exhibits explored via innovative interfaces like *Open House: If These Walls Could Talk* at the Minnesota History Center, and with gallery games played in social groups like the "ArtSort" at the Minneapolis Institute of Arts. Michael's work in museums started in the Photographic Services Department at the Museum of Fine Arts, Boston, and followed with documentaries created for the Lowell National Historical Park and Fall River Heritage State Park, in Massachusetts. As Multimedia Director at the Minnesota

Historical Society, he created documentary-based exhibits using stories from diverse communities including Native American, Asian, Deaf, Veterans, Hispanic and African American communities. As Director of Exhibits and Interpretation at the Canadian Museum for Human Rights, Michael designed and developed exhibitions that use media and technology to tell compelling human stories. He is the founder of Gamut Interactions and currently works as a media and technology consultant for museums and cultural organizations. Michael is a graduate of Tufts University and the School of the Museum of Fine Arts, Boston.

Suzanne Sarraf

Suzanne Sarraf is a Web designer at the National Gallery of Art, Washington. She is the Chair for the American Association of Museums' Media & Technology Professional Network. She graduated from New York University with a BA in Archeology, Anthropology, and Spanish. During that time she attended Universidad Nebrija and the International Institute in Madrid, Spain. She received her MA from the University of London, University College of London, Institute of Archaeology writing her dissertation on the state of museums and the Web. Suzanne attended the Getty Leadership program in 2011 and has completed two certificates programs from Georgetown University for business administration and project management.

June Sung Sew

June Sung Sew is currently the CEO and Co-Founder of Veldis Experience Pte. Ltd. with undergraduate degree in Business Information Technology and Masters degree in Business Administration. After obtaining his degree, he worked for a software company where he rose to the position of General Manager. His past working experience covered areas in general administration, business systems management, sales and marketing management as well as project management. He had been involved in a number of

IT-related projects in which his main responsibilities covered areas such as establishing project goals and targets, resources planning and allocation, project progress monitoring and review and post-project evaluation. In 2009, together with two other partners, he set up Veldis Experience Pte. Ltd., a company which deals with 3D interactive digital media solutions and services. Since then, he has been involved in a number of IDM-related projects. One of them was the collaborative R&D project with National Neuroscience Institute Singapore which was co-funded by MDA. It was an 11-month project and he took on the role of the Project Manager. Under his management, the R&D works had been delivered on target in terms of time and cost.

Leonard Steinbach

Leonard Steinbach is a technology and management consultant to museums and other cultural institutions. He teaches in the Johns Hopkins University Graduate Program in Museum Studies and recently completed an appointment as Visiting Fellow in Culture and Heritage Management at City University of Hong Kong. Prior to taking on primarily consultant and educator roles he was Chief Information Officer of The Cleveland Museum of Art where he garnered two AAM MUSE Awards, among other national and regional recognition. He was also Chief Technology Officer for the Solomon R. Guggenheim Museum (New York) and is past president of the Museum Computer Network, as well as a long-time member of the New Media Consortium's Horizon Report — Museum Edition advisory board. He has also served on committees and Boards of several museums and other cultural institutions. Mr. Steinbach is a frequent speaker at museum and related conferences and his publications include articles in AAM's Museum magazine, *Curator — The Museum Journal*, and a chapter in *Digital Museum — A Think Guide* (AAM, 2007).

Selma Thomas

Selma Thomas is an award-winning American filmmaker and a distinguished museum consultant. She was a pioneer in the introduction of digital media into museum exhibition, in the late 1980s, and continues to explore the role of digital media to create and enhance the visitor experience in museums and other physical spaces. Ms. Thomas is also recognized as a thought leader in the field of digital media and design. A 2009 Smithsonian Fellow in Museum Practice, she also teaches in the Masters Program in Exhibition Design at the Corcoran College of Art and Design, in Washington DC.

Wendy Woon

Wendy Woon is the Edward John Noble Foundation Deputy Director for Education at the Museum of Modern Art in New York and has over thirty years of award-winning experience in museum education. At MoMA she oversees all areas of MoMA Education, and has focused on transforming museum education practice for the 21st century. She has initiated, led and participated in cross institutional leadership initiatives that are key to MoMA's future. Before joining MoMA in 2006, she was Director of Education at The Museum of Contemporary Art, Chicago for ten years, starting in 1995, upon the opening of the new MCA building and Education Center, and oversaw the expansion of new programming. Woon taught and advised at The School of the Art Institute of Chicago in both the Master of Arts in Art Education and Museum Administration Programs. She is currently an adjunct professor for New York University's Graduate program in Visual Arts Administration and teaches Art Education in Museums. In addition, she has experience as an animator, filmmaker, curator, and museum and curriculum consultant. She presents nationally and internationally and joined the Community Advisory Board of WNET, and The Visiting Committee of The J. Paul Getty Museum.

GLOSSARY

Agent-Based Model	A computational model that uses distributed and autonomous software agents that mimics real world systems.
Agile Evaluation	A timely, flexible approach to analyzing the effectiveness of an educational activity that favors qualitative over quantitative measurement and does not require gathering statistically significant quantities of data. Agile evaluation is essential to the interative design process.
Ambisonic	A method of recording information about a soundfield and reproducing it over some form of loudspeaker array, so as to produce the illusion of hearing a true, three-dimensional sound-image. Ambisonics has a number of advantages over surround sound systems, the main one being that it is isotropic; i.e., the sounds arriving from all directions are treated equally (as opposed to most other surround systems that assume that the main sources of sound are frontal and that rear channels are only for ambience or special effects).

Art Pedagogy	An approach or method for teaching the subject of art, such as formalism.
Artificial Life	Artificial life, a subset of the field of Artificial Intelligence is a computational, mechanical and biochemical approach for investigating life, its processes, adaptation, and evolution.
ASEF	The Asia Europe Foundation, an organization based in Singapore with the purpose of promoting mutual understanding and cooperation between the people of Asia and Europe.
Augmented Reality	Augmented Reality (AR) is a live, direct or indirect, view of a physical, real-world environment whose elements are augmented (or supplemented) by computer-generated sensory input such as sound, video, graphics or GPS data.
Co-creative Design	A design process in which all stakeholders work together to solve a problem.
Co-evolutionary Narrative	Intelligent agents acting autonomously in response to emergent situations in consultation with their own scripted beliefs.
Cognitive Scaffolding	Describes the role of artefacts such as paper or smart phone devices to assist thinking beyond the confinement of the mind to the hand or the interface. Part of distributed cognition thinking and cognitive load theory.
Communitysourcing (see also Crowdsourcing)	Similar to crowdsourcing, but characterized by limiting outreach and participation to those most likely to best meet an organization's needs.

Complex Systems Science	Complex Systems Science is a new approach for studying science. It is a new way of looking at our world. Complex Systems Science investigates relationships between individual entities and explores how local interactions give rise to global states and behaviour such as emergence and self-organisation.
Compositional Balance	A formal quality in 2- or 3-dimensional works of art by which shapes, forms, materials, and/or colors harmonize together into a cohesive composition.
Creative Commons	A non-profit organization based in the USA and devoted to expanding the range of creative works available for others to build upon legally and to share.
Crowdsourcing	1. Collective online activities for distributed problem solving by interested groups. 2. Mustering the efforts of a virtual, online, crowd to perform specific organizational tasks.
Crowdfunding	Raising of funds through the collection of contributions from the general public using the Internet and social media; often considered a subset of crowdsourcing.
Curator	A person in a cultural heritage institution who is a specialist in the field of the institution's collections and responsible for the research, interpretation and communication of its content. In smaller museums the task often includes conservation and documentation.

Digital Native | A digital native is a person who was born during or after the general introduction of digital technologies and through interacting with digital technology from an early age, has a greater understanding of its concepts.

Encyclopedic Collection | A comprehensive universal collection, built up from a great variety of sources; for instance archaeological, ethnological and art objects from places all over the world.

Encyclopedic Museums | Museums that hold encyclopedic collections.

Enlightenment | This was a cultural movement in the 17th and 18th centuries which began in Europe with the purpose of reforming the society using reason and challenging ideas grounded in tradition and faith.

Ethnology Museum | Traditionally a museum that collects and exhibits material from an ethnological viewpoint. However many ethnology museums have been or are in the process of being restructured to communicate a broader concept leading to the enhancement of understanding between different cultures.

Facilitative | An important characteristic in teaching practice whereby the instructor supports observations and elicits contributions from students to communicate ideas rather than delivering them directly her/himself.

Flow | The experience of pleasurable absorption in a task that takes priority over other tasks. The term was created by Mihály Csíkszentmihályi in 1990.

Freemium   Freemium is a business model by which a
                            proprietary product or service (typically a
                            digital offering such as software, media,
                            games or web services) is provided free of
                            charge, but money (premium) is charged
                            for advanced features, functionality, or
                            virtual goods.

Geo-location   Geo-location is the identification of the
                            real-world geographic location of an object,
                            such as radar, mobile phone or an Internet-
                            connected computer terminal. Geo-location
                            may refer to the practice of assessing the
                            location, or to the actual assessed location.

Global Audience   The part of the general public all over the
                            world that is interested in a specific source
                            of information and/or entertainment.

HCI   Human Computer Interaction (HCI) is a
                            term that explains a broad field of research
                            that utilizes scientific methods to the design
                            and evaluation of computer-based artifacts,
                            services and systems. Examples are usability,
                            computation, interface design and software
                            systems. See Special Interest Group of the
                            Association for Computing Machinery
                            http://www.sigchi.org/.

Identifier   A string of characters that identifies a specific
                            resource in a digital library or on a network.

Image Manipulation   A tool that allows digital images to be
    Software   changed in a numerous ways and saved for
                            alternate use.

In-app Purchase

In-app purchases are purchases made from within a mobile application. Users typically make an in-app purchase in order to access special content or features in an app such as power-ups, restricted levels, virtual money, special characters, boosts, etc. The purchasing process is completed directly from within the app and is seamless to the user in most cases, with the mobile platform provider facilitating the purchase and taking a share of the money spent (usually in the range of 30 percent or so), with the rest going to the app developer.

Interactive Cinema

Transforms passive viewers into active participants. Interactive cinema as described by UNSW iCinema Centre encompasses three strategies: Interactive Narrative Systems (the exploration of narrative systems that allow the viewer to interact with a wide range of cinematic materials including autonomous narrative agency); Immersive Visualisation Systems (the investigation of multimodal environments that provide settings for the exploration of diverse, mixed-reality scenarios); and Distributed Interface Systems (the integration of distributed multi-user virtual environments within local and globally networked systems).

Intergenerational Collaboration

People of all ages, especially family members, working together to create something of value or sharing in a goal-driven experience.

Interoperability

The tasks of building coherent services for users from components that are technically different and independently managed.

Iterative Design	A development process that incorporates, in rapid and repetitive succession, stages of design, testing, and adjustment.
Kinesthetic	A body in motion is one endowed with kinesthetics, derived from the Greek *kinein*, meaning "to move", and *esthesia*, "to perceive."
Large-scale Interactive Immersive Visualization Environments (IIVES).	IIVES are interactive display systems that situate the user and visitors at the core of the experience. Often they include 3D projection inside a 360° screen providing a panoramic enclosure inside which the visitor is present or, 180° fields of view which encompass the visitor peripheral vision. IIVES can be used to show objects at real-world scale which causes the viewer to "suspend disbelief" and be inside the scene. IIVEs promote a sense of being present and or "being there" in the presented scenario that is separate from ordinary experience. Interaction with these digital environments can create levels of immersion as users direct their own narrative unfolding of the content.
LCCN	A serially based system of numbering cataloguing records in the Library of Congress in United States.
Learning Modalities	The multitude of ways people learn, for example: via the five senses, with the assistance of actions, and/or with adaptive devices.
Metadata	Data about other data, commonly divided into descriptive metadata such as bibliographic information, structural metadata about formats and structures, and administrative metadata, which is used to manage information.

Mixed Reality Narrative	Augmented reality provides opportunities for the conjunction between the "actual" and the overlay of the "virtual."
Mobile Augmented Reality	Mobile Augmented Reality Applications utilize camera equipped mobile devices as platforms for sensor-based, video see-through mobile augmented reality. Modern mobile augmented reality systems use one or more of the following tracking technologies: digital cameras and/or other optical sensors, accelerometers, GPS, gyroscopes, solid state compasses, RFID and wireless sensors.
Monoscopic	The term used to describe a viewing modality that involves a single projector for a single image rather than paired stereo images.
Multimodal Interaction	A form of human-machine interaction using multiple modes of input and output.
Native Mobile App	A native mobile app is a smartphone application that is coded in a specific programming language, such as Objective C for iOS and Java for Android operating systems. Native mobile apps provide fast performance and a high degree of reliability. They also have access to a phone's various devices, such as its camera and address book. In addition, users can use some apps without an Internet connection. However, this type of app is expensive to develop because it is tied to one type of operating system, sometimes forcing the company that creates the app to make duplicate versions that work on other platforms.

OAI	An attempt to build a "low-barrier interoperability framework" for archives containing digital content. It allows service providers to harvest metadata from data providers.
Participatory Evaluation	Participatory evaluation or participatory design is a process that integrates users/audiences/visitors involvement in the design and decision making process in analysis and or problem solving. It is acknowledged that users participation and agency in the project generates insight and knowledge to the problem context. Methods are usually design led.
Peer-to-Peer Learning	A method of information transfer that does not originate with an expert, such as a teacher, but is a result of students helping one another and discovering new information together. Peer-to-peer learning has been a cornerstone of progressive educational practice since the 1950s and is essential to most forms of online learning.
Perspective Painting	An approximate representation on a flat surface of an image as it is seen by the eye.
Phablet	A phablet is a smartphone class featuring screen sizes from around 5.0˝ to 6.9˝, designed to combine or straddle the functionalities of a smartphone and a tablet, eliminating the need for two devices.
Phenomenology (Archaeology)	Phenomenology is the study of conscious human sensory experience, frequently applied in landscape archaeology as the study of perception through embodiment within particular places such as monuments to aid in their interpretation.

Polychronic Narrative	A synthesis of multi-branched and algorithmically determined navigable systems.
Post-processual Archaeology	In a simple definition, archaeology is a study balanced between anthropology (the study of human cultures), history (the study of human historical and prehistoric past) and archaeometry (the science of decay and its measurement). Post-processual archaeology (the term first coined by Dr. Ian Hodder in 1999) criticises processualists for getting too involved with the science of archaeometry at the expense of understanding the behaviours of man, genders and the culture of people in general. Post-processual archaeology is characterised (among many other things) by the tension of hermeneutics (as the art of understanding "texts," artefact assemblages, landscapes, historical periods and other peoples) and the technical, theoretical tasks of interpretation. Another defining feature is related to phenomenology and embodiment that defines the relationship between people and the material world.
Prosthetic Vision	Instrumental magnification such as telescopes and microscopes, that allow perception to go where it has not gone before.
Protocol	A set of rules that describe the sequence of messages sent across a network, specifying both syntax and semantics.
QR Code	QR code (abbreviated from Quick Response Code) is the trademark for a type of matrix barcode (or two-dimensional barcode) that is an optically machine-readable label that is attached to an item and that records information related to that item.

RDF	A method for specifying the syntax of metadata, used to exchange metadata.
Reanimation Library	An artist project by Andrew Beccone that provides public access to books with unusual illustrations that have been de-accessioned by New York City Libraries (see www.reanimationlibrary.org).
Scenographic Spatial Narrative	The bodily journeying of 3D scenographic spaces that is at synchronous scales. The practice of design that unites the visual, auditory image and environment into a single, artistic form of communication.
Scopic Regime	Scopic regimes are culturally specific ways of seeing. Christian Metz (1981) is usually credited with the first using the concept "scopic regime." He distinguishes, for instance, film from theatre. According to Martin Jay (1988) there are three scopic regimes of modernity (cartesian perspectivalism, narrative art and baroque). Identifying the scopic regimes specific to cultural groups replaces the traditional definition of "vision" as a universal phenomenon.
Semantic Differential	A visual rating scale to measure the connotative and semantic meaning of artefacts, events and ideas. A way to describe and measure the qualitative and abstract.
Server	Any computer on a network, other than a client, that stores collections or provides services.

Social Practice

An important focus of many contemporary artists who engage audiences in the art-making process with the goal either of creating something that is widely valued or of changing perceptions that lead to creation of a better world.

Spatial Located Narrative

Narrative that unfolds at a particular location. Spatial located narrative is appropriate to all forms of story-telling using locative media and can be applied to such this as scroll paintings.

Stereoscopic

The term has to do with twin imaging camera techniques, technologies of stereo-capture and the use of twin projection systems to create 3D images as opposed to "stereographic" which is the result of the stereoscopic projection of a solid object onto a planar surface.

Synchronous/ Asynchronous

A characteristic of online and onsite learning environments describing whether students and teachers are present and interacting in real time (synchronous) or not (asynchronous). Students participating in a typical physical classroom discussion or live video chat are learning synchronously; students who are posting to an online discussion board or reading a textbook at home are learning asynchronously.

Telepresence

Is a technique that allow a person to feel as if they were present in a virtual space.

Theory of Multiple Intelligences	First proposed by Harvard professor Howard Gardner in late 1970s, this landmark theory proposes that effective teaching should appeal to more than one learning modality and that individual learners often favor some modalities over others. Most of these modalities cannot be measured by standardized instruments, such as Intelligence Quotient (IQ) tests (http://howardgardner.com/multiple-intelligences/).
Transcriptive Narrative	Is beholder-initiated, editorial actions involving the manipulation of duration and movement in the reassignment of eventfulness to episodic media content.
Universal Design	A characteristic of both industrial products and software interfaces by which creators consider the wide range of potential users — especially those who may not be able to move, speak or hear as well as others — and develop a single tool or interface that works well for all or most of those users.
User-centred Design	User-led agency and application for solving a problem with stakeholders.
Web App	A web-based application is any application that uses a web browser as a client. The term may also mean a computer software application that is coded in a browser-supported programming language (such as JavaScript, combined with a browser-rendered markup language like HTML) and reliant on a common web browser to render the application executable.

Wikiproject   A WikiProject is a group of contributors who want to work together as a team to improve Wikipedia. These groups often focus on a specific topic area (for example, women's history) or a specific kind of task (for example, checking newly created pages).

XML   A simplified version of SGML intended for use with online information.

Z39.50   A protocol that allows a computer to search collections of information on a remote system, create sets of results for further manipulation, and retrieve information: mainly used for bibliographic information.

INTRODUCTION

Steven Wu and Herminia Din

Digital heritage today leverages on leading-edge information technologies and is underpinned by a host of processes including digital asset management and digital preservation. This burgeoning digital heritage ecosystem enables art, culture and technology professionals to co-create novel fusions of new media with historical and cultural artifacts. As one may expect, museums and other heritage institutions are being metamorphosed rapidly to deliver advanced visualization, interactive and social-media services. In these dense, rapidly developing digital ecosystems, new media and mobile platforms are becoming the new drivers of online culture experience. It is pertinent to ask if a digital heritage ecosystem could ever be stable or sustainable. One suspects "no" to the first and a "possible yes" to the second goal.

This anthology aims to address many of the issues and challenges outlined above whilst proposing several working solutions in the form of real-life projects and exhibits. Professionals and managers with years of practice in their respective fields have contributed their well-honed lessons and knowledge on many emerging issues confronting digital heritage and its ecosystems. To deliver these concepts and lessons to targeted groups of readers, this book is segmented into four parts:

(1) Strategy and Policy
(2) Applications and Services
(3) Business and Partnership Models
(4) Emerging Concepts and Directions

Strategy and Policy

Increasingly, museums with their wealth of digital assets and meta-data have a pivotal role to play in the transition to a knowledge economy and the development of a digital content sector. To be effective in this role, these influential museums need a clear mandate to develop medium to long term innovation strategies. Museums therefore must be cognizant of the broader government agenda for funding purposes and to ensure alignment with the national agenda as well as global developments. What are the elements of an IT-innovation strategy for museums? How can these be fine-tuned to address the imperative for innovation and concurrently position the museum to be competitive vis-à-vis other global players? Digital ecosystems are constantly evolving in response to internal policies and external forces. Which model has been shown to be effective in a specific situation and how should the participants contribute their respective roles for optimal results? Emerging digital ecosystems participants will also benefit from lessons on how collaborations and technology applications in the service of cultural heritage can be enabled. The three essays in this grouping encapsulate knowledge and experience in museum IT strategy and implementation, digital heritage ecosystem development and lessons from curatorial practices. They will be valuable to senior management and policy makers who are envisioning the future of their digital heritage strategies.

Museums with the wherewithal to craft and execute a medium to long term innovation strategy are few and far between. Chapter 1,

IT-enabled Innovative Services as a Museum Strategy: Experience of the National Palace Museum, Taipei, Taiwan, elaborates on how the National Palace Museum (NPM) has developed its IT-enabled innovative services as a museum strategy. In envisioning its innovation strategy, NPM has responded to the global trends in developing a knowledge economy and nurturing a digital content industry. It saw the need to create a digital museum and to position itself for global competition. For NPM, the digitization of cultural artifacts has been beneficial in the internal planning of exhibitions, management of the collection, training of staff, utilization of images and texts, and design of web pages. The author reminds that digitization of artifacts is but a small step in the journey as subsequent work such as digital asset management is even more critical.

The development and sharing of digital heritage know-how and services today are necessarily cross-organizational and usually spearheaded by a non-profit institute or center with a cohesive network of resources and expertise. Chapter 2, *Designing Digital Heritage Competencies Centers: A Swedish Model,* highlights the activities and processes at the Digital Heritage Center (DHC) in Stockholm, Sweden, which supports advancement within the digital heritage sector as well as communication between cultural heritage institutions and its participants. Several of DHC's initiatives have focused on enabling this type of collaboration and the implementation of new technologies in the service of cultural heritage.

Chapter 3, *7 Lessons Learnt for Digital Culture,* presents a number of useful lessons on digital culture distilled from the author's years of curatorial experience at leading museums. Digital content should be discoverable and accessible online so as to foster long term engagement with the public and researchers. The author advocates the use of social media to engage with the worldwide audience, and reminds the reader that digital content needs to be maintained and tools need to be upgraded to keep up with the fast changing technology. The chapter concludes that "digital technology should not be thought of as a burden; but rather, as a powerful extension of your organization."

Applications and Services

Exhibitions are the staple deliverables of most, if not all, cultural institutions including museums. Exhibitions serve to engage and educate the public on the institution's collections as well as those of others. Museums want to create memorable, inspiring and, hopefully, transformative experiences. Few, however, are ready to draw useful lessons from the emerging online behaviors and visitors expectations. To be able to conceptualize, plan and deliver a virtual or blended exhibition is also becoming a requisite skill for curators. Beyond engaging the public through exhibitions and user participation, museums also need an education strategy. The six essays in this grouping offer a breadth of implementation details on real life heritage projects and museum education initiatives. Through these case studies, the reader gets an insight into how digital technologies have been integrated with culture and the arts, giving a new spin to user experience and learning.

New pedagogical approaches are essential to making cultural experiences relevant and meaningful to today's museum participants. In Chapter 4, *Reinventing MoMA's Education Programs for the 21st Century Visitor*, the authors posit that emerging online behaviors and equally evolving onsite visitor expectations can complement, and even inform, each other. The chapter presents the thinking behind how MoMA builds connections and stimulates dialogue across multiple venues — onsite, online and offsite — with web-based and social media-powered communications. This chapter will be particularly relevant for education and evaluation staff working in a variety of cultural heritage sites and museums.

Museum collections were once limited to one-way communication in which static entries were delivered with little opportunity for interactivity. In Chapter 5, *OneMillionMuseumMoments*, the author expands on this relationship; the goal is to preserve, extend, and enhance a collaborative space in order to extend collaborative learning and understanding. Museum goers and museum professionals are invited to share their "museum moments": their experiences and projects, thoughts and ideas. The mission is to create a participant observer virtuous circle, where both professionals and the public inspire and draw inspiration from one another.

In Chapter 6, *Documentary Storytelling Using Immersive and Interactive Media,* case studies from projects using immersive experiences are used to showcase powerful human stories that visitors find engaging and memorable. All of this work is based on the documentary film approach to storytelling, but with a range and variety of museum experiences made possible by the availability of creative technology tools that allow visitors to interact and engage with exhibits, to learn in new ways. The chapter offers suggestions and guidelines to readers about using documentary methods to create interpretive projects for heritage sites.

The Buddha Tooth Relic Temple and Museum (BTRTM) is not only a temple but also an iconic museum in Singapore with more than 300 statues currently being displayed, representing the heritage of many different eras of Buddhism. Chapter 7, *Making of Buddha Tooth Relic Temple and Museum Virtual Temple,* explains that the project's objective is to create a virtual 3D replica of this heritage building and to showcase it to the world via the internet. The project was completed in over a one year by adopting an incremental project management cycle in which the external structure would be first created and the rooms would then be added by the development team one by one until they were fully completed. The virtual temple can be used to enhance both the pre- and post-visit experience. Visitors can first familiarize themselves with the layout and contents before their visit. Subsequently, visitors can re-experience and share their visits with others.

Presenting a personal perspective in Chapter 8, *Digital Media in Museum,* the author expands on the changes to exhibition planning and design experience over the past 30 years, and the evolving role of digital media — as artifact, content and process — as it has played an increasingly central role in that experience. The chapter explores what digital media has meant to the museum (as institution and as workplace), to the visitor and to the exhibition process; and the core of this discussion also examines the growing significance and impact of digital media inside an institution that originally defined itself as a collecting institution. Because exhibitions are designed and produced by multi-disciplinary teams from different museum departments, they present a convenient vehicle to explore the essential relationship between visitor and museum, museum and content, and visitor and content.

Chapter 9, *Using New Media for Exhibit Interpretation: A Case Study*, focuses on core concepts of digital storytelling in preserving cultural heritage. The authors explain the process of planning, developing, and organizing the *Yuan Ming Yuan — Qing Emperors' Splendid Gardens* exhibit, as an example of a comprehensive approach in applying new media technology for interpretation. Although three dimensional computer simulation techniques have been used to visualize heritage sites, this exhibit goes further by using digital tools to represent archaeological artifacts and historical events in developing a "fully integrated" exhibit narrative.

Business and Partnership Models

Digital heritage partnerships are not uncommon amongst institutions from different parts of the world. The commercialization of digital assets may not be the primary goal as there are often other more fundamental challenges to be overcome. How do business models and partnerships impact the outcome of a project and its value to online visitors? How do they provide the support framework for specialized knowledge, practices and skills to be shared with less experienced partners? The three essays in this grouping highlight the collaborative nature of digital culture projects and the business models of personal devices. Museums across the world may collaborate to pool digital assets online in order to showcase a thematic collection. Cultural heritage project initiators may also pull resources and funding from their partner organizations. As personal devices become ubiquitously relevant to the digital culture space, effective business models that integrate mobile computing into the user experience with due attention to revenue generation (to offset development costs) are discussed through case studies.

Chapter 10, *The Virtual Collection of Asian Masterpieces: A Universal Online Museum*, introduces an online museum set up as an "encyclopedic" collection of digital art of distinction "masterpieces" from Asia and several other non-Asian countries. It is open to each participating museum to select what it deems to be a masterpiece. The author discusses quality of content issues as it is not possible to digitize artworks to the same standard across so many participating museums. The contents of the Virtual Collection of Asian Masterpieces (VCM) website are licensed under a Creative Commons "Some Rights Reserved" License. Another hurdle is that English language has been a major barrier as language skills are inadequate especially in Asian museums. Nonetheless, the VCM has taken off successfully as it offers visitors the chance to view, learn from and enjoy the rich variety of masterpieces from all over the world.

In Chapter 11, *A Tale on a Leaf: Promoting Indonesian Literature and Culture through the Development of Lontar Digital Library*, the authors trace the conceptualization and implementation of a digital library system for Lontar Foundation, an independent and non-profit organization established in 1987. The primary aim is to promote Indonesian literature and culture through the publication of translations of Indonesian literary works. Lontar and its partners believe that many aspects of culture can be codified and be well managed. By optimizing the Lontar Digital Library's assets, cultural information can also be re-purposed and disseminated all over the world for the purposes of promotion and education.

Smart phones and tablets are becoming globally ubiquitous and it is foreseeable that in the future mobile computing will become increasingly relevant to digital heritage. What is the potential of mobile technology in preserving and promoting heritage? What are best practices to integrate mobile media into the overall museum or heritage site experience design? In Chapter 12, *The Future of History is Mobile: Experiencing Heritage on Personal Devices*, the author examines these issues and presents case studies of benchmarked mobile heritage projects, including an in-depth examination of the growing field of mobile augmented reality.

Emerging Concepts and Directions

Technology innovations seed the development of new paradigms in exhibition design and presage novel ways of curating exhibits. Increasingly, curators are eager to blend new technologies such as new media, visualization and mobile computing to augment their exhibits. The four essays in this grouping cover the conceptual and technical development of large-scale interactive and immersive museum installations, and the use of visualization in the process of heritage site reconstruction. In addition to enhanced interactivity, digital heritage encounters and museum visits have also been elevated to a more personal, mobile experience. As more aspects of museum visits are being impacted by technology innovations, user experience evaluation has also evolved to capture and analyse the expanded range of user inputs. Crowdsourcing in digital heritage has also emerged recently and it is opportune to delve into the effectiveness of various forms of crowd-engagement.

In Chapter 13, *A Cultural Heritage Panorama: Trajectories in Embodied Museography*, the authors chart trajectories of the philosophical, conceptual and technical development of six large-scale interactive and immersive museum installations based on significant tangible and intangible world heritage from Hong Kong, China and India. Each one of the display systems exploits a combination of mixed reality and multi-modal interfaces, designed to promote kinesthetic and interactive participation of users. The installations described encompass four main ways of seeing: panoramic, hemispheric, linear spatial navigation, and augmentation. The interactions of the visitors to these installations are conceived of as performances, three-way relationships between user-system-spectators. Each installation is briefly described in a framework of content and the user-experience.

Recent decades have seen an exponential rise in the application of computer visualization to heritage sites and landscapes. In some ways this may be seen as an improved approach to illustration. In Chapter 14, *From Product to Process: New Directions in Digital Heritage*, the authors propose that there has been a growing realization that the actual process of digital visualization involving computational methods can offer much more than traditional approaches. For example, in addition to facilitating new ways of engaging with virtual environments, the process of visualization offers new ways of interrogating archived data and raises new hypotheses that drive further research. This essay focuses on process guidelines on visualization as first a process and then a product for capturing, reconstructing and visualizing heritage sites for the phenomenological interpretation of sites.

Technological innovations are rapidly changing the way we experience and interact with information, enabling museum visitors to engage with cultural heritage in transformative ways through interactive and embodied digital interfaces. In Chapter 15, *I Sho U: An Innovative Method for Museum Visitor Evaluation*, a new method for museum visitor evaluation is proposed. Research into how new digital experiences are received and understood by the public has been largely limited to quantitative data analysis and observation. In response to the need for new evaluation tools, I Sho U (literally "I Show You") significantly advances traditional visitor studies by providing: tactile interfaces, real-time upload of visitor responses, automatic data analysis and, real-time visualization of aggregated data for museum stakeholders and participants alike. I Sho U is an interface paradigm that could transform visitor evaluation, with implications for how we design, manage and invest in our museums.

In Chapter 16, *Digital Cultural Heritage is Getting Crowded: Crowdsourced, Crowd-funded, and Crowd-engaged*, the author examines the new evolving relationships between the "the crowd" and cultural heritage institutions as the public is encouraged to participate in projects, contribute talents, service, and knowledge, and generate financial support. Starting with brief historical and theoretical contexts, the discussion covers how institutions or special projects can successfully engage and reward crowds using specific tools and techniques designed for that purpose. Successful examples in cultural heritage from around the world provide information and inspiration. The author proposes that crowd-based activities can be an effective strategy in the creation, preservation and promulgation of cultural heritage knowledge, although some institutional and regional challenges may need to be met.

In conclusion, this book presents some recent initiatives as well as challenges, policy and strategy issues in developing a digital heritage ecosystem within the broader context of an emerging digital culture. Case studies are drawn from USA, Europe and Asia to showcase the breadth of innovative ideas in delivering, communicating, interpreting and transforming cultural heritage content and experience through multi-modal, multimedia interfaces. It is our hope that the end result would be a practical reference book for policy makers, business people, researchers, curators and educators as well as the culture-minded public seeking to understand how the field of digital heritage and culture may impact our social, cultural and recreational pursuits.

PART 1
Strategy and Policy

1

IT-ENABLED INNOVATIVE SERVICES AS A MUSEUM STRATEGY: EXPERIENCE OF THE NATIONAL PALACE MUSEUM, TAIPEI, TAIWAN

James Quo-Ping Lin

Introduction to the National Palace Museum

The National Palace Museum (NPM) is a world-class institution with a collection of over 695,000 objects comprising renowned ceramics, calligraphy, painting, ritual bronzes, jade, lacquer wares, curio cabinets, enamel wares, writing accessories, carvings, tapestries and embroideries, and rare books and documents spanning over 8,000 years of Chinese history (List of Categories in the Collection, n.d.). The collection of cultural artifacts held inside the NPM consists of an enormous treasure trove of objects from the Song, Yuan, Ming and Qing Dynasties. Development of the NPM is closely connected to the social changes of modern China. In 1925, thirteen years after the founding of the Republic of China, the last Qing Emperor, Puyi, was exiled from the Forbidden City. The cultural artifacts left within the palaces were collectively itemized, and the NPM, a new museum atop the old palace, was born. However soon after its establishment, following the deteriorating situation of an impending Sino-Japan War, the NPM collections started their "drifting" years. Most of its holdings were moved into the inner land of mainland China to avoid damage from gunfire. In autumn 1948, fighting between the

3

Nationalist and Communist armies took an adverse turn, and the Central Government made the decision to send its most precious objects in the collections to Taiwan. A total of 2,972 crates were shipped; while these accounted for only 22 percent of the items originally transported south from Beijing. In 1965, a new museum was built in the Taipei suburb of Waishuanxi. The new museum site was named the "Chung-Shan Museum" in honor of the founding father of the nation, Dr. Sun Yat-sen, and first opened to the public on the centenary of his birthday (Brief Chronology, n.d.).

Achievements of the IT-enabled Innovative Service in the NPM

As prize winners (Awards, n.d.) of several international museum competitions on digital products, the NPM in Taipei, Taiwan has much experience to share with museum colleagues world-wide in terms of strategy, possibilities, and challenges of introducing IT-enabled innovative services into a museum context in a broad sense. All these achievement will not be possible without support from a series of national IT-enabled innovative projects, as pictured in Figure 1. These projects started with the *E-Taiwan Initiative* introduced in 2000 with emphases on construction of information and communication infrastructure. In short, these include the Digital Archives, Digital Museum, E-learning, Ubiquitous Network Society (UNS), and Cultural Creativity projects. Hundreds of thousands of museum objects have been saved in digital forms, which have brought significant benefits to the museum and the society. In the aspect of museum operations, the digital images can enhance curatorial practices, conservation research, learning resources dissemination, cultural marketing, and so on.

In summary, the achievements of these projects include:

1. Extensive metadata systems for all collections;
2. Launch of websites in nine languages to provide wide knowledge of various subjects;
3. Installation of wireless network system;

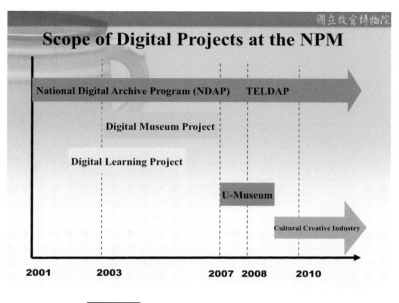

Figure 1.   National projects of the NPM.

4. Publication of e-newsletter with a circulation of 250,000 copies both in Chinese and English;
5. Providing e-learning and online exhibitions;
6. Application of various electronic media, including films of all types, mobile apps, interactive kiosks, and new media art into museum operation.

From the public standpoint, these achievements provide ubiquitous opportunities to learn the museum collections via a variety of approaches. It is expected that IT-enabled innovative services could bring more positive impacts to society, especially in terms of educational and economic benefits.

The Strategic Implication of Adopting IT-enabled Innovative Service at the NPM

The strategic implication of adopting IT-enabled innovative service at the NPM includes the rationale of adopting IT-enabled innovative service, structure and relationship among these projects, and the development stages of these projects.

The Rationale of Adopting IT-enabled Innovative Service

The reason why the NPM eagerly adopted IT-enabled innovative services can generally be divided into five aspects. The first was in response to the global trend in developing a knowledge-based economy and specifically the nurturing of digital-content industries. The second was in response to the trend in developing the digital museum. The third was the acceptance of central government policy directions. The fourth derived from the practical needs of the museum itself. And finally, the fifth was to face steepening competition the global museum industry. The rationale of adopting IT-enabled innovative services can be further elaborated as follows (Lin, 2007a).

First of all, in 1996, the Organization for Economic Co-operation and Development (OECD) issued the *Knowledge-Based Economy Report*, which became an important reference for countries around the world. The emergence of a knowledge-based economy has caused businesses to place greater focus on content and creativity, further highlighting the significant role of cultural content in economic development. Today, museums not only serve the long-established functions of storage, display, research, and education, but have also become an indispensable medium in the development of a knowledge-based economy, especially with respect to digital content industries.

Secondly, the Japanese scholar Sakamura (2000) discussed the evolution of physical museum to digital museum. He brings up several reasons museums in the 21st century use technology to integrate virtual and physical parts into digital museums:

1. Digital collections can provide more information than real collections.
2. By using hyperlinks, people can broaden their readings.
3. Faster communication speed.
4. Using 3D or planar technology to process relic information.
5. It can show the process of relic repairs.

In step with the development of computers and the Internet, museums are also moving toward the digital world. Digital museum can certainly spread the information all over the world — as, for example, online news would — in order to achieve the strategy of market expansion.

Thirdly, in accordance with the strategy of the central government in Taiwan, the Council for Cultural Affairs was responsible in the project *Challenge 2008: Digital Taiwan* for completing the digitization of all public museums' collection in Taiwan by 2007. This, combined with the fact that Taiwan has already become the place in Asia with the highest broadband Internet penetration, shows that Taiwan already possess an environment of widespread information technology and communication, with Internet and telecommunication providers offering a plethora of services. Along with the robust development of the electronic information industry, Taiwan is truly taking off in the digital-content industry (Lin, 2007b).

Fourthly, we should also look at the actual need for digitizing the museum collections in order to further assist to serve the museum functions. As already mentioned, the four main functions of a museum are collection, exhibition, education, and research. However, they are often hindered by various factors, such as the inherent fragility of artifacts, limited exhibition space, set opening and closing times, the difficulty of database searching, and the inconvenience of using value-added applications. These obstacles also become impediments to the museum's role as an educational institution. Only by removing these obstacles will the museum's role as a provider of services, education, and cultural exchange be enhanced. In this regard, digitization offers a comprehensive solution to these problems. As far as the NPM is concerned, the digitization of cultural artifacts has been beneficial in the internal planning of exhibitions, management of the collection, training of staff, utilization of images and texts, and design of web pages. For the public, it has also been invaluable in providing educational services, supporting research, aiding the licensing and management of images, increasing value-added applications, encouraging innovative and content-based industrial developments, enhancing the upholding and protection of domestic culture, and inspiring the creation of digital information. Therefore, digitization of the collections in the NPM plays a significant role in the national development plan (Lin, 2007a).

Finally, through Michael Porter's "Competitive Forces Model," we can also observe the dramatic change in the overall competitive environment of the museum industry worldwide (Porter, 1980). Judging from the sheer number of competitors within this industry, the dramatically increasing number of museums around the world results in far greater direct competition compared to the past. Furthermore, on the customer level, various new trends — such as changes in consumer taste, reduction in the number of visitors, and the rise in popularity of traveling abroad — have created another crisis for the museum industry. From the viewpoint of suppliers and upstream industries, the awareness and study of art and culture requires a long period of investment to create something of limited quantity, therefore making it difficult for museums to display contents to satisfy the ever-changing needs of the marketplace. Furthermore, considering that the threshold for entering the museum field is not very high in Taiwan, the many newcomers have only intensified the already existing competition. Many substitute products and new services have become available, such as the rise of new leisure and entertainment means, including television, movies, arcades, and Internet games. This, when combined with other factors such as the recent economic downturn, political instability, stiffening of regulations, and the fast-paced and temperamental nature of the social and cultural environment, have all had a considerable effect on the museum industry. Faced with this difficult environment for management, most museums around the world have vigorously pursued any effective means of solving these problems. The digitization of museum collections is one of the most promising. Presently, many museums and institutions around the world are promoting the task of cultural digitization, some of the more prominent examples being the British Museum, the Louvre, the UN's Memory of the

World, the US's American Memory, and Canada's National Digital Collections (Lin, 2007a).

In summing up the above five issues — the new trend towards a knowledge-based economy, the trend in the development of the digital museum, accepting the direction of central government policy, the need for digitizing collections of artifacts, and acute changes in the overall competitive environment in the museum industry — the primary motivations behind the trend of developing digitization in museums around the world are clearly evident. In Taiwan, the task of museum digitization began in May of 1998 with the National Science Council of the Executive Yuan promoting the project "Towards the New Millennium — Humanistic Concern as the Focus of Technological Development for the New Century," which included "Digital Museums" as one of its sub-projects. At the time, the NPM participated in this project under the theme of "The Beauty of Cultural Objects in the National Palace Museum." Afterwards, through several changes and overhauls, the NPM proposed the three projects of "Production of a Digital Archives of Art at the National Palace Museum," "Establishment of a Digital National Palace Museum and Value-added Applications," and "National Palace Museum E-learning" as its plan to deal with the age of digitization.

Structure and Relationship Among These Projects

The strategies adopted by the NPM to the above ends will affect the distribution and utilization of its resources, and will also directly influence the achievement of its goals in digitization. When our digitization plan just started, a coherent plan was not yet in place for the long term outlook regarding such a plan for the NPM. It was undertaken mainly to cooperate with the government policies in which certain projects that fulfilled specific goals were developed. However, during yearly management meetings, we constantly reflected over each single step and eventually came up with a more developed outlook. Similarly, after much discussion and brainstorming, in the museum's digitization plan, we concretely drew up a long term outlook for a digitization project and decided upon a yearly execution plan accordingly. This long term outlook is "based on the belief of combining culture and technology, set a model of the digitization for museums, create an example of digitalized collection industry, build a comprehensive economic system for museums" (Lin, 2007a).

Based on the long term outlook planned above, with regard to the execution strategy, due to the limitations in terms of budget and human capital, the NPM is adopting a strategy to "use a chain to divide work into yearly projects so that a solid result can be seen year after years" (Lin, 2007a). That is, in order to push for a smooth digitization, the digitization of our collection is divided into three categories. They are Digital Archives, Digital Museum, and lastly, Digital Learning, Knowledge Economy and Cultural Artifact Education. By combining all three categories, it is hoped that the greatest possible effect of digitization can be seen.

After several years of experimentation and discussion, the NPM has now formulated its strategies for proceeding with digitization, its principal missions being:

1. Effectively supporting studies and research,
2. Developing a digital museum and utilizing value-added applications,
3. Effectively supporting online exhibitions,
4. Focusing on services, value, and promotion, and
5. Effectively supporting an environment of stress-free and efficient learning of cultural, historical and artistic information.

With these missions in mind, the NPM has designed a three-tier strategy for digitization. From bottom to top, they are (as shown in Figure 2) Tier I represented by digital archives; Tier II by digital museum; and Tier III by digital learning, knowledge-based economy, and the promotion of education in art. It is hoped that through the seamless integration of these three tiers, that the results of the efforts in the digital archives in Tier I and the digital museum in Tier II will be promoted and utilized, achieving the goals of promoting art and culture while enhancing the knowledge-based economy (Lin, 2007a).

Figure 2.   Strategy for implementing digitization.

Development Stages of These Projects

The digitization of the collection of the NPM is a project involving all departments within the Museum, along with critical technical support from Academia Sinica and National Taiwan University, financial sponsorship from the National Science Council, Council for Economic Planning and Development, and the Council for Cultural Affairs, as well as research efforts by relevant suppliers. Owing to constraints of funding, personnel, and technology maturity, the whole process of implementing the 3-tiered strategic plan need to be divided into several stages. From our observation, this process may be roughly divided into four stages: seeding, germination, growth, and diffusion (Lin, 2007a).

The "seeding stage" commenced in 1999 when the NPM began a cooperation with IBM on a digitization project. At that time, the project focused on constructing a preliminary system framework and creating a small volume of high-resolution files. The successes in this stage formally established the foundation for the digitization of the NPM.

The "germination stage" began in 2001 with the "Digital Initiative Project," which completed the planning and preliminary construction of the NPM Digital Archives System. This was followed in 2002 by two national-level mid-term projects: "The Digital Archives National Technology Project — Research and Development of the NPM Cultural Artifacts Digital Archiving System" and "The Project for Establishing and Developing Internet Culture — The Construction and Utilization of the National Palace Digital Museum." In 2003, work continued with "Cultural Artifacts E-learning at the NPM" as part of "Challenge 2008: Digital Taiwan — E-learning National Technology Project." These three intermediate range projects set the pace for the continued digitization of the NPM.

Following the "germination stage," the NPM aimed to complete the digitization of its collection by the year 2007. Therefore, in 2004, the NPM accelerated its digitization efforts in order to officially enter the "growth stage." In the meantime, the application of these raw material produced by the digital archive program are aggressively embedded into the digital museum and E-learning projects.

It was hoped that the task of digitization would enter the "diffusion stage" by 2007, so that the results of digitization of its collections could become evident. Currently, the NPM has the capability to collect all the outcomes from those three national projects and place them into a platform for further use. These include internal use for research and education outreach and also for commercial licensing in various models and this is where the UNS project and cultural creativity project took its place in 2010.

Possibilities: Showcase IT-enabled Innovative Service Achievement

According to the above mentioned 3-tier strategic plan, the NPM successfully launched three national level mid-term projects including the National Digital Archive Program (NDAP), the National Digital Museum program, and the National E-learning program. And, later on lead to the success of UNS project and cultural creativity project in 2010. All these projects reveal the broadest possibilities of adopting IT-enabled innovative service in the museum context (Fung and Lin, 2012).

Digital Archive Program (2002–2012)

NPM has participated in the NDAP starting from 2002 and accomplished various missions including extensive database building for key collections. The goal of phase one of the NDAP is to start the groundwork for digitization of the nation's cultural resources, a task which is similar to setting the foundation for building the pyramids. Likewise, the scope of work is wide and grand and the impact difficult to foresee. The NPM began to plan its first five-year plan for Digital Archives in 2001, and the following year (2002) it became a main institution for the NDAP (Fung and Lin, 2012).

Regarding the division of work, the plan requires three of NPM's curatorial departments, Department of Antiquities, Department of Painting and Calligraphy, and Department of Rare Books and Documents, to provide artifacts for digitization. The digitalized materials also include bookkeeping records, films, X-ray films and maintenance records from the registration office, the publication office and the technology office, and the information center is responsible for providing information technology support and project management. In addition, during the initial stage of this plan, assistance from Computer Center of Academia Sinica, Institute of Information Science and Information Team of the Digital Collection Technology Plan were also gratefully received.

In terms of output, this project carefully selects artifacts from NPM's collections to build metadata and high quality digital images that match up with the latest world standard. Those that are set up included the following; "The NPM Antiquities Metadata System," "The NPM Paintings and Calligraphy Metadata System," "The NPM Ch'ing Archival Documents Metadata System," and "The NPM Rare Books Metadata System." All the afore-mentioned systems are available for public use. In addition, this plan aims to continuously expand the management system for the artifacts warehouse, set up and improve the digital collection backup system hardware as well as create a high-speed, safe and high-quality sophisticated image viewing system. Now, a large part of the collection has been digitalized and, via the World Wide Web, to allow free access for browsers around the world. Our aim is to spread knowledge of the collection in the museum so that it can be acquired by the general public, so that this facility can enhance education and that value can be added to business practice.

Digital Museum Program (2003~2007)

Our Digital Museum Program hopes that by the means of technology, the concept of the museum is no longer a restraint and that the beautiful artifacts and educational resources they contain are more accessible to the public, be it local, national or global. The first step is to create the NPM web site which can be read in many different languages including Chinese, English, Japanese, German, French, Spanish, Korean, Russian, and Arabic. It is also hoped that through the real-time provision of information concerning the museum and the actual displays, an overall top service quality in the museum will be achieved. Since 2000, a dozen of theme-based digital museums have been successfully completed (Lin, 2007b).

In addition, various multimedia films and interactive DVDs have been successively created and appropriate presenting facilities were built. So far, those which are now available for use by the general public are as follows: *The Beauty of Famous Paintings, The Essences of Paintings and Calligraphy,* and *The Beauty of Calligraphy* — which are all multimedia films. Interactive DVD in various languages that have been created include the following: *The Beauty of Enamel; Treasured Paintings and Calligraphy; Treasure Hunts in the National Palace Museum; Convergence of Radiance; Age of the Great Khan; The Garden of Books and Paintings; The Fashionable vs. The Antiquarian; The Spirit of Jade; Emperor Sung Hui Zheng;* and, *Northern Sung Paintings and Calligraphy.* In order to utilize high-tech multimedia technology to the best advantage and to fulfill the expectations the general public have for a multi-functional, technological and digitalized museum, all these DVDs and films were also been presented in many public venues including Taoyuan International Airport and Taipei Metro-Rapid-Transportation system.

Moreover, in order for the general public to see and understand the NPM from different angles, our plan includes the production of a series of films, which is a truly creative and interactive experience. The first in the series, entitled *The New Life Behind History*, Director Wang Xiaodi invited creators from throughout the country to come to the NPM and then started on the creative process, and feel a sense of achievement in their creative works. Not only this, he then recorded the process. The entire movie pushes us to rethink what artifacts inside the display case actually are, to reconsider the experience to be gained inside a museum, and to ponder the question, "do the objects just sit still in the same time and space or they do have another fresher life waiting for us to discover?" Film number two *The Passage*, funded by the NPM and directed by Cheng Wentan, is the first drama of its kind to be played in theaters. Through the famous calligraphic work *The Cold Food Observance* of Su Dongpo, people from three different walks of life are woven together, bonding intimately with historical pieces of the NPM in order to express a friendly and beautiful story. This film was nominated in many Film Festivals including the Tokyo Film Festival and won the Best Sound Effect Award in the 41st Annual Golden Horse Film Festival (in Taiwan). Film number three, *The Craftsmen's Skills in a Prosperous Era* is a documentary directed by Ho Xiaoxian, reveals just how skillful and extraordinary the craftsmen's skills are, their conceptual and thematic framework being the Ming and Ching artifacts collection in the National Palace Museum.

In addition, director Pon Wenchun was asked to produce *Old is New* — a 90-second commercial film. The content and inspiration for this film was drawn from Sung Dynasty's Huang Tingjian's famous *Poem in Seven-Character Verse: Hua Ki Xun Ren Tie* and a local electronic music composer Ling Qiang was invited to perform it anew. In the film, the elegant poem is read in old Taiwanese with a background of soft and tranquil electronic music. Not only does it bring to life on the screen the beautiful writing from thousands of years ago, but it also combines the aesthetics of thousands of years of living history. This film, incidentally, won the Gold Medal for the category of Promotional/Marketing film in 2006 AAM Muse Award in the USA.

Lastly, in terms of value added usage, the digital resources created by the digitization programs of the NPM have the capability to incorporate the design, production, and marketing ability of private sectors to develop all kinds of value-added usage. By means of digital publishing, all kinds of publications such as artifact catalogues, CD-ROMs and replicates of paintings, via Internet and E-commerce, the National Palace Museum's artifacts can be viewed all over the world. Furthermore, a value-added global market can be created so that the development of nation's digital content industry and creative culture industry can be further enhanced and increased revenue can be brought to the nation's state treasury.

E-learning Program (2003–2007)

The NPM's E-learning Project aims to use the abundant cultural resources of the museum to create multiple digital learn resources so that the benefits and ethos of digital learning can be widely spread and a demonstrative digital learning model for museums can be set up. This project utilized output from Digital Archives program as the raw materials to create four museum e-learning models, namely: on-site interactive digital learning, off-site digital learning, online digital learning, and on-site wireless guided learning (Lai and Lin, 2006).

Firstly, the on-site interactive digital learning model aimed at creating a situational museum learning environment. We applied the state-of-the-art information and multimedia technology to develop an interactive digital learning and display system to provide a creative and friendly museum digital learning experience so that learners become increasingly interested in the content of the museum's collections and, through interactive learning, the learning process can be more efficient and engaged. For example, by combining the round shape fans often used in Sung Dynasty with an infrared sensing device and a large screen, viewers can each hold an imitated fan and lightly touch the wings of flying butterflies on the screen while learning about the content of the artifacts interactively and therefore enjoy the precious artifacts the NPM has to offer.

Secondly, the off-site digital learning model aimed at bringing the above situational museum learning environment beyond its walls. According to the idea of creating a mobile and digital museum, the NPM has, since 2005, hosted "Digital Learning in the NPM" themed display and activities. Emperor Sung Hui Zheng's poem *Dancing Butterfly Chasing Breeze* was used to create an exhibition of *Dancing Butterfly Lost in the Path and Gracefully Chase the Night Breeze: Digital Learning in the National Palace Museum,* and it showed that abundant multiple digital learning resources can be displayed comprehensively. Since it's opening, it has been displayed in many cities around Taiwan.

Thirdly, the online digital learning model aimed at establishing a digital learning web site with all kinds of digital learning courseware which have been designed for various levels of learners. From the easiest to the most challenging, through a strict step-by-step learning process, a self-motivated learning environment has been created so that learners are able to learn the most in-depth knowledge of the NPM collections by themselves. Additionally, various educational activities have been held so that aims of spreading cultural, historical, artistic, educational as well as digital learning can be achieved in tandem with an enhanced enjoyment of the beauty of the NPM's collection.

Lastly, for constructing the on-site wireless guided learning model to provide museum visitors with a personalized digital guided service, the NPM has develop a digital guided system based on handheld computer, wireless network, and RFID technology. Text, pictures, and audio are incorporated into the system. The handheld equipment includes pocket PC, earphones, RFID label reader, and shoulder straps. Viewers can choose either the pre-defined mode or self-defined mode. In the pre-defined mode, viewers follow the predefined route with a choice from 30-minute, 60-minute, or 120-minute program. In the self-defined mode, viewers can use the sensor to read the RFID tag alongside the artifact and bring up the related information.

Challenges

The above-mentioned projects not only bring major changes and unlimited opportunities to the museum, but also carries difficulties and challenges. First of all, it has been a struggle to get the necessary funds from the central government for digitization. Progress has been slow due to current budget restrictions by the government. Second, besides implementing the budget already allocated, one must also simultaneously handle outside tasks and face various levels of management pressure. Third, regarding personnel, government regulations in terms of employment also creates difficulties in the acquisition of digitization specialists and their efficient training. Differences of digital understanding also exist among those assigned to the task of digitization. Combined with the difficulty of communication between departments, achieving a consensus in the goals of digitization is not always easy. Fourth, the problem of managing temporary employees on digital projects; and the recent discovery of a severe issue with the lack of artistic and cultural understanding by information technology specialists in general. Fifth, the task of integrating the upstream and downstream parts of the digital content industry still needs to be reinforced. The value-added chain throughout the digital-content industry also requires time to yield results. Sixth, in terms of technology, many key digital technologies have yet to mature (such as the application and verification of watermarking), thus digital authorization cannot fully proceed. Finally, the digital-content industry sometimes slows down to a crawl while waiting for the legal system and regulations to catch up with the times (Lin, 2007a).

Conclusion

The collection of the NPM consists of world-class Chinese cultural treasures, and its digitization is extremely beneficial to the functions of exhibition, education, research, management and publication. It is also important to protect and promote ancient art works with the help of technologies available today, the additional benefits being the enrichment of our cultural heritage and enhancement of economic development. Accordingly, the strategy of adopting

IT-enabled innovation into the NPM will have a great impact on both inside and outside of the museum walls. These endeavors, besides bringing major changes and opportunities to the museum, also carries unlimited difficulties and challenges.

In conclusion, it is evident that the definition and role of museums are changing. Rather than a mere archive of human cultural treasures, it is now a multi-purpose social-economical hybrid. We can also conclude that the trend of using technology in a museum context is inevitable and a must-use strategy to not only survive but also to excel in its competitive environment. In doing so, a museum needs cross-departmental and cross-institutional collaboration to compensate for its limitation of personnel and funding. In the meantime, we must emphasize that using technology in a museum context is not just a technical issue. It must be based on a holistic strategic plan and executed with a careful combination of art, technology, imagination, and creativity for optimal results.

The analysis and discussion of the NPM's efforts in digitization in this chapter illustrates the experiences, achievements, and potential that lie within the field of digitizing the museum industry. It is thus hoped that other museums in the process of or planning digitization will benefit the above discussion and learn from the many issues and challenges faced by the National Palace Museum.

References

Awards (no date). *Administration.* Available online at: http://www.npm.gov.tw/en/Article.aspx?sNo=02000043 [Last accessed on August 13th, 2013].

Brief Chronology (no date). *About the NPM.* Available online at: http://www.npm.gov.tw/en/Article.aspx?sNo=03001502 [Last accessed on August 13th, 2013].

Fung, MC and QP Lin (eds.) (2012). *A Special Report on the National Digital Archive Program of the National Palace Museum* (in Chinese). National Palace Museum, Taiwan.

Lai, TS and QP Lin (2006). The Development of "Digital Museum" and the Innovative Applications of e-Learning at the National Palace Museum.

World Scientific and Engineering Academy and Society (WSEAS) Transactions on Computers Research, 1(1), 37–44.

Lin, QP (2007a). An Overview of the Digital Projects of the National Palace Museum. *The National Palace Museum Monthly of Chinese Art*, No. 286, 112–124 (in Chinese).

Lin, QP (ed.) (2007b). *Fashionable NPM* (in Chinese). Digital Life, National Palace Museum, Taiwan.

List of Categories in the Collection (no date). *About the NPM*. Available online at: http://www.npm.gov.tw/en/Article.aspx?sNo=03001524 [Last accessed on August 13th, 2013].

Porter, ME (1980). *Competitive Strategy: Techniques for Analyzing Industries and Competitors*. New York: Free Press.

Sakamura, K (ed.) (2000). *Digital Museum 2000*. Japan: The University Museum, The University of Tokyo.

2

DESIGNING DIGITAL HERITAGE COMPETENCE CENTERS: A SWEDISH MODEL

Halina Gottlieb

Motivation

The need to bridge the gap between ICT research and cultural heritage is becoming increasingly important. Although, there has been a wealth of research and great technological advances in the field, relatively little investment in sharing resources between those involved, coordinating diverse efforts and cultivating the culture of competence centers has been made (Kanellou *et al.*, 2008). Our R&D work at the Interactive Institute Swedish ICT in Stockholm, between 1999–2010, has focused on the development of services that support the implementation of digital technology in the cultural heritage sector and knowledge transfer between active members (www.tii.se). This research is based on knowledge fields such as digital heritage, museum studies, interaction design and management, and innovation (Gottlieb, 2011).

When we began our work, there was limited exchange between existing fora and there was undue emphasis placed on technology. A few established, but isolated fora focused on broad issues and the implications of digital technology in the museum and heritage sector. A lack of collaboration between museums and related digital media environments was evident.

Furthermore, there was a general lack of knowledge in the museum community about the aesthetic, pedagogical and interpretative use of digital technologies. There was a lack of experience within the museum and heritage community regarding collaboration with external knowledge partners, as well as research and concept development partnerships. Therefore, it was important to instill curiosity among museum and heritage professionals in how to creatively use digital technologies in museum exhibitions, programs and interpretation, as well as the need to advocate the value of conference participation (Gottlieb, 2006).

In trying to bridge this gap, the center has identified several key areas. With the support of several foundations and EU grants, contributions from the Interactive Institute Swedish ICT, as well as time and materials offered by valued partners, the center has been able to develop over the years, conducting important research and development in the field of digital heritage (see Figure 1).

Designing Modes for Co-Creation and Collaboration

The Digital Heritage Center Sweden AB was a spin-off from the research studio Vision for Museums (1999) within the Interactive Institute Swedish ICT in 2010. It focused on development of new modes for interface and interpretation (Gottlieb and Simonsson, 2006; Beck and Cable, 2002, pg. 82–84; Gottlieb *et al.*, 2005; Black, 2005; Dewey, 1980; Laurel, 1993).

The Digital Heritage Center Sweden AB has grown both in scale and scope by establishing itself as an expertise center and expanding into Europe and beyond. Since its inception in 1999 and being renamed in 2007, the Digital Heritage Center Sweden AB has been drawing on experience from years of collaboration with a host of researchers, small and medium sized enterprises (SMEs), government agencies and organizations. Through a number of initiatives, the center has sculpted its mission to support the implementation of new technologies in cultural heritage (see Figure 2).

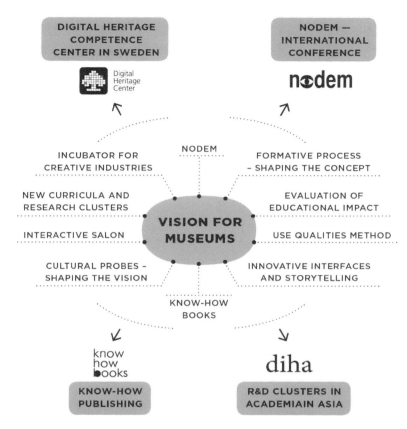

Figure 1.   © Halina Gottlieb. A Selection of R&D Activities at the Digital Heritage Center and Outcomes.

The center has served these goals through a variety of activities and initiatives, including multidisciplinary projects, the development of cross-disciplinary methodologies, by initiating specialized laboratories, an ambulating conference, research clusters, academic and vocational training, workshop publications, such as know-now books and research papers, by organizing and curating exhibitions, demonstrations and other outreach events.

Apart from our interest in developing models of technology for improving visitor interpretation of museums, considerable effort

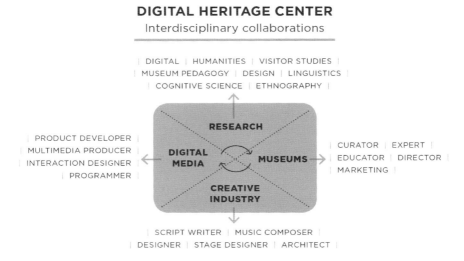

Figure 2. © Halina Gottlieb. Stakeholders in the digital heritage sector participating in activities initiated by the Digital Heritage Center.

has been put into introducing new practices for developing regional competences in the field, along with methods for training and assisting digital heritage participants in the transfer of new knowledge.

The center has started organizing workshops, interdisciplinary and international conferences, practical seminars, incubator programs as well as putting together academic and on-site courses, the publication of research studies, know-how books and new academic curricula such as "New Technologies and the Exhibitions" (2003–2005).

Collaboration of this type signifies exchange of specialized knowledge, practices and skills across various disciplines and sectors. What is more, the actual process of research and prototyping generates, besides end-use products, valuable know-how that needs to be continuously documented and systematized for the purpose of future applications in new projects, thus securing the growth of this young field.

Interactive Salon for Sharing know-How

In 2006/07, we initiated the *Interactive Salon,* a showroom for technologies that promotes and interprets cultural heritage. The *Interactive Salon* was a touring exhibition showcasing innovative technologies and concepts for communication with visitors in different museum environments (Gottlieb, 2006/2007). The project was the result of the collaboration between the Interactive Institute Swedish ICT AB, Stockholm City Museum and European Network of Excellence in Open Cultural Heritage (EPOCH) and received support from Culture of the Future, The Bank of Sweden Tercentenary Foundation and EPOCH. Various projects from European research institutes, universities, the creative industry and museums were invited to demonstrate how new technology and concepts can enhance the visitor experience, interpretation and communication in museums and similar environments.

These projects offered examples of the main types of digital media technologies that have been applied to museum environments. They demonstrated the broad spectrum of partnerships involved, including government authorities, SMEs, IT companies, foundations, museum content providers, heritage sites, media producers and research institutes.

The initiative was the first of its kind in Sweden and it created a forum for discussion about technologies that promote and preserve cultural heritage. Meetings, evaluations, scenario labs, seminars and workshops were organized during the exhibition in order to support cultural heritage institutions in their dialogue with other professionals working in the field. Also, the exhibition allowed the public to take part in ongoing research projects in the fields of ICT and cultural heritage.

Incubator Model for Supporting SMEs in Creative Industry

The Incubator program, the first of its kind, was primarily directed at companies within the creative industry (artists, designers, architects, media producers, etc.) that are in their startup phase. It was aimed at

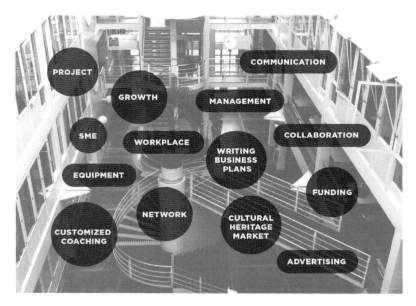

Figure 3.   © Halina Gottlieb. Framework for the Incubator Program.

promoting the use of digital media for cultural heritage purposes. The Incubator model included infrastructure resources, network support, individual coaching, as well as a host of training activities (see Figure 3).

Startup companies were offered a workspace two days per week. In this stimulating and supportive environment, surrounded by experts in cultural heritage, design, IT, and R&D, SMEs could grow and develop by directly participating in projects initiated by the center at the Interactive Institute Swedish ICT within its Incubator program, as well as in projects commissioned by third parties.

Through the Incubator, the SME had access to knowledge and a variety of skills, via entrepreneurs, decision makers in the field of culture, IT companies and venture capitalists. What is more, individual coaching, expertise in IT, business and advertising, was tailored to the specific needs of the SME. Startups within the Incubator regularly participated in lectures, workshops, and study visits.

The Incubator program aimed to help SMEs learn such skills as project management and coordination, business plan development, becoming proficient in communicating with customers and collaborating partners as well as developing extensive knowledge about the cultural heritage market. The Incubator model also acted as an instrument to facilitate the process of making an experimental prototype into a commercial product.

The first company to emerge from the Incubator was Evoking Spaces in 2006. The company specializes in designing audio-visual experiences for visitors at museums and other cultural heritage sites. Evoking Spaces was involved in the development of the Interactive Salon exhibition in Stockholm.

Touch of Kandinsky, Breathing Life into a Painting and *Old Masters Paintbrushes* were Evoking Spaces' commercial projects. Orders were placed for these projects by the Universal Forum of Cultures, the B.A.N.G. Exhibition at Planetarium ALFA in Monterrey, Mexico, 2008; the Papalote Children's Museum, Mexico City, Mexico in 2008; Stockholm City Museum, Sweden in 2008; and, the Science Centre in Singapore in 2009.

Practical Seminars — Bridging Research and Practice

During Museum week, 2002/03, in collaboration with the Swedish Arts Council (Kulturrådet), the center, then named "Vision for Museums", initiated a series of practical seminars for museums and other cultural and educational sites. The seminars focused on introducing to culture professionals and educators a new interdisciplinary field of visitor studies as a theoretical and practical tool for developing the communication of cultural content to audiences. A number of key international guests were invited to give lectures and provide practical training.

The topics discussed during the seminars focused on methods for getting access to visitor understanding and needs in the context of cultural experiences. A range of approaches was also suggested to be used in the preliminary, conceptual stage of planning an exhibition, approaches employed during the development of a prototype or program, as well as approaches aimed at the final assessment of a cultural product.

Designing and Deploying Research Methodologies

Over the years, the practical and conceptual approach endorsed within this framework encompassed Digital Heritage as the main field of R&D, as well as two other fields: Interaction Design and Museum Studies, all of which are of an interdisciplinary nature. This methodological framework gains knowledge through the process of designing, implementing and evaluating experimental prototypes in relevant environments and by involving relevant actors and end-users (see Figure 4).

Design-Oriented Research

Design-oriented research, commonly used in the field of Human Computer Interaction and Interaction Design, aims to develop novel applications of technology, styles of interaction and communication, and interface solutions. It also provides a framework which facilitates

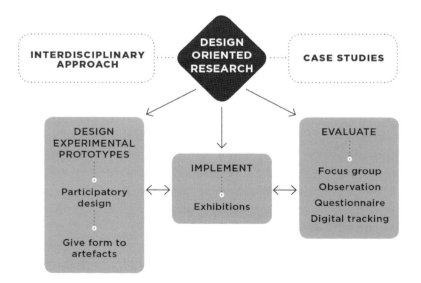

Figure 4. © Halina Gottlieb. An outline of the methodological framework used at the Digital Heritage Center/Interactive Institute Swedish ICT.

the exploration of possibilities and solutions outside current paradigms, including paradigms of style, technology or economic boundaries.

Zimmermann *et al.* (2007) identifies the following potential outcomes of a design-oriented approach:

- The creation of new interfaces or advancements of current solutions;
- The identification of gaps in existing models;
- The discovery of unanticipated effects;
- The creation of templates for bridging theory and practice (in terms of problem space, use context and users).

Living Lab

Originally built by Professor William J. Mitchell in 2003 with the aim of studying the interaction between people and new technologies in a living environment, the Living Lab model was later picked up by Nokia and the European Network of Living Labs (ENoLL) and adapted to their own research needs.

The Living Lab method brings together interdisciplinary experts from universities, businesses, research institutes, venture capital firms and intermediating organizations to test and co-create innovative products and services that respond to our changing world. This methodology was implemented at Vision for Museums at the begining of 2000 because, due to its interdisciplinary and pragmatic nature, the approach provides the perfect conditions to undertake integrative R&D operations. It also stimulates knowledge sharing and speeds up learning and real-life problem-solving processes (Gejer *et al.*, 2006; Westerlund and Leminen, 2012).

Cultural Probing Approach in Prototyping New Concepts for Museums

Nowadays, great emphasis is laid on creating customized experiences that take into consideration the visitor's identity as well as their interests, education, preferences, goals and needs. In this new context, cultural probes are indispensable from the very first stage of the project development, when the vision of the future exhibition begins to take shape (Gaver *et al.*, 1999).

Vision for Museums and Interactive Institute Swedish ICT came up with an innovative approach in 2001 that connected the cultural probing methodology used in design research with the front-end evaluation methodology used in museum studies. By integrating research tools from the field of interaction design and museum studies, valuable insights into visitor behavior, attitudes and motivation can be gained and, ultimately, incorporated into the development process before investing too many resources into a project. Cultural probing can be implemented through structured questionnaires, interviews, focus groups, workshops or with the help of digital tracking of behavior (Gottlieb, 2002).

This approach not only guarantees a good start to a planned exhibition, but it also opens up the possibility of dialog between museum staff and advisors which helps us to gather systematic knowledge about various target groups.

Visitor Study Lab

With the emergence of new paradigms in cultural heritage thinking, and according to the post-modern conception of museum design, everything in an exhibition should revolve around the visitor.

The Visitor Study Lab (1999–2000) has been created exclusively to assess visitor interaction patterns in exhibitions using digital, interpretive installations, their impact on the visitor experience, as well as knowledge acquisition. The lab contains digital tracking and digital recording equipment which can be installed in various cultural heritage environments.

Sociocultural Perspective 1999–2004

The greatest challenge remains to find an effective and accurate way of evaluating the educational impact of an exhibition and enabling knowledge acquisition. We pioneered an innovative methodology for evaluating the educational and cognitive impact of digital media in cultural heritage sites by integrating a sociocultural perspective with a multimodal approach inspired by social semiotics (in the process of assessing learning in the context of an interactive museum exhibition).

Adopting this approach means focusing on the dialog between the exhibited artifacts and visitors. Meaning is viewed as emerging multimodality from the interaction between the individual and contextual resources that surpasses traditional linguistic communication, adding elements such as text, photographs, images, animation, color, light, music, sound etc. Consequently, artifacts represent the mediating tools of inner transformation or learning (Gottlieb and Henningsson, 2004; Gottlieb *et al.*, 2005).

This approach can be put into practice by applying quantitative (questionnaires) and qualitative (focus groups, observation, interview) instruments. The data collected and analyzed by the Vision for Museums highlighted and confirmed the potential of digital artifacts and applications in mediating learning. Two important criteria must be satisfied in the assessment of the educational impact of digital prototypes: mastery and appropriation. More specifically, in order to verify whether the novel experience will have a lasting impact on knowledge acquisition, we need to test if visitors master the matter and see if they have appropriated the content, through a more complex processing of meaning that involves negotiation of previous knowledge, be it formal or informal, together with the new content provided by the exhibition.

Use Qualities Approach 2004–2012

Originally employed in the field of interaction design, the use qualities approach was also adopted by the Digital Heritage Center Sweden AB and the Interactive Institute Swedish ICT for the summative evaluation of digital exhibits in museums (Löwgren and Stolterman, 2004; Gottlieb, 2011). Such an approach can provide systematic access to the very intimate process of experiencing cultural content and measure how it relates to the visitors' own interests and everyday references, as well as to what extent it can provide a space for social action (Khaslavsky and Shedroff, 1999; Lundequist, 1995).

The most effective use qualities for engaging with interpretive content and intellectual accessibility are those that connect to a user's sense of motivation, for example, elements of playability, seductiveness, relevance and usefulness or transferability of use. The use qualities approach can be successfully implemented with the help of both quantitative (questionnaires, digital tracking) and quantitative methods (observation, focus groups, interviews), or a combination of both.

With a focus on interface and interpretative evaluation, the method identifies not only the properties of a digital prototype relevant in achieving the objective of improving visitor engagement, but also aspects that concern the degree of flexibility, fluency or autonomy of a given interface in the hands of visitors, as well as intuitiveness and accessibility. By using an integrated methodology that mixes focus on the visitor (as in museum studies) with focus on interaction modes and interfaces (as in human-computer interaction), we can see whether the exhibited collection has met its goal, whether it has any shortcomings and if any changes need to be made (see Figure 5).

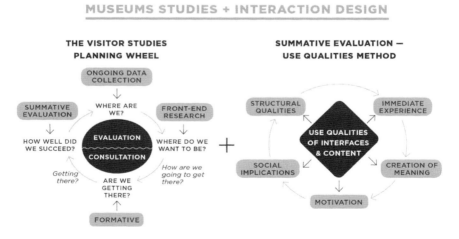

Figure 5. © Halina Gottlieb. Evaluation methodology which bridges museum studies with interaction design used between 2004–2012.

Sustainable Outcomes in Europe and Asia

The Digital Heritage Center Sweden AB has been devoted to supporting the use of new technology mainly in Scandinavia through activities that foster sustainable know-how transfer. However, there is a need for these activities to be more cost-effective to reach a wider range of people. The center has introduced numerous initiatives and participated in novel research on the development of digital interfaces and interpretative content that enhance visitor engagement.

Know-How Publications as Experiment in Knowledge Transfer
from Research to Practice

The center participated in facilitating training for leaders of competence centers run by the Centre for Research in Innovation Management (CENTRIM) at the University of Brighton. A group of senior researchers from CENTRIM led the Network of Expertise Centers at EPOCH 2006–2008. The EPOCH partnership provided the opportunity to develop the concept of know-how books, based on the scenarios idea introduced within the EPOCH program (see Figure 6). Know-how books bridge the gap between research findings and the practical aspects of professionals working in the cultural heritage sector. Using illustrations and step-by-step instructions, the books highlight functional information covering the design, development and implementation of ideas and their solutions, and give thoughtful suggestions for alternative applications within cultural heritage.

The Interactive Institute Swedish ICT's work behind the idea, content coordination, editing, design, publishing and promotion of the know-how books series gave us insight into how to improve future versions. There has been valuable feedback from cultural heritage professionals, who have commented on how much this sort of information is needed in the field.

The know-how book series will be continued in 2013–2014 with a new collection focusing on individual knowledge transfer between research and academia, cultural professionals and industry. The development of the new know-how books, which will function as

Figure 6.   Know-how books published in the context of EPOCH.

publications to introduce individual research results and creative industry solutions to museum professionals, is part of the knowledge transfer actions in the field of digital heritage of "The Nordic Knowledge Triangle" project, supported and funded by the Nordic Council of Ministers between 2011–2014.

Nordic Conference Forum (NODEM)

Like any other NODEM initiative, the Conference series promotes collaboration between scientists and cultural professionals, in order to stimulate new insights and innovative solutions. Each conference is centered on a core theme allowing participants to systematically contribute ideas and discuss issues aimed at consolidating the interdisciplinary grounds of employing digital technology in the field. The themes range from the discussion of more abstract and theoretical topics to very specific issues concerning the actual implementation of digital media in sites of cultural experience.

The NODEM Conference in 2012 explored Intangible Heritage, particularly in relation to cross-media and design issues. The City University of Hong Kong was chosen as the location to host this international encounter, considering the prominent position of intangible heritage in Asia in recent times, as well as the richness of topics and perspectives that Asian scholars could offer.

NODEM also functions as an interdisciplinary portal bringing together knowledge, know-how, best practices, innovations and insights that emerge in the context of such collaboration. This valuable repository is freely available at http://repo.nodem.org and will expand over time. It is envisaged as the virtual meeting place of researchers, SMEs, artists and cultural professionals from all over the world, providing an interface between cutting-edge research in the field of digital technologies, arts and education.

Digital Intangible Heritage of Asia (DIHA) — Research Cluster in Asia

In 2009, the center developed an embryonic research cluster at Nanyang Technological University (NTU) in Singapore as a result of the collaboration between the Institute for Media Innovation (IMI), Professor Martin Reiser and the School of Humanities and Social Science (HSS), Nanyang Technological University, Singapore, Dr. Bee Chin Ng and Dr. Francesco Cavallaro. The focus of the research cluster was to connect intangible and tangible heritage through digital media and become an Asian center which actively works with centers in Europe. The aim is to bring together students and senior researchers with those associated with the digital heritage sector outside of academia.

DIHA was developed as a thematic research cluster with the aim to encourage interdisciplinary collaboration and knowledge exchange in the field of intangible cultural heritage by strengthening connections between cutting-edge research, new curricula within academia, and society (http://diha.ntu.edu.sg).

The research cluster is supported by an extensive network of relevant actors in Europe and South-Asia-Pacific, including researchers, SMEs, government agencies, academia, museums, science centers, artists, designers and creators, regional and national heritage boards, libraries and other memory institutions (Ng *et al.*, 2011).

The projects promoted by DIHA always unfold collaboratively, as an interdisciplinary process that connects ICT, cultural heritage, R&D and the Creative Industries. Such teamwork is governed by principles of flexibility and tolerance, and by the view that members of the teamwork are, first and foremost, investigators involved in a long-term and collaborative work process, rather than being experts in their respective fields.

The future vision of DIHA is to build frameworks for digital cultural heritage projects and engage interest groups at NTU, arrange collaborative workshops at NTU for researchers and students, identify new possibilities and partners in Singapore within cultural heritage and ICT, and Creative Industries, and establish collaboration and participation in European Union programs.

Future Growth Ambitions

In the upcoming years, the goal is to expand and refine the model of an international competence center and to build bridges between partners with similar initiatives. Building sustainable competence centers, which include a wide network of cultural heritage institutions, ICT organizations, SMEs, researchers, foundations and government bodies, is vital for a thriving digital cultural heritage. This can be achieved by nurturing long-term collaboration between already existing centers and initiatives in order to avoid fragmentation of knowledge and duplication of existing ideas. It is important to generate common resources in order to create a dynamic European knowledge-sharing network of competence centers.

We will continue to develop the interdisciplinary and cross-sector approach employed so far. Its methodological and theoretical framework will be augmented by making use of related fields such as cognitive and affective sciences, as well as cognitive semiotics, a newer discipline dedicated to extending a thorough understanding of meaning-making processes. One area of study that will receive particular attention is intangible cultural heritage. Our ambition is to investigate several components of intangible cultural heritage from a variety of perspectives.

We will also continue to support the process of knowledge exchange and transfer in the field of digital heritage, by developing a flexible transfer system that will be customized to suit the specific needs, ambitions and requirements of all of those involved in the field. The Digital Heritage Center Sweden AB will do its utmost to share and transfer the experiences accumulated over a decade of laboratory work and prototyping in the field. We will focus primarily on museum design and on providing a framework for interpretive content for new museums.

At present, we hope that our competence center will make a truly useful contribution to the field of Digital Heritage, and will provide a resource and inspiration for future practitioners and researchers in this exciting, emerging field which is still looking for its own individual identity.

References

Beck, L, and T Cable (2002). *The Interpretation for the 21st Century: Fifteen Guiding Principles for Interpreting Nature and Culture.* Urbana, IL: Sagamore Publishing.

Black, G (2005). *The Engaging Museum: Developing Museums for Visitors Involvement.* London: Routledge.

Dewey, J (1980). *Art as Experience.* New York: Perigee.

Gaver, W, A Dunne and E Pacenti (1999). Cultural Probes. *Interactions,* 6(1), 21–29.

Geijer, L, E Insulander and H Gottlieb (2006). *It Felt as if One was There — Visitor Response to an Interactive Museum Exhibition as an Example of Learning in Informal Settings.* Danish Research Centre on Education and Advanced Media Materials (DREAM) Conference 2006, Odense, Denmark. September 21st–September 23rd, 2006.

Gottlieb, H (2006/2007). *Interactive Salon 2006/7 Catalogue.* Stockholm: Interactive Institute.

Gottlieb, H (2006). *Visitor Focus in 21st Century Museums.* Stockholm: Interactive Institute.

Gottlieb, H (2011). *Designing Engagement for Art: Exploring Interfaces and Interpretive Content of Digital Heritage Artifacts in Museum Environments.* PhD Dissertation, University College Dublin, Ireland.

Gottlieb, H and P Henningsson (2004). *Digitala medier för besökare på museer.* Stockholm: Dramatiska Institutet.

Gottlieb, H and H Simonsson (2006). Designing Narrative and Interpretative Tools. *Engage,* 18.

Gottlieb, H, H Simonsson, L Gävert-Asplund and S Lindberg (2005). Audio Guides in Disguise: Introducing Natural Science for Girls. *Re-thinking Technology for Museums Workshop.* 15 June. University of Limerick, Ireland.

Gottlieb, H (2002). *Digitala medier i besökarens tjänst. Rapport från seminarium.* Visions for Museums. Stockholm: Interactive Institute.

Gottlieb, H, H Simonsson and H Öjmyr (2005). Virtual Touch of a Sculpture. *2005 Electronic Visualisation and the Arts Conference,* 27–29 July. London.

Kanellou, D, A Grantham, K Rodríguez Echavarria, H Gottlieb and D Pletinckx (2008). Bridging the Knowledge Gap between Cultural Heritage and Information and Communication Technologies Professionals: The Network of Expertise. In Posluschny, A, K Lambers and I Herzog (eds.), *Layers of Perception: Proceedings of the 35th International Conference on Computer Applications and Quantitative Methods in Archaeology* (CAA), Berlin, Germany. April 2nd–April 6th, 2007.

Khaslavsky, J and Shedroff, N (1999). Understanding the Seductive Experience. *Communications of the ACM,* 42(5), 45–49.

Laurel, B (1993). *Computers as Theatre.* Wokingham, UK: Addison-Wesley.

Löwgren, J and E Stolterman (2004). *Thoughtful Interaction Design — A Design Perspective on Information Technology.* Cambridge, MA: MIT Press.

Lundequist, J (1995). *Design och produktutveckling: Metoder och begrepp.* Lund, Sweden: Studentlitteratur.

Ng, BC, F Galli and H Gottlieb (2011). Asian Heros in Cultural Heritage Context: An interactive installation for children combining language and mythology. *Re-thinking Technology in Museums 2011,* 26–27 May. University of Limerick, Ireland. Available online at: http://www.idc.ul.ie/techmuseums11/paper/paper11.pdf

Westerlund, M and S Leminen (2012) Editorial: Living Labs, *Technology Management Review*. Available online at: http://timreview.ca/issue/2012/september [Last accessed on June 20th, 2013].

Zimmerman, J, J Forlizzi and S Evenson (2007). Research Through Design as a Method for Interaction Design Research in HCI. *Proceedings of the SIGCHI Conference on Human Factors in Computing Systems*. San Jose, California, USA. April 28–May 03, 2007. New York: ACM.

3

7 LESSONS LEARNED FOR DIGITAL CULTURE

Christine Kuan

The digital landscape has changed radically in the past decade, and so has institutional thinking about the Web. As recently as the 1990s, museums were terrified of other websites *linking* to their websites without their express permission. Some cultural institutions and libraries were apprehensively putting thumbnail images of their works online — for reference only (certainly not for reuse or publication). When websites started making high-resolution images available online, many cultural heritage institutions saw this as a foray into dangerous territory and took all possible measures to lock down and "protect" their digital assets. Fast forward to now, and many museums are giving away high-resolution TIFF files as part of their newly minted open access policy.[1] In a slow but certain sea change, museums today are aggressively vying for visibility and users on the Web through as many channels as they can possibly manage — Facebook, Twitter, Pinterest, YouTube, Google Art Project, Flickr, Weibo, Tumblr, and others.[2]

---

[1] National Gallery of Art, Washington, DC; Walter Art Museum; Yale University Art Gallery; Los Angeles County Museum of Art; Rijksmuseum; Library of Congress. See also, Siegal (2013).
[2] Small museums like the Andy Warhol Museum have more than 625,000 Twitter followers.

Schooled in the history of art and the spirit of avant-garde, I am always game for breaking new ground and challenging the status quo. In summer of 2012, I left my position as Chief Curatorial Officer and Vice President of External Affairs at ARTstor (artstor. org), a nonprofit digital image library founded by The Andrew W. Mellon Foundation, and joined Artsy (artsy.net).[3] Artsy is a startup technology company that, at the time, had not yet launched its website to the public. After more than a decade of working at prestigious not-for-profit cultural institutions — The Metropolitan Museum of Art, Oxford University Press, and ARTstor — I gave up what some might consider to be one of the most rewarding jobs in the cultural sector to work in a startup that could fail at any moment. Why? Because it was a once-in-a-lifetime chance to create a new online experience for art.

Just as the Internet has disrupted our concepts and experiences of music, shopping, dating, research, publishing, TV, and communication (to name a few), the art world is also ripe for disruption. Artsy's mission is to make all of the world's art accessible to anyone with an Internet connection. With The Art Genome Project[4] and the latest advances in engineering and user experience design, Artsy is attempting to provide a library of images, a social media blogging platform, and an e-commerce and auction service all via one free website. By bringing together content from museums, galleries, foundations, and artists' estates, Artsy is erasing the boundaries we have long upheld in the analog realm. In reality, however, these boundaries evaporated when the Internet was invented.[5]

---

[3] In its early days, ARTstor was also considered a radical concept by daring to put up high-resolution images for teaching and research.

[4] The Art Genome Project is a way of providing pathways for discovering collections. Each "gene" has a value of 0 to 100 and enables terms like Abstract Expressionism, City Life, Splattered/Dripped, Food, Landscape, Bright/Vivid to have various values to enable sophisticated relevancy ranking in search results.

[5] All Internet browsers automatically search across commercial and non-commercial websites. Google Image search and other for-profit technology platforms already deliver search results from nonprofit and for-profit sources on the same web page. Museums already use Facebook, Twitter, Pinterest, and other for-profit platforms to promote their exhibitions, programs, and collections.

While working at The Metropolitan Museum of Art during the directorship of Philippe de Montebello, I absorbed his unwavering commitment to excellence in terms of art historical scholarship, building encyclopedic collections, and serving the public. These lessons from the Met have shaped all my subsequent thinking, whether as Editor-in-Chief of Grove Art Online, Chief Curatorial Officer at ARTstor, or Chief Curator at Artsy. For over a decade, I have worked across international borders with hundreds of museum and gallery directors, administrators, marketing experts, technologists, curators, artists, educators, scholars, students, librarians, publishers, and others — some in their 80s and some in their teens. This chapter is not a scientific study or a list of required reading (there are plenty of those out there), but it is a list of a few things that I have learned along the way that might be helpful in thinking through some of the challenges facing all of us as we strive to disseminate our collections, reach new audiences, and impact the future of digital culture.

1. Curation Is the New Black[6]

Don't Digitize Everything Plus the Kitchen Sink

When you are deeply knowledgeable and passionate about your collection, you will wish to digitize everything because you want the entire collection to be digitally preserved. I have worked with many museums, libraries, and archives that have insisted on digitizing all the objects, transparencies, folders, scraps of paper, notebooks, etc. Aside from the staggering costs of such a gargantuan undertaking, there are two additional considerations that are too important to be overlooked — time and user experience. Even if you have all the money in the world to digitize absolutely everything A to Z, for the first few years you will undoubtedly only get through a small fraction of your collection. This initial set of digitized content may make little sense if published to the Web (e.g., all the contents in folders A to C).

When undertaking a multi-year digitization project in this way, you and your team may not see meaningful results for a very long

---

[6] Oates, G (2010) as quoted in Cope (2010).

time and that can be very frustrating for your board, your staff, and you. Then, let us suppose you do successfully digitize everything and you are able to publish all of these materials online. There is also the daunting challenge of enabling users to navigate and make use of this digital content, which may require incredibly sophisticated interaction design and engineering. Instead, I would recommend a short-term strategy of curating highlights from your collection to be digitized at high quality and published as soon as possible. There should also be a long-term strategy of tackling subsequent groups of high priority collections. This two-pronged approach allows for your institution to see immediate results while working toward the long-term goal of a more comprehensive digital collection on the Web.

2. Design, Design, and Design!

Technology Is Not Enough; UX Is Critical to User Engagement

Recently, I attended a digital culture conference in Europe and one of the leads of a major digital culture initiative said that they are not concerned about user experience (UX) but only concerned with serving up their data to the public. When I relayed this information to Artsy's Head of Design, Robert Lenne, he said, "That's like saying, we'll just take you to the storage room and you can look at the art there!" Institutions must recognize that increasingly the "public face" of the institution and the visitors' first (or only) experience of its collections may very well be its Web presence rather than its physical spaces.

Placing strong emphasis on UX and allocating adequate resources to website design and user experience should be just as important as how you prioritize exhibition design and onsite visitor experience. While some institutions might feel that the Web is peripheral to their core activities, the Web is, in fact, central to the public's experience of your institution. Don't let internal departmental politics muddle your UX design. Focus on the end-user religiously. Allow experts in this area to lead the way so that you don't wind up with a website that only your human resources director can navigate!

3. A Picture Is Worth 1,000 Words

Without Useful Metadata, Digital Content Has Little Value

I cannot count the number of times I have met with artists, photographers, archivists, curators, and museum staff who said that they have thousands of beautiful images to share but none of them are cataloged. Invariably, I am shown dozens of boxes with the assurance that it will be a piece of cake to look up the information in books or, even better, that they can easily recall the information and write it down for me. Regretfully, this enthusiasm does not make for a scalable method of sharing digital collections. Not only is it critical to create high-quality image files in an organized way (for example, filenames should be numerical without any metadata in the filename), it is equally essential to have corresponding metadata in a fielded electronic format (such as Excel, XML, CSV, etc.), which is critical to your collections being discoverable on the network.[7]

In addition, it is increasingly important to capture more than just tombstone metadata (Creator Name, Title, Date, Medium, Dimensions, Rights Information,[8] etc.). If you are also able to capture descriptive information for your objects (such as wall text, educational information, conservation history, or curatorial commentary), it will allow you to share and reuse rich and engaging contextual information with the public, researchers, marketing, and others. Metadata creation is the most labor-intensive and expensive aspect of digitizing cultural materials and many projects are experimenting with crowdsourcing metadata, including the Steve project and the very successful BBC Your Paintings project, which has over 8,000 individuals tagging

---

[7] Linked Data is the hot topic of the moment, but this requires a separate in-depth discussion of metadata sharing. There are numerous Web resources on this topic, for starters see: http://linkeddata.org/

[8] Digital rights management is a whole separate topic and navigating the challenges of distributing copyrighted content on the Web requires a separate work. There are numerous studies and guides for dealing with copyright, including the College Art Association Intellectual Property resources: http://www.collegeart.org/ip/

artworks in UK public collections.[9] There is already substantial data proving that crowd-sourced data are nearly as accurate and as useful as data generated by expert catalogers.[10]

4. Think Sustainability

Infrastructure Is Critical to the Longevity of Digital Heritage

One of the most wonderful aspects of digital content is its potential to be reused and repurposed. Too often, cultural institutions plan for a single exhibition catalog, one-time use wall labels, new photography for a single project, etc. without implementing the infrastructure to capture this digital content for future use. I have also worked with mega-institutions that have invested millions in digitization and archiving only to have tossed out their post-production image files to save on storage space. These institutions were short-sighted in thinking that standards for images on the Web would remain static. They archived their raw files and tossed out the high-resolution post-production files after they had created low-resolution derivative files for their website. A few years later, high-resolution, zoomable image files have become the new normal; and many institutions now give away their high-resolution post-production files for free as part of their institutional mandate to serve the public.[11]

The cost to re-crop and redo post-production work on hundreds of thousands of raw image files is far more exorbitant and time-consuming than it would have been to simply store the post-production files. Whether for marketing, publication, commercial use, or content partnerships, institutions should anticipate that digital standards will change and, thus, avoid creating circumstances where the institution will have to recreate high-quality digital content. The management of your digital content is critical to your institution's

---

[9] steve. museum The Social Tagging Project: http://www.steve.museum/ and BBC Your Paintings: http://www.bbc.co.uk/arts/yourpaintings/

[10] See Galaxy Zoo project, which has successfully trained more than 150,000 people to classify astronomical details in images: http://www.galaxyzoo.org/

[11] Not to mention the fact that with gigapixel images and other imaging technology, digital images have already surpassed "print-quality" images.

ability to disseminate and repurpose that content for future exhibitions, publications, multi-media, and special projects. The savings over the long run will more than pay for the effort and it will benefit your institution in terms of press, marketing, and communications as well because you will have more digital content at your disposal.

Both a content management system (CMS) and a digital asset management system (DAMS) are necessary for ensuring that the work of creating digital collections will not result in merely a one-time-only use, and this infrastructure can guarantee that you will have provided a long-term trajectory for all your digital assets. It is also critical to have the editorial tools to modify your content on the front end and back end. If everything your team delivers requires a hack or a last minute duct-tape job, you will burn through a lot of expensive efforts and irritate your staff who will have to redo a lot of painstaking work. Always plan for infrastructure and tools for the long-term management of your digital content. Do not treat digital media like you are working with papyrus — those days are over! Take advantage of the digital medium — maximize its potential for education, research, marketing, and fundraising.

5. Do Not Turn Your Collections into Fossils

Locking Up Your Digital Content Will Ossify Your Institution

A core mission of any cultural institution is to properly steward its physical collections — to protect, preserve, and conserve objects. Understandably, many institutions have transferred this protectionist philosophy to their digital strategy. It is important to recognize that making the digital versions of your collections discoverable to the public and to researchers online is a fundamental part of fostering long-term interest in and ongoing engagement with your collections. Do not allow the mirage of money, or image licensing, to prevent you from taking full advantage of the Web for promoting your exhibitions, collections, and programs and engaging with the public. Studies have shown (Tanner, 2004) that the net income from image licensing is, in general, nominal (with a few exceptions). Digital media offer wonderful tools for reaching new donors, younger audiences, scholars, and people who may not have been familiar with your collection before.

As James Cuno, President and CEO of The J. Paul Getty Trust, has written, "Acquiring, preserving, and providing access to works of art is the basis for an art museum's contract with the public and the foundation of the trust that authorizes that contract" (Cuno, 2006, pg. 52). Enabling online access to your collections on the Web allows for your institution to remain vibrant and relevant — which is obviously important for sustaining the core activity of stewarding your collections well into the future. Many institutions that have kept their collections under wraps have not only lost visibility and relevance among the public, but have also become invisible among their peers. In a recent conversation with a German art museum director, he said that he was guiding some art historians through his collections and the art historians were stunned that they have never seen most of the objects before. Needless to say, the museum is pouring a great deal of effort into digitizing the collection and making it accessible online. Don't allow your museum to morph into a mausoleum — use new technology to keep your institution and your collections alive.

6. Make New Friends, But Keep the Old

Social Media is Here to Stay

As the old Girl Scout song goes, "Make new friends, but keep the old. One is silver and the other is gold." The traditional means of making friends through events, mailings, lectures, memberships, and so on continue to serve institutions extremely well. Now social media platforms enable you to make thousands, if not millions, of new friends who can learn about your exhibitions, collections, and programs no matter whether they are down the street or halfway around the world in a yurt. Social media is shockingly powerful — it changes governments; it changes lives. This is communications on steroids, and most importantly, it is fundamental to the way people under 25 engage with each other and with culture. Being able to share, discuss, and interact with digital content is a way that people connect. Empowering your institution to take part in the conversation is a way of fostering continued dialogue between your institution and the public.

So many institutions have only one person or an intern dedicated to social media, and no other staff are on social media channels. There is a whole other world out there that is important and relevant. It is not going away, and saying social media is not for your institution is like saying the radio or the telephone is not for your institution. I recently worked with one of the executors of a powerful artist's estate who was keen to partner with Artsy but faced opposition from his colleagues because of the potential problem of people sharing the artist's works on social media and other outlets. As the executor explained, "No, you do not understand. The problem is if people *do not* share her works. We *want* people to want to see her work. That is the mission of the Foundation, to promote her legacy." In the end, this point of view prevailed and the estate signed the agreement.

7. Nothing is Forever

Iterative Technology Development is Efficient, and Perhaps, Unavoidable

Jean Monnet, the founding father of the European Union, once said, "Nothing is possible without individuals. Nothing is lasting without institutions." Individuals instigate new technologies: some technology lasts and some technology dies, but all of it changes. In some ways, digital media is the antithesis of the institution and of the very intent of cultural heritage. Institutions are designed to stand the test of time and thus, create multi-year digital strategies and assemble large task forces to oversee digital technology with the same intent. Unfortunately, technology changes far too rapidly for any plan to fully anticipate all of your institutional needs. Case in point, Pinterest (pinterest.com) launched in March 2010, and it is now standard for websites to have Pinterest buttons (just like Facebook, Twitter, or Tumblr, buttons among others). Even if you did not plan for it five years ago, too bad, users are still demanding it.[12] We also could not

---

[12] As of January 2014, Pinterest had over 70 million users.

have known just a few years ago how dominant mobile technology would become, but now we live and breathe by our smartphones.

It is highly likely that months after you have launched your website, blog, mobile app, CMS or DAMS, it will be time to maintain it, upgrade it, evolve it, or maybe even trash it and start over because you realize your institution now needs something entirely different. I have worked with several major museums that within two years of having implemented their expensive DAMS had determined that they needed a total overhaul and planned to adopt a new system. I have also worked with smaller institutions that have been plodding along with simple Filemaker databases or Excel spreadsheets for collections management and are now able to implement affordable new Web-based solutions that are low maintenance and low cost.

Monumental digital projects are heavy investments and colossally difficult to tweak if circumstances should change — and they will change. It is also important to note that while some see open source engineering as a cost-saving solution, very few institutions have the engineering expertise to customize open source code for their institution.[13] Today, technology companies emphasize "agile development" — that is, constant iteration on smaller pieces of the technology and frequently assessing progress and reevaluating priorities. It is more cost-effective, but it is also a luxury few institutions have unless they have a team of talented developers and designers under their roof. If you do not have the means to work in this way on your technology projects, you should be simply be wary of extra expensive, long-term technology projects because it is certain that digital technology in year five will look nothing like it did when you embarked on the adventure.

Institutions should consider utilizing free platforms and tools where it makes sense for the organization, and focusing on technology efforts that deliver the most bang for the buck. Plan your core infrastructure carefully so that you will have full control and the tools to manage your digital assets safely and securely, but assess

---

[13] Open source code also comes with a numerous intellectual property issues which your institutional counsel should review very carefully before incorporating any open source code.

your options based on your own institutional needs (do not simply copy the decisions of the wealthiest institutions; they do not always know best). Once we accept that digital technology does not promise forever, only the immediate future, it is easier to identify priorities and the technologies that are the best fit for your institution.

Conclusion

Finally, impact is the ultimate measure of our efforts. Think twice about investing in projects that are intended to serve a handful of scholars in an obscure area of interest. Digital culture is of rising importance and will dominate the future of our institutions, our communities, and global arts exchange. The digital technology we have at our fingertips is so sophisticated and user-friendly that we are all capable of being content creators and our institutions can easily participate in cultural dialogues taking place all over the Web. Engaging international users, serving students, scholars, and educators, and fostering future interest in your collections is critical to the longevity and relevance of your institution, collections, and mission. Digital technology should not be thought of as a burden; but rather, as a powerful extension of your organization. Now is the time to share the wealth of your digital content with the world. Enjoy this remarkable privilege and opportunity.

References

Cope, AS (2010). Buckets and Vessels. In J Trant and D Bearman (eds.) *Museums and the Web 2010: Proceedings.* Toronto: Archives & Museum Informatics. Available online at: http://www.archimuse.com/mw2010/papers/cope/cope.html

Cuno, J (ed.) (2006). *Whose Muse? Art Museums and the Public Trust.* USA: Princeton University Press.

Oates, G (2010). They're Watching You, with Heather Champ and George Oates. Tummelvision, January 29th, 2010. http://tummelvision.tv/2010/01/29/tummel-vision-episode-3-wheather-champ-and-george-oates-theyre-watching-you/

Siegal, N (2013). Masterworks for One and All. *New York Times*, May 28th, 2013. Available online at: http://www.nytimes.com/2013/05/29/arts/ design/museums-mull-public-use-of-online-art-images.html?_r=0 [Last accessed:

Tanner, S (2004). *Reproduction Charging Models and Rights Policy for Digital Images in American Art Museums.* Available online at: http://www.kdcs. kcl.ac.uk/fileadmin/documents/USMuseum_SimonTanner.pdf [Last accessed on].

PART 2
APPLICATIONS AND SERVICES

4

REINVENTING MoMA's EDUCATION PROGRAMS FOR THE 21st CENTURY VISITOR

Jackie Armstrong, Deborah Howes, and Wendy Woon

> MoMA is dedicated to the conversation between the past and the present, the established and the experimental. Our mission is helping you understand and enjoy the art of our time.[1]

When The Museum of Modern Art (MoMA) was founded in 1929, the first director, Alfred H. Barr, Jr., conceived of the fledgling museum as a "laboratory" for experimentation with art exhibitions and pedagogy. The very premise of modern and contemporary art, design, film, and architecture is to question — to disrupt and push the boundaries of tradition. This pioneering spirit of curiosity and debate has fueled our re-envisioning of MoMA Educational programs, and digital technologies have enabled us to engage publics with art, ideas, and cultural experiences that are complementary with the way people all around the world communicate and learn in this digital age. MoMA's Department of Education has re-embraced experimentation, informed by research and iterative design, in order to move beyond traditional educational

---

[1] About MoMA (2013).

formats drawn from primary, secondary, and higher-education models and to serve people of all ages and abilities over a lifetime.

MoMA's educators[2] are not alone in this evolution of museum education from a didactic to a more facilitative role. Museums and cultural heritage sites worldwide are developing more responsive and innovative education methods that empower visitors to challenge assumptions and inspire creative thinking that can be models for, or complements to, formal education. For example, the 200-plus member institutions of The International Coalition of Sites of Conscience[3] create programs that "engage the public in connecting the past and present in order to envision and shape a more just and humane future." Visitors to the Lower East Side Tenement Museum[4] in New York City, a founding member of ICSC, participate in group discovery and conversation about the daily life of immigrants in

---

[2] The Museum of Modern Art's Department of Education, under the leadership of Wendy Woon, The Edward John Noble Foundation Deputy Director for Education, consists of the following staff members, all of whom are instrumental to the programs described herein: Jackie Armstrong, Emily Fischer Landau Fellow; Jessica Baldenhofer, Associate Educator, School Visits; Laura Beiles, Assistant Director, Adult Programs; Sara Bodinson, Director, Interpretation & Research; Susannah Brown, Associate Educator, Courses and Seminars; Francis Estrada, Assistant Educator, School Visits; Cari Frisch, Associate Educator, Family Programs; Deborah Howes, Director, Digital Learning; Pablo Helguera, Director, Adult and Academic Programs; Laurel Humble, Assistant Educator, The Alzheimer's Project; Sarah Kennedy, Associate Educator, Lab Programs; Maren Lankford, Assistant to the Deputy Director; Mary Malaythong, Department Manager; Elizabeth Margulies, Assistant Director, Family Programs; Lisa Mazzola, Assistant Director, School & Teacher Programs; Carrie McGee, Associate Educator, Community & Access Programs; Stephanie Pau, Associate Educator, Interpretation & Research; Sheetal Prajapati, Assistant Director, Learning and Artists Initiatives; Francesca Rosenberg, Director, Community, Access, and School Programs; Lara Schweller, Coordinator, Community & Access Programs; Meryl Schwartz, Assistant Educator, The Alzheimer's Project; Allegra Smith, Assistant Educator, Digital Learning; Madeleine Witenberg, Coordinator, Education Administration; Wendy Woon, Deputy Director for Education; and Calder Zwicky, Associate Educator, Teen & Community Programs.
[3] About Us (2012).
[4] The Lower East Side Tenement Museum website can be found at: http://www. tenement.org

19th- and early 20th-century New York City and then take part in open discussion about whether the economic and social realities of immigrant workers have improved. In order to succeed in this style of unscripted and interactive programming, educators develop skills in engaging people through dialogue, respecting cultural exchange, and personalizing learning experiences. In her book *The Social Work of Museums* (Silverman, 2010), museum educator and scholar Lois Silverman documents many such museum programs that serve as catalysts for social change and personal growth. As Silverman (2010, pg. 16) explains, "[…] by making meaning of objects, people in museums are actually developing — and sometimes even changing — meanings and aspects of themselves, their relationships, and the society in which they live."

Museum Education as a Creative Process, Informed by Research

When applying these and other innovative teaching methods to learning about art in a museum context, MoMA's educators see themselves as "cultural producers" or "co-creators." We work with people (visitors as well as artists) and environments and technologies to create new methods of engagement and meaning that are relevant to today and ready to evolve with the future. Because MoMA's collection embodies and exemplifies provocation and creative thinking, MoMA's educators embrace that spirit of innovation and play a dynamic role in designing learning experiences that are open-ended and process-oriented. The musician Brian Eno (1996) captures the inspiration for this new role when he writes:

> Stop thinking about art works as objects, and start thinking about them as triggers for experiences. (Roy Ascott's phrase.) That solves a lot of problems: we do not have to argue whether photographs are art, or whether performances are art … because we say, "Art is something that happens, a process, not a quality, and all sorts of things can make it happen."

This chapter will illustrate that when MoMA invites visitors into a creative process, it offers a learning experience that not only mirrors artistic process but also encompasses a variety of learning modalities, such as listening, sharing, making, comparing, and critiquing.

Another signature influence in the evolution of MoMA's educational programs is the importance of research. Many new program ideas are informed by studies on neuroscience and memory processing. Howard Gardner (2011), the John H. and Elisabeth A. Hobbs Professor of Cognition and Education at the Harvard Graduate School of Education and the developmental psychologist who pioneered the landmark Theory of Multiple Intelligences, as well as a Member of MoMA's Board of Trustees and Trustee Committee on Education, encourages educators to broaden the Museum's learning experiences in order to reach a diverse public in a more effective way. Today, educators must take into account not just visitors' developmental stage or preferences, but also their motivations, interests, and settings. Museum researchers John H. Falk and Lynn D. Dierking theorize that a museum experience is multifaceted and constructed from overlapping sociocultural, personal, and physical contexts, which evolve in a fourth dimension, over time. Falk and Dierking's (2013) extensive visitor research on the impact of motivating factors shaping museum experiences has been influential to MoMA's educators as they develop programs and resources.

For example, because museums are social spaces, MoMA educators create programs and environments that allow people to learn from one another. These new models of "peer-to-peer" learning often occur among participants of different ages and abilities and even evolve into enduring communities of learners that meet locally or globally online. At the same time, there is an increasing interest in the use of play as a strategy for engagement. This is a common approach for artists such as Marcel Duchamp and the Dadaists and Surrealists in the first half of the twentieth century who were interested in games of chance and exchange, as well as for artists today working in social practices and digital games. Cognitive science confirms that short-term memories become long term when combined with an unexpected element, like surprise (Pink, 2009). As a result, MoMA's educators are incorporating serendipity, playfulness, and social interaction into their program designs.

With the mindset of the "laboratory," we have woven prototyping, testing, and innovating into our practice, involving both staff and visitors in the process. Agile evaluation plays a key role in our understanding of how to foster productive gallery learning behaviors such as closer looking, social engagement, critical thinking, meaningful revelations, documenting, sharing, and building community. Having a full-time, dedicated evaluation fellow in the Department of Education who collects both quantitative and qualitative data helps inform the decision-making to support these goals in quick iterations. Over the past six years we have collected a prodigious body of knowledge about our visitors, information used not only for gaining insight into past successes and failures and making improvements, but also for predicting our visitors' responses to new programs or initiatives. Our growing dependence on continual program assessment reminds us that there is always room for improvement and that no program or installation is really ever complete. This perpetual self-assessment is also necessary in a world of seemingly rapid and constant change: Like our participants, we must grow as they grow to continue to be relevant.

The Digital Role in Museum Learning

The kind of learning that will define the twenty-first century is not taking place in the classroom — at least not in today's classroom. Rather it is happening all around us, and it is powerful. We call this phenomenon the new culture of learning (Thomas and Brown, 2001, pg. 17).

Esteemed educators Douglas Thomas and John Seely Brown provide a view of 21st century learning opportunities that is optimistic and in sync with MoMA's approach, not only because of the evolution of digital technology, but also because of our more expansive thinking about how learning can take place (Thomas and Brown, 2001). As images of our collections become available online and information can be sought out from multiple sources by an increasingly digital native public, we must ask ourselves: Why are museums relevant? What types of cultural experiences will people want inside the walls of the museum? What makes a satisfying museum learning experience on the web? The possible answers to these questions are varied and numerous: Educators with typically limited resources must make strategic decisions about when and where digital tools can optimize their success.

An approach that MoMA has found useful (reflected in the experiments described below) is to prioritize two criteria:

1. The trajectory of lifelong learning: We continually develop learning opportunities appropriate to needs of participants as they evolve from child to senior, and we strive to make these experiences accessible; and
2. The opportunity to inspire and enhance art experiences: These include providing behind-the-scenes expertise, fostering dialog with MoMA staff, supporting creative activities, and designing engaging, relevant, and easy-to-use resources of information with built-in opportunities for dialogue and social exchange.

Traditional notions of museum content authority are broadening to recognize and value the experience and knowledge visitors of all kinds bring with them. Personalization of learning experiences, when enabled by digital technologies, allows us to incorporate this information exchange among museum staff and visitors in elegant and productive ways. Harnessing the power of digital tools (such as apps, blogs, videos, webinars, and/or social media sites), we can build wide and varied communication networks and then populate them with well-framed ideas geared to inspire meaningful and authentic exchanges.

Three Experiments

To better understand what some of the aforementioned ideas look like in practice, here are three (among many) categories of recent experiments in educational programming that are reshaping the 21st century museum experience at MoMA.

MoMA Art Lab and MoMA Studio

A visit to a large museum like MoMA can be overwhelming for adults and small children alike. Traditional museum behavior requires a level of decorum that discourages people from touching objects, making loud sounds, and moving energetically. John Falk's research has indicated that family visits are important to museums because they are the greatest predictor of future museum visitorship (Falk and Dierking, 1992). MoMA educators wanted to create an environment that is a gateway to the collection, allowing both kids and adults to go beyond looking and talking about works of art to interacting with art in new ways.

In 2008, we created a temporary hands-on laboratory space for families, adjacent to the Museum's Abby Aldrich Rockefeller Sculpture Garden, where visitors of all ages experiment, play, and create as they make connections between their own explorations and the ideas, tools, and techniques of modern and contemporary art. Now a regular feature with rotating "themes," this 700 sq ft "Art Lab" (Figure 1) provides space for families to learn together while participating in a range of interactive play-based experiences: exploring first-hand a range of materials, creating shadow puppets and collaborative stories, matching shapes and materials with images of art works, designing chairs, and using a computer touch screen to create paintings. Art Lab participants share their experiences online through photographs, blog posts, and tweets and join MoMA's social-media network to stay in touch with program schedules. Public response and regular feedback from Art Lab facilitators informed each of the five MoMA Art Lab iterations to date: Color, Line, Shape, Material, and People.

We know from our evaluation studies that adults have a strong desire to share the MoMA gallery experience with children, and MoMA Art Lab was cited by visitors as an excellent way to support this joint engagement with art and culture (Armstrong, 2012a). Art Lab visitors appreciate the design of the light-filled and colorful environment that is carefully organized for their use. Hands-on activities guided by open-ended prompts and selected materials foster creative innovation, often inspiring intergenerational collaboration.

Figure 1.   Material Lab, installed from February 10, 2011 to August 31, 2012, invited visitors to touch and explore traditional and non-traditional art making materials through specially designed discovery boxes, collage, assemblage and drawing stations, and a light table.

…[I]n the galleries they see what artists have done and [Art Lab] gets them closer to thinking about the hand of the artist, what materials they work with and how they work with materials, the way artists layer and shape things — this helps us to connect to the art after we've looked at it (Material Lab visitor, 2012).

The MoMA-trained facilitators foster a warm, supportive atmosphere that visitors truly value. People tell us that being greeted and invited into the space is an important part of their visit. When challenged to create an app-based experience patterned after successful activities tested in several Art Labs, MoMA educators wanted to replicate this welcoming environment filled with engaging activities for the electronic tablet format. The award-winning MoMA Art Lab App (Figure 2) appeals to people of all ages because it supports many of the playful art-making

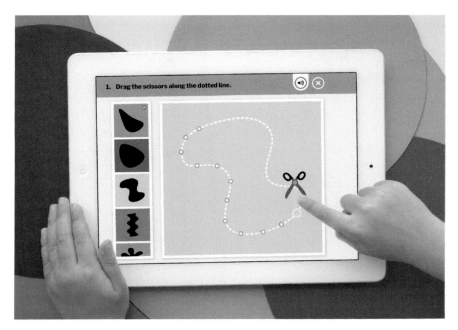

Figure 2.   Launched in June 2013, the MoMA Art Lab app is an iPad app
intended for children ages seven and up where users can create their
own artworks using shapes, lines, and colors.

experiments that motivate children and their parents to take part in
creative activities that are fun for everyone. A select number of artworks
from MoMA's collection are featured for their innovative approach to
art-making — collage layering, line drawing, cut-out silhouettes — as
well as their connection to other expressive forms such as music and
words. The MoMA Art Lab App's tablet-size surface and large toolbars
support collaborative play as easily among peers as with adults — just
like the thoughtful universal design of the child-sized chairs, tables, and
activities in the Labs. Observations of the Art Lab App[5] installed for
public use in Café 2 at MoMA have shown us that visitors of all ages enjoy
using the app, particularly those in their 20s and 30s. The installation

---

[5] MoMA, Dept. of Education. Summary of MoMA Art Lab App Observations in
Café2. Unpublished report, 2013. MoMA Art Lab iPad app can be downloaded at
http://www.moma.org/explore/mobile/artlabapp

features a large monitor that mirrors whatever someone is creating with Art Lab on the iPad below to everyone else around them. Despite the well-trafficked location, visitors spend an average of 8 minutes using the Art Lab App, inspiring an energetic social environment in which sometimes even strangers begin a conversation about the Art Lab activity.

Another act of inserting creative, collaborative art-making spaces into the museum experience is the series of MoMA Studios, also located in the Education building and accessible to the public for free. Like MoMA Art Lab, MoMA Studios drew some inspiration from past experiential and creative-learning environments at MoMA. Three prominent programs providing alternative ways for people to interact in a participatory way in the Museum were: the annual Art Carnivals (Figure 3) — featured internationally as models of

Figure 3. The Children's Holiday Carnival, on view from December 10th, 1956 to January 13rd, 1957, was one of multiple interactive learning spaces that demonstrate MoMA's history of innovative and participatory art education.

innovative art education between 1942 and 1963 (Newsom and Silver, 1978); The People's Art Center (1948–60); and The Institute of Modern Art (1960–69). MoMA Studios have become a hub of activity for drawing new communities of makers and artists into the Museum, and they also are places that invite people to slow down, explore the materials and themes, and make connections to their own lives. "I like how the space creates possibilities for creativity, collaboration — you can create something artful without being an artist" (Common Senses Studio visitor, 2012).[6]

Although each Studio installation differs in content and structure, all are designed to prioritize visitors' opportunities for discovery, self-expression, and engagement in a creative process, the way professional art studios or research laboratories do. Artists and designers have been asked to participate and help shape these spaces. Print Studio invited visitors to explore a variety of different printmaking approaches using a range of digital tools such as copy machines, scanners, and computers with image-manipulation software. With artist Andrew Beccone's Reanimation Library relocated to the Studio, a wide-ranging series of books of images was available to copy and reuse. Visitors could experiment with these tools and images on their own and consult with facilitating artist educators when they needed help. Participants shared printmaking techniques and were able to display their results. "There is something very satisfying about this … one gets inspiration from seeing the work of other people and being around other people and seeing what they are doing" (Visitor to Print Studio, 2012).[7]

The Studios initiative has fulfilled the goal set by MoMA's founders to be a space designed for exploration and experimentation. MoMA educators work closely with artists and curators to develop and determine programming for the Studios so that the learning objectives align with gallery themes. MoMA re-embraced and built

---

[6] See Armstrong (2012c; 2013a)

[7] MoMA, Dept. of Education. Print Studio: Lessons Learned from a Creative Experiment, Visitor Interview, Unpublished report, completed in 2012.

upon its founding identity as an institution dedicated not only to the creative expression of artists but also to fostering creativity in its visitors.

From Gallery Talks to Gallery Sessions

Since 2010, MoMA educators have developed and refined alternative gallery pedagogies that offer opportunities for multi-model content exchange and experimentation in order to make learning more meaningful and accessible to our large and varied audiences. While there had always been an emphasis on in-gallery experiences that involve some form of exchange — Q&A at the very least — initiatives that incorporate multisensory experiences such as art making were primarily used in programs designed for children and people with disabilities.

With the goal of expanding the pedagogical possibilities to incorporate new ways of participating more fully, MoMA educators began rapid prototyping of ideas for in-gallery engagements, known as "interventions," that might work across audience areas (e.g., families, teens, adults) as a way for people to make new and unexpected connections to the art as well as with other visitors. Beginning in 2010, MoMA Education staff began informal, unscheduled experiments with in-gallery interventions. Two years later, formal documentation of the gallery interventions program began using mixed methods approach (observations, informal visitor interviews educator reflections, and follow-up online questionsaires with visitors). The results of these assessments were compelling: visitors responded very positively to the concept as a whole and especially appreciated the "surprise" element. These "guerrilla" interventions, now called "Gallery Sessions" and expanded to one-hour, open-ended events, have replaced traditional gallery tours and include diverse activities such as: arranging colored bars and squares while observing a Mondrian painting to better understand compositional balance; a collective reading of a work by poet and Picasso art collector Gertrude Stein in the Cubism galleries; re-enacting Yoko Ono's Grapefruit Scores performance in the exhibition *Tokyo 1955–70: A New Avant-Garde*, a variety of drawing (e.g., a Surrealist "Exquisite Corpse" game) and writing exercises; and asking visitors about what they would like to discuss and then allowing the conversation to unfold naturally. Our extensive research indicates that participants find these sessions highly memorable, original, and fun.

> The experience was memorable because it was unexpected and a welcome communion with strangers in what can often be a quiet and subdued environment. I think it's important to have more interactive ways to experience art (MoMA Program attendee, 2013).[8]

Other variations on the participatory-strategies theme include "Agoras," or drop-in debates, on topics such as "Is everyone an artist?" These have fostered active conversations in the Sculpture Garden, while stimulating simultaneous, live Twitter conversations with our social-media followers.

> The [MoMA's program raised] concern/awareness/interest in social and world issues within the restrictions of popularism/ capitalism[.] [I] was impressed by MoMA's attempt at breaking down the walls of the art world and creating something refreshing. (@MoMATalks Twitter follower, 2013).[9]

Launched in the fall of 2013, a role-playing game brochure, called *Everyone's a Critic*, can be played by visitors with their friends and family, or perhaps even with strangers. While assuming the role of an artist or critic, participants are challenged to examine nearby artworks and formulate reasonable arguments with each other about which ones belong to a selected theme. Once we've piloted and evaluated the game for gallery use, we will experiment with an online version or distributing through a mobile app.

---

[8] See Armstrong (2012b; 2013b).

[9] MoMA Talks Tumblr can be found at http://www.momatalks.tumblr.com. @MoMATalks is the Twitter handle to follow. See Armstrong (2013c).

Lifelong Learning and Online Communities

Whether motivated by curiosity or career enhancement, visitors of all ages are more regularly using digital means to fulfill a range of learning needs, as well as to feel a part of a community of learners. Many people look to digital solutions, which are usually available at any time and from any place, to escape or enhance their busy lives, limitations of geographic location, and in some cases disability, in order to connect to something meaningful. Although museum websites have long been popular destinations for finding collection facts and schedules of events, few of them provide deeper engagement for online visitors seeking mentorship, inspiration, exchange, and community. Over the past few years, some art museums adapted many of the existing web-based and social media tools such as Facebook and Twitter for educational purposes, thereby creating a more dynamic environment for all learners. MoMA has been actively exploring web-based and social media tools to support a range of educational opportunities including streamed and recorded lectures, interactive experiences and peer-to-peer learning.[10] These efforts have engaged new and increasingly global audiences in substantial and long-term learning activities.

Social Media as a Tool for Museum Learning

The 2012 Horizon Report stated, "The most effective social media services encompass the aspects of face-to-face interactions that we cherish" (Johnson *et al.*, 2012). Motivated by the realization that millions more visitors browse MoMA.org than explore our physical museum in New York City every year, MoMA launched the *MoMA/PS1 Inside/Out Blog* in 2009 as a way of breaking down formal communication barriers and welcoming the public to learn more about what happens "behind the scenes" at the Museum.[11] After four

---

[10] MoMA Learning website can be found at http://www.moma.org/momalearning. See Armstrong (2012d).
[11] MoMA Inside/Out Blog can be found at: http://www.moma.org/explore/inside_out

years of operation, this blog has become one of the most important ways that the Museum documents its history. Similarly, the *MoMA Talks* Tumblr site, started in 2012, contains the most up-to-date information about a wide range of mostly art-related topics — not just schedules of Museum events but visual and text documentation of past activities and transmissions of live programming in combination with live tweets, some of which simulate inquiry-based learning conversations that might otherwise be able to take place only in the gallery.[12] Followers of the *MoMA Talks* Tumblr page like the range of content, only some of which is directly related to MoMA, and take part in lively discussions on current themes with visitors from all over the world. Because of the great success of the MoMA Talks Tumblr site, it has been integrated into MoMA's main Tumblr site and Education staff members continue to play a key role in contributing content to the site.

> I feel more of a personal connection [to MoMA through visiting the *MoMA Talks Tumblr* site] than [from] just visiting the MoMA website. You're sharing things that you think other like-minded people would like, and not just promoting things that are at the museum. Seeing you [MoMA] in Tumblr, it puts you in my mind more, so I visit your website more, and I've purchased things from the website, because you were in my mind to look there… and you get me thinking I need to get back to New York! (Anonymous quote from *MoMA Talks Tumblr* site, 2013).

Some of MoMA's social media activities are organized by age in order to bolster familiarity among the participants and to tailor design and content to audience interests. After the success of the MoMA Talks Tumblr page, the MoMA Teens Tumblr site was launched in Summer 2013 with a completely different look and design.[13] We hope that seeing archived images of teens engaged in art-making activities from our myriad of past and present

---

[12] MoMA Talks Tumblr can be found at: http://moma.tumblr.com/

[13] MoMA Teens Tumblr site can be found at http://www.teens.moma.org

classes — along with pictures of their artwork — will instill pride in current students and will inspire new teens to connect with our programs. In 2012, we collaborated with the Selfhelp's Virtual Senior Center program in Queens, NY, to conduct interactive conversations about art for home-bound seniors.[14] This synchronous program welcomes seniors to join a Google Hangout with group members who talk together (with some guidance from MoMA educators' questions) about ideas brought up after looking at a slide show of artworks. Participating seniors love the informal conversation and the company, just as they would during a museum visit with friends, and they are appreciative of MoMA's providing this social and educational opportunity. The following represent a small sampling of the feedback the program received from seniors who participated:

> Stella: Classes are very interesting, she's (MoMA Educator) very good — she explains a lot of things that I didn't know.

> Patty: Fabulous, wonderful! I was raised in a family that went to museums and enjoyed the arts but when I was older and had a family didn't have time. As someone who can't get to the museums now to be able to see art right at home is wonderful. She not only explains about the artist but in context of what's going on in the world.... To have someone who is so knowledgeable, articulate and willing to interact with us is great. I've learned so much.

> Blanche: Enjoy[ed] this class very much — it's very challenging. She presents well and extracts from us what we see about the art. She gets the most out of us so we get the most out of it.[15]

Online Courses

After many years of success in offering courses onsite at MoMA, and after running up against the limitations of the size and number of

---

[14] Selfhelp's Virtual Senior Center program in Queens, NY, http://www.selfhelp. net/virtual-senior-center. Quotes from participants are taken from email exchange with Carmella Chessen, Outreach/Volunteer Coordinator, July 2013.
[15] ibid.

Museum classrooms, MoMA's staff began experimenting with delivering courses online.[16] In the fall of 2010, MoMA piloted its first fee-based online courses: a Modern Art history survey class, and an abstract-painting materials and techniques studio course, which later garnered generous support of a funding partnership with Volkswagen of America that allowed us to expand the offerings. Each course features videos of in-gallery lectures, behind-the-scenes interviews (Figure 4), narrated slide shows, readings, and/or studio demonstrations depending on the course topic. Visitors can register for either a "self-guided" version of the course that allows only

Figure 4. MoMA Conservator Glenn Wharton in front of *Untitled* (1993) video sculpture by Nam June Paik during interview by MoMA Educator Deborah Howes for video featured in online course: "Catalysts: Artists Creating with Sound, Video and Time."

---

[16] MoMA online courses can be found at http://www.moma.org/coursesonline. Observations of online courses students taken from MoMA's Dept. of Education unpublished reports.

independent review of all materials, or an "instructor-led" version (with a common start and end date) that also includes asynchronous conversations and/or critiques of studio work in process, guided by the MoMA-trained educators and artists. The online course materials also supported a "flipped" classroom in which students consult the online materials on their own, and on-site instructors use the courseware as a "blackboard" to review videos and other media elements with students in the physical classroom. This is how 200 students over the past two years have learned with MoMA in Jakarta, Indonesia, under a licensing agreement with the American cultural program provider @America.[17]

Since their debut, MoMA Online Courses expanded to cover six different course topics and attracted over 4,500 enrollments from over 60 countries. A look at the results of our online student surveys reveals some differences in how students engage with the courses: Some are primarily interested in digesting the information at their own pace; others like to engage in peer and instructor conversations as they learn, often putting tremendous effort into the assigned weekly discussions. In particular, students attending the instructor-led studio courses frequently bond as a learning community. Some have even organized into enduring affinity groups with the help of social-media platforms like Facebook, and they invite Museum staff to participate in their online conversations. They exchange art-related news, support each other's art-making, share images from personal travels and occasionally even make plans to meet up in person. Many do not live close to major modern art collections, so these online communities become important sources of inspiration for their artistic interests.

> I liked the ability to see the exhibits from my armchair ... many miles away from MoMA, but without compromising the quality of my learning (MoMA online courses student from Glasgow, UK).

These early successes inspired MoMA educators to expand our online reach even further by creating a "Massively Open Online Course" (MOOC) in partnership with Coursera, as this pioneering

---

[17]@America cultural programs can be found at http://www.atamerica.or.id/

company was beginning a professional development program for primary- and secondary-school teachers. In July 2013, MoMA launched "Art and Inquiry: Museum Teaching Strategies for Your Classroom," a free, four-week course that explores object-based learning and discussion as a classroom activity.[18] Chief among our objectives in offering this course is raising teachers' awareness of MoMA's comprehensive online resources on Modern and Contemporary Art, including the MoMA Learning website,[19] and to contribute to the effectiveness of primary- and secondary-school education worldwide. From a pre-course survey, we discovered that the majority of registrants are emerging professionals (in their 20s and 30s) and that many of them are non-teachers. This global platform allows thousands of students from around the world to participate in discussions about teaching cultural heritage in the classroom. MoMA could never connect with so many people from so many different countries and backgrounds without the power of these ubiquitous and inexpensive digital platforms.

Conclusion

> Given the accelerating economic, social and educational changes of the 21st century, today's libraries and museums face dramatic shifts in the population they serve and the communities in which they operate.[20]

The concept of museum — named for the Ancient Greek mouseion, a dedicated place for the Muses who inspired the arts — as a physical temple for contemplation has now transformed into an agora, or community space, spanning the digital and physical realms and open to virtually every citizen of the planet. Creating memorable and satisfying learning experiences for this wide range of needs is

---

[18] Coursera website can be found at http://www.coursera.org; "Art and Inquiry," MoMA's Coursera MOOC, can be found at http://www.coursera.org/moma
[19] MoMA Learning website can be found at http://www.moma.org/momalearning. See Armstrong (2012d).
[20] See Museums, Libraries and 21st Century Skills (2009).

not about choosing a particular platform or going with the most current trend or technology; it is always about crafting the best learning environments possible and framing the experiences in the most accessible ways. Collection objects are central to this effort, and curators and artists must be part of the ongoing dialogue with our publics. Museum educators play a key role in facilitating these conversations, providing much-needed insights into visitor learning and engagement, and also managing the iterative process of experimentation, evaluation, and refinement of programs and learning environments. Finally, museum directors are expanding their focus to redirect resources to prioritize the museum experience in all of its variety — onsite, online, blended — on a global scale. As MoMA Director Glenn D. Lowry explains:

> Museums in the 21st century are rapidly becoming highly social and participatory spaces that enable people to engage in an ongoing conversation about art onsite and online. Central to MoMA's history and mission is the need to continually challenge ourselves to experiment with new approaches to education, with the goal of creating dynamic learning experiences that catalyze the connection between art and people's lives.[21]

References

About Us (2012). *International Coalition of Sites of Conscience.* Available online at: http://www.sitesofconscience.org/about-us/ [Last accessed on June 22nd, 2013].

Armstrong, J (2012a). Material Lab is a Happening Space. *MoMA/PS1 Inside/Out Blog,* [blog] August 21st, 2012. Available online at: http://www.moma.org/explore/inside_out/2012/08/21/material-lab-is-a-happening-space [Last accessed on].

Armstrong, J (2012b). A Rovin' We Will Go! Roving Gallery Guides at *MoMA. MoMA/PS1 Inside/Out Blog,* [blog] November 1st, 2012. Available online at: http://www.moma.org/explore/inside_out/2012/11/01/a-rovin-we-will-go-roving-gallery-guides-at-moma [Last accessed on].

---

[21] Lowry, G. Email exchange with Wendy Woon, July 2013.

Armstrong, J (2012c). MoMA Studio: Common Senses Welcomes Families After Hurricane Sandy. *MoMA/PS1 Inside/Out Blog*, [blog] November 8th, 2012. Available online at: http://www.moma.org/explore/inside_out/2012/11/08/moma-studio-common-senses-welcomes-families-after-hurricane-sandy [Last accessed on June 23rd, 2013].

Armstrong, J (2012d). MoMA Learning – Evolving to Meet the Needs of its Users. *MoMA Learning Blog*, [blog] December 31st, 2012. Available online at: http://www.moma.org/learn/moma_learning/blog/moma-learning-evolving-to-meet-the-needs-of-its-users [Last accessed on June 23rd, 2013].

Armstrong, J (2013a). Invitation to Explore: The Challenges of Getting Visitors to Touch the Art. *MoMA/PS1 Inside/Out Blog*, [blog] February 13th, 2013. Available online at: http://www.moma.org/explore/inside_out/2013/02/13/invitation-to-explore-the-challenges-of-getting-visitors-to-touch-the-art [Last accessed on June 23rd, 2013].

Armstrong, J (2013b). From Idea to Pilot to Program: Roving Gallery Guides at MoMA. *MoMA/PS1 Inside/Out Blog*, [blog] February 20th, 2013. Available online at: http://www.moma.org/explore/inside_out/2013/02/20/from-idea-to-pilot-to-program-roving-gallery-guides-at-moma [Last accessed on June 23rd, 2013].

Armstrong, J (2013c). Evaluating the MoMA Talks Tumblr: Some of the Cool Things We've Found Out So Far. *MoMA Talks Tumblr Archive*, [blog] May 13th, 2013. Available online at: http://momatalks.tumblr.com/post/50348563392 [Last accessed on June 23rd, 2013].

Eno, BA (1996). *Year with Swollen Appendices: Brian Eno's Diary*. London, England: Faber and Faber Ltd.

Falk, J and L Dierking (2013). *The Museum Experience Revisited*. Walnut Creek, CA: Left Coast Press.

Gardner, H (2011). *Frames of Mind: The Theory of Multiple Intelligences*. New York, NY: Basic Books.

Johnson, L, BS Adams, H Witchey, M Cummins, V Estrada, A Freeman, and H Ludgate (2012). The NMC Horizon Report: 2012 Museum Edition. Austin, Texas, USA: The New Media Consortium. Available online at: http://www.nmc.org/pdf/2012-horizon-report-museum.pdf

Mission Statement (2013). About MoMA. The Museum of Modern Art (MoMA). Available online at: http://www.moma.org/about [Last accessed on June 23rd, 2013].

Museums, Libraries and 21st Century Skills (2009). Institute of Museum and Library Services. Produced by the Office of Strategic Partnerships under the Direction of Marsha Semmel, Deputy Director for Museums Services, and Director for Strategic Partnerships. (IMLS-2009-NAI-01) Washington, DC. Available online at: http://www.imls.gov/about/21st_century_skills_home.aspx [Last accessed on June 23rd, 2013].

Newsom, BY and AZ Silver (1978). *The Art Museum as Educator: A Collection of Studies and Guides to Practice and Policy.* Berkeley, USA: University of California Press.

Pink, DA (2005). *Whole New Mind: Moving from the Information Age to the Conceptual Age.* New York, NY: Riverhead Books.

Silverman, LH (2010). *The Social Work of Museums.* New York, NY: Routledge.

Thomas, D and JS Brown (2001). *A New Culture of Learning: Cultivating the Imagination for a Word of Constant Change.* Create Space Independent Publishing Platform.

5

ONEMILLIONMUSEUMMOMENTS: A CULTURAL INTERTWINGLING

Suzanne Akhavan Sarraf

OneMillionMuseumMoments (Sarraf and Din, 2013) invites museum[1] visitors and museum professionals to share their own "museum moments" — their experiences interacting within the museum environment and the projects developed to interpret the museum environment. Utilizing and integrating channels of social media and other technologies, *OneMillionMuseumMoments* engages the community by simply asking, "what is your museum moment?"

A museum moment happens when the viewer is moved, touched, informed, awed, shocked, puzzled, confused, excited, transported, inspired, or enlightened during a museum visit. This project perpetuates the reader-response (Rosenblatt, 1938) scenario in which the museum visitor acts as an active agent and imparts a real existence to a work of art thus completing its meaning through interpretation and the sharing of that unique experience. Because of this phenomenological approach, it is the interpretation and involvement of the "reader," or visitor, as an

---

[1] The term "museum" as used within this essay is defined in the broadest sense. It includes all types of cultural heritage environments, e.g., aquariums, science centers, galleries, heritage sites, ecomuseums, etc.

accomplice or collaborator that is essential in communication and for providing meaningful engagement. Such a relationship creates an environment that is "not only a distribution of knowledge from those who have it to those who do not, but a more profound sharing of knowledge, an implicit and sometimes explicit dialogue from very different vantages about the shape, meaning, and implications", (Frisch, 1990, pg. xxii) of what is observed and experienced. The *OneMillionMuseumMoments* project mission is to create a participant-observer (Kawulich, 2005, pg. 43) virtuous circle — be inspired and inspire others.

These experiences will showcase the role of museums' continued relevance in the global community, as well as integrate the diasporic created by museums through the numerous discrete media projects developed to interpret collections and exhibitions. This project will present a more holistic approach to the museum environment and venture to give the myriad of projects a sustained and useful online presence.

The project will comprise a multifaceted approach through the integration of social media interactions with this environment, accompanied by the interpretive work created by museums. The strategy envisages a virtual environment that facilitates the essence of human nature — the need for connection — wherein the conversation about and of museums is generated and maintained by cultural advocates and consumers. As "the meaning of things lies not in the things themselves, but in our attitude towards them" (de Saint-Expupery, 1948, pg. 154), this type of collaboration is a continual and evolving process that directly involves user groups, their observations, experiences, interpretations, and reinterpretations. In the evolution of the project, *OneMillionMuseumMoments* taps into the diversity of the global community and its collective intelligence and varying perspectives, thus ensuring that these cultural spaces maintain continued relevance. Using these resources we will demonstrate the value of our global virtual citizen curators while ensuring the continued relevance of museums as viable sources of information and repositories of knowledge in the 21st century.

Background

The "museum" is storied and defined by restricted access and limited permission to the manifestations of human culture. "For 2,000 years museums have held an exalted place in society, built on the belief that through objects, they tell the history of how humans shape the world — and have been shaped by it" (Peel, 2013). The term *mouseion*, coined by the Greeks, originally referred to an institution founded for the philosophical pursuit of scholarship.

The early Renaissance saw the revival of the term, yet began the transformation into the concept of museum as we know it today. Of particular importance to this development were the grand patrons of the arts, such as the Medici family of Florence, Italy, whose prolific and comprehensive patronage and collecting laid the foundation for the modern museum. The "museum" of 17th century Europe saw the cabinet of curiosity — "a microcosm or theater of the world, and a memory theater" (Fiorani, 1998, pg. 268). These cabinets "displayed an encyclopedic collection of all kinds of objects of dissimilar origin and diverse materials on a universal scale" (Collecting for the Kunstkammer, 2013) and "conveyed symbolically the patron's control of the world through its indoor, microscopic reproduction" (Fiorani, 1998). The cabinet of curiosity demonstrated the patron's status and interpretation of his environment, while highlighting that he had the means to create and maintain these collections. These collections were built upon the largess of many of these patrons and are the foundation of many of the institutions that we visit today.

However, the physical structures that housed these objects defined access, interpretation, and interaction with the collections. This closed aspect of museums needs to evolve and reinvented. Museums must become a place of universal access. "A museum is the memory of mankind as it preserves pieces of history," (de Montebello, 2008) and through technology there need not be physical boundaries or geographical or social limitations.

Project Description

Museums today are known for their online presence as much as or more so than their physical site. Without question, the Internet and World Wide Web have changed the way we define and extend our personal impressions of the world. *OneMillionMuseumMoments,* a project conceived by Herminia Din and myself, exploits the vastness of the virtual and online environments facilitating dynamic access and exchange, "migrating ubiquitously, via communication and computing technology, without regard to borders, class, or age. In effect … a municipality whose currency is information and access" (Freedman, 2000, pg. 2).

"Museums are already demonstrating their comfort manipulating a digital environment", as noted in 1995 by Katherine Jones-Garmil. She observed that museums have had "a long courtship with technologies," but never before has this relationship been so exciting and conducive for increasing the reach of museums and their collections. As Jones-Garmil concluded of that thirty-year relationship, that "[t]hese are exciting times for museums … . Through new technologies like digital imaging and local and global networks, [museums] are able to capture and share information on their collections in ways that have only become possible in the last few years." (Jone-Garmil, 1995).

Almost three decades later, in 2013, the spectrum of technological resources available has become even more vast and broadly accessible to the general public, mirroring the evolution of access to physical museums. These technological advancements have allowed museums to provide open access to their collections through a myriad of initiatives.

Facebook, Flickr, Google+, Google Maps, Open Street Maps, Instagram, Tumblr, Twitter, Youtube, and Vimeo are but a few of the resources museums are using to evangelize and share the immense compendium of knowledge and holdings that have previously been universally inaccessible. Just as museums are using these online environments to bring new interpretations to their collections, so too is the global populace. By 2015, according to Stefan Ferber's projections, "not only will 75 percent of the world's population have access to the [In]ternet. So will some six billion devices. The fact that there will be a global system of interconnected computer networks, sensors, actuators, and devices all using the [In]ternet protocol holds so much potential" (Ferber, 2013). This potentiality, this smarter web, can be exploited to evoke a new means of interaction with the volume of material being produced by the establishment and by those consuming and reinterpreting this material is staggering.

OneMillionMuseumMoments aspires to create a portal that is a repository of personal moments, essentially creating a "meta-museum" in its own right, linking and integrating different museums, patrons, objects, and experiences. Aggregating these disparate streams into one resource is seminal to this project, allowing participation by any conduit that is most comfortable for the user.

Drawing from John Dewey's pragmatic approach to aesthetics, it is the personal moments and experiences we wish to preserve, extend, and enhance, thus creating a collaborative space intended to develop and promote collaborative learning and understanding. As Dewey (1935, pg. 14–15) explains,

> As we manipulate, we touch and feel, as we look, we see; as we listen, we hear … . The eye attends and reports the consequence of what is done. Because of their intimate connection, subsequent doing is cumulative and not a matter of caprice nor yet of routine. In an emphatic artist esthetic experience, the relation is so close that it controls simultaneously both the doing and the perception. Such vital intimacy of connection cannot be had if only hand and eye are engaged. When they do not, both of them act as organs of the whole being, there is but a mechanical sequence of sense and movement as in walking that is automatic. Hand and eye, when the experience is esthetic, are but instruments through which the entire love creature, moved and active throughout, operates. Hence the expression is emotional and guided by purpose.

As participant observers, we are mediators of our environment and can contribute a richer nuanced interpretation that can influence and augment the interpretations by others. It is with the integration of social media that we can facilitate a dialogue with the global community; through the democratization of knowledge and information, we can contribute to the larger dialogue. Each of these forms of distribution can continually build a more cohesive and viable resource for users. Through this we can educate, preserve and archive global cultural holdings, creating a living resource and record of human knowledge and experience with which to educate. As noted by Nicolas Negroponte learning "comes from exploration, from reinventing the wheel and finding out for oneself … . By playing with information … the material assumes more meaning." (Negroponte, 1995, pg. 199).

Purpose

Utilizing the tools and resources available on the web defines *OneMillionMuseumMoments* as a comprehensive aggregator of experiences of the global community in concert with the materials created by museums. The gestalt of this project is to create an extensible repository — in essence, a central location housing the interpretation of our shared global culture. It "is not about supplanting the quasi-religious experience of seeing Rothko's RED in jpeg format. Nor is it calling for the demise of the physical museum … . It's about bringing the assets of museums to unprecedented numbers in unprecedented ways" (Peel, 2013).

This project is built upon the "open" ideals as defined by OPENGlam: "an initiative run by the Open Knowledge Foundation that promotes free and open access to digital cultural heritage held by Galleries, Libraries, Archives and Museums." (OpenGLAM, n.d.) In this shared system, "[a] piece of data or content is open if anyone is free to use, reuse, and redistribute it — subject only, at most, to the requirement to attribute and/or share-alike." (Open Definition, n.d.) The philosophy behind *OneMillionMuseumMoments* is based on openness; the tools used to contribute are free and accessible allowing for read/write access by all — even if the commercial environments and tools used to create or contribute these experiences are not (Tate, 2012). "The main idea underlying collaborative projects is that the joint effort of many actors leads to a better outcome than any actor could achieve individually" (Kaplan and Haelin, 2009, pg. 63). Thus the project adheres to the fundamental ideals upon which the World Wide Web was conceived, "a powerful, ubiquitous tool ... built on egalitarian principles and because thousands of individuals, universities and companies have worked, both independently and together as part of the World Wide Web Consortium, to expand its capabilities based on those principles." (Berners-Lee, 2010). It is with the concept of open standards that this project's portal system has been conceived.

OneMillionMuseumMoments is built upon the premise behind syntactic and semantic interoperability while utilizing open standards. "Interoperability, like openness, is something that we generally think of as a 'good thing' in the context of information and communications technologies ... [as]we believe it leads to innovation" (Gasser and Palfrey, 2007, pg. ii).

Method

Each avenue of social integration is based upon self-selected content communities (Kaplan and Haelin, 2009). A user can navigate and contribute using the means with which he/she is most comfortable. The contribution will automatically be incorporated into the larger environment creating a limitless participatory space. By connecting each disparate group to a larger whole, the benefit to that "collaborative projects enable the joint and simultaneous creation of content by many end-users ... in this sense, probably the most democratic manifestation of UGC [User Generated Content] — which enable the group-based collection and rating of Internet links or media content." (Kaplan and Haelin, 2009).

The social media outlets used currently and those which will be available in the future will be able to integrate seamlessly — each will feed data into the other. This repository will grow and evolve to mediate the social environment while integrating new methods of social media as they evolve and gain prominence and popularity in the market. Each entry will endeavor to follow the open standards and the philosophical ideals of "The Internet of Things," (IoT) (European Commission — Information Society and Media DG., 2009). The IoT is "a dynamic global network infrastructure with self-configuring capabilities based on standard and interoperable communication protocols where physical and virtual 'things' have identities, physical attributes, and virtual personalities and use intelligent interfaces, and are seamlessly integrated into the information network."

Implementation

OneMillionMuseumMoments (see Figure 1) project is in its gestational phase, with a clearly defined mission and vision; and the requirements scoped are in an iterative process of identifying resources for future developments. The domains and site have been purchased and designed. Social media channels — Facebook, Flickr, Google Maps, YouTube, Twitter — have been established. Exploiting the native

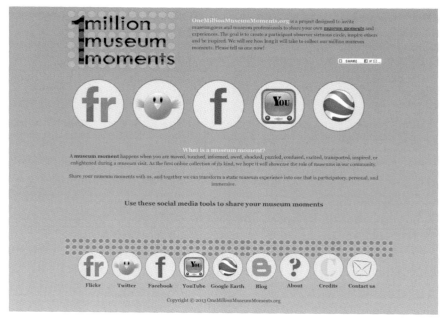

Figure 1. *OneMillionMuseumMoment* site.

APIs of these tools is key in integrating each to make a referential system where any material posted feeds the others seamlessly — reaching disparate audiences where they feel most comfortable as each of these bespoke outlets feed into the other. Each of these forms of distribution can continually build a more cohesive and viable resource for users.

The site and associated channels will grow organically within the online environment, adding in features and outlets as resources become available and to accommodate for market expansion based on geography and social media trends. Localization is a key aspect of growth to accommodate an expanding global audience — an integral aspect of creating a holistic representation of our global cultural heritage. Entering into the online environment slowly will also give the opportunity to learn how to traverse the environment in an effective and informed way.

Aggregation of projects produced by institutions would be progressive and adaptive wherein this material can be pulled in based on the resources/limitations of the contributing institution. The disparate data sets from visitors and institutions would conform to standards purported by the W3C to create a more "Sematic Web" by adhering to the tenets of "Web of Data," (W3C, n.d.) to help data integration, collection of interrelated datasets "to have the huge amount of data on the Web available in a standard format, reachable and manageable" (W3C, n.d.). At the core of this multi-layered and multifaceted project is the communication technologies interoperability and "the ability to transfer and render useful data and other information across systems ... enriched by adding context-specific definitional elements ... given life by the viewpoint of a variety of stakeholders" (Glasser and Palfrey, 2007).

Conclusion

OneMillionMuseumMoments, a project created by museum visitors and museum professionals, ensures that our shared cultural heritage enjoys a continued thriving and inspiring existence online. "By embracing technology and forging innovative partnerships, museums will become the fiery muses that set the world's innovation alight, and not the mausoleums where art just goes to die" (Peel, 2013). Using open technologies and social media tools we can engage with online communities and tap into their diverse collective intelligence to create an unbounded repository that exploits the use of an un-tethered technological interaction to transcend artificial barriers. Museum collections were once limited to one-way communication, in which museums delivered static entries with marginal interactivity. Museum-visitor interaction is approaching a dynamic equilibrium, in which a steady state is reached and a new social contract created between the institution and the public (Sarraf, 2009). This state should need not be limited to a static experience but "[a]n experience is something that personally affects your life" (Dewy, 1935), that flows globally.

The virtual walls that silo niche social media tools and projects created by institutions will dissolve and the distinct artificial institutional constructs that define these closed systems will open, to create an open integrated intelligent semantic system, allowing the mingling of data from multiple fragmented data sources. "In order to secure our relevance in the 21st century, we need to break free from the idea that museums are constrained by physical wells" (Shogger, 2000, pg. 10).

This project considers the transclusion of resources from our global visitors other cultural institutions, taking a passive experience and making it an active experience creating a common culture through art. "We build it now so that those who come to it later will be able to create things that we cannot ourselves imagine" (Berners-Lee, 2010).

"Let us do something, while we have the chance!" (Beckett, 1949)

References

Beckett, S (1949). *Waiting for Godot*. Act II. Available online at: http://samuel-beckett.net/Waiting_for_Godot_Part2.html

Berners-Lee, T (2010). Long Live the Web: A Call for Continued Open Standards and Neutrality. *Scientific American,* [online] November 22nd, 2010. Available online at: http://www.scientificamerican.com/article.cfm?id=long-live-the-web&print=true [Last accessed on May 1st, 2013].

Collecting for the Kunstkammer (2013). Heilbrunn Timeline of Art History. *Metropolitan Museum of Art.* Available online at: http://www.metmuseum.org/toah/hd/kuns/hd_kuns.htm [Last accessed on May 1st, 2013].

de Montebello, P (2008). A History Of Museums. *The Memory Of Mankind.* Available online at: http://www.npr.org/templates/story/story.php?storyId= 97377145 [Last accessed on May 1st, 2013].

de Saint-Exupery, A (1948). *The Wisdom of the Sands.* New York: Amereon Ltd.

Dewy, J (1935). *Art as Experience.* New York: Minton, Balch & Company.

European Commission-Information Society and Media DG. (2009). Internet of Things-Strategic Research Roadmap. Available online at: http://www.internet-of-things-research.eu/pdf/IoT_Cluster_Strategic_ Research_Agenda_2009.pdf [Last accessed on May 1st, 2009].

Ferber, S (2013). How the Internet of Things Changes Everything. *Harvard Business Review Blog Network,* [blog] May 07th, 2013. Available online at: http://blogs.hbr.org/2013/05/how-the-internet-of-things-cha/ [Last accessed on May 1st, 2013].

Fiorani, F (1998). Reviewing Bredecamp 1995, *Renaissance Quarterly,* 51(1).

Freedman, Gordon (2000). The Changing Nature of Museums. *The Museum Journal,* 43(4).

Frisch, M (1990). A Shared Authority: Essays on the Craft and Meaning of Oral and Public History. New York: State University of New York Press.

Gasser, U and John P (2007). Breaking Down Digital Barriers — When and How ICT Interoperability Drives Innovation. *Berkman Publication Series.* Available online at: http://nrs.harvard.edu/urn-3:HUL.InstRepos:2710237

Jones-Garmil, K (1995). Museum in the Information Age. *Archives & Museum Informatics,* 2.

Kaplan, AM and Ml Haenlein (2009). Users of the World, Unite! The Challenges and Opportunities of Social Media. *Business Horizon,* 53, 59–68.

Kawulich, Barbara B. (2005). Participant Observation as a Data Collection Method. *Forum Qualitative Sozialforschung/Forum: Qualitative Social Research,* 6(2).

Negroponte, N (1995). *Being Digital.* New York: Vintage Book.

Open Definition (n.d.), http://opendefinition.org/ [Last accessed on May 1st, 2013].

OpenGLAM (n.d.) http://openglam.org/ [Last accessed on May 01, 2013].

Peel, Y (2013). How museums can transform the art of learning. *CNN* [online] January 24th, 2013. Available online at: http://business.blogs. cnn.com/2013/01/24/how-museums-can-transform-the-art-of-learning/ [Last accessed on May 1st, 2013].

Rosenblatt, LM (1938). *Literature as Exploration.* London: Heinemann.

Sarraf, S (2009). The Internet, the Web, Social Media, and Museums: Ubiquity and Power; Omnipotence, Omnipresence, and Omniscience. *International Symposium on Art Museum Education, Innovation in the Art Museum Education Tradition.* Taipei: Taipei Fine Arts Museum Press.

Sarraf, S and H Din (n.d.) http://www.onemillionmuseummoments.org/.

Schogger, D (2000). Making the Old Look New: British Museums Need to be More Interactive and Entertaining to Appeal to a Wider Market. *Design Week,* [online] January 27th, 2000. Available at: http://www. designweek.co.uk/news/making-the-old-look-new/1123202.article [Last accessed on May 1st, 2013].

Tate, R (2012). Mr. Zuckerberg, Tear Down This Wall. *Wired,* [online] December 12th, 2012. Available online at: http://www.wired.com/business/ 2012/12/internet-napoleons/ [Last accessed on May 1st, 2013].

W3C (n.d.). Linked Data. Available online at: http://www.w3.org/standards/ semanticweb/data [Last accessed on May 1st, 2013].

6

DOCUMENTARY STORYTELLING USING IMMERSIVE AND INTERACTIVE MEDIA

Michael Mouw

Documentaries offer tremendous opportunities to emotionally and intellectually connect museum visitors to stories and interpretive content. Though we often think of documentaries as films, these projects may also take alternate forms such as gallery learning games, interactive exhibits, immersive storytelling theaters, applications on mobile and wearable devices, and even a thrilling ride experience in the museum. This chapter will address a documentary approach to storytelling using examples from a variety of different platforms.

My career is focused on working collaboratively on documentaries created with talented museum team members who have wide, varied skill sets. The goal of each team is to make new forms of media and technology-driven exhibitions, as they meld interaction design with experience design. As a creative and technical director, I lead multidisciplinary teams of museum staff and talented vendors to design and develop deeply immersive and highly interactive experiences to showcase powerful human stories. The desired outcome is museumgoers will find their experiences with stories emotionally engaging and memorable. The body of work created with the project teams is based on a documentary filmmaker's approach to storytelling, yet it uses a range and variety of interactions and experiences only made possible by new creative technology tools. These tools offer a wide range of options for free-choice learning in museums to allow visitors to interact with exhibitions, and with each other, in meaningful new ways.

At the core of this collaboratively created body of work are the photographs, written accounts, audio and video interviews, objects, and historic films from museum collections. These form a solid foundation for any documentarian who wants to tell compelling stories by using new technology tools. In this chapter, I will offer examples and suggestions to readers who want to use documentary storytelling methods to produce interpretive projects for museums. I will use the work of the Minnesota Historical Society (MHS) as a case study — the organization has over two decades of experience creating a gamut of projects which show an evolution of storytelling approaches. From 1991 until 2009, I worked on staff at MHS and helped to develop many of these varied documentaries. Now I look in from outside of the organization, still doing some commissioned projects for the museum. I believe this array of work from one organization, so firmly rooted in human storytelling, will be useful to readers interested in cultural heritage. The documentary method-ology and mindset can be applied to immersive installations, highly interactive exhibits, mobile and gallery learning games, the Web, and to more familiar narrative media productions, like documentary films.

Story is Key

A compelling story is at the core of any interpretive media and technology experience that hopes to offer accessible information for museum visitors. This is true whether we are discussing projects for history museums, science centers, contemporary or encyclopedic art museums, children's museums, institutions of contemporary culture (like human rights), or organizations that focus on nature and the environment. Over time, I have been asked for media and technology tips and tricks from museum colleagues after they toured completed exhibits projects. The answer is always the same and it rarely involves technology: start with a good story and don't make anything up. Sticking with facts in documentary-based storytelling is important, even if the project's content research doesn't reveal everything the team hoped to find. A documentary, in whatever form it takes, needs the firm foundation that an interesting and fact-based story provides — this strong foundation allows the technology and the learning scaffolding to be built in solid, conceptual layers. With a documentary approach to storytelling, the final project will have "the ring of truth" as a story resonates with museum viewers and users. Good documentary stories are timeless as they continue to feel fresh to a museum audience for many years. At MHS, the *Home Place Minnesota* multimedia object theater was a compelling, immersive, documentary storytelling experience for museumgoers from opening day in June 1993, until it closed nineteen years later, in June 2012.

Why be concerned about making up parts of a story to fill in gaps revealed by research on a documentary as it goes forward, when the discovered facts don't pan out as expected? Museums are often well stocked with highly trained experts. Experts sometimes determine they know what the subject of a documentary would have said, what the subject might have been thinking, what inspired the subject, or how the subject felt at certain time and place. If factual source material can't be found in written accounts, through photographs, or in audio, film, or video interviews to support a proposed story, why not write dialog? Can't you make up part of the story to achieve hoped-for interpretive points in a media and technology project? The answer lies in the lack of experience museum staff and most production companies have with writing good quality dialog and the thin resources available for this approach in most museum projects, especially when they are compared to commercial films and stage plays. It is almost impossible for museums to compete with dramas coming out of Hollywood, New York, or London with their large budgets and dedicated staff who produce believable dramatic experiences for film and stage. When museums go down the path of dramatic dialog for films or other media and technology projects, the quality of the visitor experience usually suffers. Additionally, museums are a highly trusted source of information for the public, so vetting a story through factual research fits within the missions of our organizations. Yes, it can be difficult to research documentary projects and find materials to support required content and interpretive points. Sometimes research will point the stories under development in a new direction — this is the organic nature of making documentaries. The best plan is to let research lead where the story will go, and then plan media and technology platforms to best support the storytelling. Putting technology first is putting the cart before the horse. If technology is the only consideration at the start of a project, the story may turn out to be a poor fit for a preselected media and technology platform, and it may be ill-suited for the interaction design or visitor experience the museum wishes to create.

Process Comes Next

One way to ensure that the story experience and technology progress together smoothly is to write a short and concise narrative treatment for the documentary project. This allows the team, stakeholders, and potential vendors have an overview of the story, the proposed technology, and project goals. A treatment can be as simple as a one-page document listing these essential items. Treatments used with my teams have evolved to include additional project details in a text document with sections for: a statement about the museum and its mission, a short list of the proposed media and technology platforms, one page narrative description of the story with its proposed interactions and visitor experience, key messages, experience and learning objectives, target audiences, desired response, look and feel, project constraints, accessibility parameters, prototyping and testing plans, project deliverables, technical requirements, proposed software and hardware, a list of relevant background documents from the museum, preliminary budget, and major milestones in the project schedule. This level of detail supports a wider understanding of the project proposal, but the most important aspect of any treatment is to articulate in one page a description of the story with the proposed interactions and experiences for museum visitors, and a clear, short list of objectives. If ideas cannot be articulated on one page with clear goals, the framework for the proposed documentary project is weak and probably needs to be revisited.

I believe the documentary approach to storytelling is reductive rather than additive, as research needs to reveal a good selection of source materials with text, audio, image, and video assets. I affectionately call this "the pile of stuff" every documentary project needs to move forward. Of course, these materials are carefully researched media assets pulled together by skilled subject matter experts, researchers, and curators to support the creation of a compelling story. This precious pile of stuff informs the documentary's storyline and media and technology choices, as things move forward. The difficult work at the front end of any documentary project is to find quality source materials to allow a team to carefully craft a story through the substantial editing process which usually starts rough, gets smoother, and ends with a finely polished production — only after the work goes through many project iterations.

At the center in understanding how story elements of a documentary are selected, are the written transcripts from audio, video, and filmed interviews. The transcripts of interview subjects are some of the most important working tools of a documentary maker, as audio and video are time-based media. If twenty hours of audio interviews are available for the project, it takes much more time than twenty hours of work to carefully listen to and take notes of the original interview material. A written transcript in a digital format can be searched for key words to allow sections of source media to be skipped over, to more quickly find story elements. It is important to listen to audio for quality or watch video segments in the interview media material. While a selection in the written transcript may be compelling, you may find that it has unintelligible audio or unusable video, after reviewing the recording.

While working on a recent commissioned documentary film project, we obtained more than sixty transcripts of audio interview subjects who grew up during WWII. These interviews had potential to include train travel stories which was the subject of the film. After searching the written transcripts for key words connected to rail travel, just over thirty interviews had story segments that looked interesting, after reading the text. Using the written transcripts as a guide, we searched and listened to digital audio recordings of interviews for the selected story segments. Five interviews were eventually included as story elements in the half hour documentary film production. Though this may be one example, this is not unusual math for a documentary project. Research needs to also locate photographs, graphics, and film and video segments that can be sequenced to the audio to bring a story to life. In addition, an immersive storytelling theater will add objects and theatrical settings lighted in synchronization with the story, to illustrate the narrative. In documentary productions, the work of illustrating the story with visuals is called "covering" the audio. This overarching work of gathering research materials that are then refined through a careful editing process, is why I think of documentary making as reductive rather than additive. These projects require gathering of ample source materials, the selection of meaningful story segments, and careful editing of audio and visuals, along with the installation and lighting of objects and settings for an immersive storytelling theater. The goal is to craft a documentary experience that flows through a dramatic and understandable story arc, with a clear beginning, middle, and end. A compelling story carried by a strong narrative is key if the project is highly interactive, an immersive installation, a mobile experience, or if it is time-based, like film.

Changing Story Platforms

Over the past two decades, media and technology platforms have allowed documentary stories to break the linear time-based progression of narrative film or video — stories can be placed into small, succinct segments offered through a menu of choices to visitors. This allows online users and museumgoers to experience stories as unique sequences they mentally construct into larger themes and overarching narratives. Documentary story segmentation started with the introduction of interactive computer kiosks and CDROM programs. The segmented approach has progressed with improvements and developments in the Web, through the growth of learning games, and in electronic books and publications.

Now, with transmedia trends, we see stories designed to work across multiple media and technology platforms. A story, often originating from a concept for a commercial film or video game (and documentaries), may be experienced from a variety of angles through media channels including cable or broadcast television, video games, graphic novels or print media, electronic publications, films, live theater, radio, billboards, toys and merchandise, online experiences, and social media interactions on mobile or wearable devices. All of the channels may be used to explore a single storyline reinforced through the use of disparate media and technology platforms. The story may also be delivered as smaller, unique narrative segments through each channel. With this approach to transmedia, users need to construct narrative segments in their minds, as building blocks, to construct and understand a larger, complex story universe. The larger story can only be pulled together by a curious and motivated consumer of multiple channels, as the user explores the variety technology platforms connected to the project. As it placed into multiple channels, the transmedia approach adds layers of complexity to the creation of a documentary story, as the narrative is delivered in new forms. Even with the additional layers of choice and interaction, the key is to stay grounded in a fact-based, compelling story. This is the foundation of every documentary project.

Storytelling Evolution

Documentary stories from MHS have been delivered through a variety of media and technology platforms starting with documentary films from the 1970s, like *The Last Log Drive*. The film uses footage of early 20th century lumberjacks at work in northern forests, as they cut down trees by hand to float rafts of logs downriver to sawmills. The film is a fascinating look at a lost way of life and it still interests new audiences. The construction of the Minnesota History Center as the headquarters of MHS in 1992 brought new staff hires. Developments in technology allowed staff to create *V is for Voices* and other pioneering interactive documentaries delivered on touchscreen computer interfaces, in the new galleries. These documentary programs presented visitors with a menu of concise one to two minute stories drawn from audio interviews in the museum's collection. The segments were illustrated with historic photographs and films from the collection and archives to visualize short narratives. Exhibitions at MHS also featured video documentaries accessed through menus of buttons which allowed visitors to select short segments — originally these stories were delivered from LaserDiscs, then from digital video discs (DVDs), and currently from digital video players. Projects on the Web proved the Internet was also a venue for powerful human stories with the *Duluth Lynchings Online Resource*, followed by *Share Your Story in the Minnesota's Greatest Generation* initiative, and *The US-Dakota War of 1862* oral history project. Immersive theater projects at MHS began with *Home Place Minnesota* which inspired many others to follow. Smaller, more focused installations used documentary videos and museum objects lighted in sequence to illustrate stories, including the groups featured in the *Minnesota Communities* exhibit. In *Open House: If These Walls Could Talk*, the museum's approach was expanded to create a large interactive exhibit focused on the stories from families who lived in one house. Cell phones were used as a platform for documentary stories at the organization's historic sites and for the *Minnesota River Valley Scenic Byway Mobile Tour* project. Gallery learning games started with the eighteen-player *Minnesota 150 Challenge* and the subsequent four player quiz show in the *1968* exhibit, followed by *Play the Past* mobile learning game currently in development — these games all have documentary stories woven into social learning and play. Finally, documentary films have been a staple in the storytelling realm of the organization. They are used as short segments woven into exhibition design or as stand-alone films featured in dedicated theaters, like *Minneapolis in Nineteen Minutes Flat* at the Mill City Museum.

As the Minnesota Historical Society is an organization with a statewide network of over two dozen museums and historic sites, staff have had unique opportunities to gather in-house teams to collaborate with a variety of vendors to explore new methods to deliver diverse, documentary-based stories.

Immersive Storytelling

As I mentioned, immersive storytelling theater projects at MHS began with *Home Place Minnesota*. The show seated an audience of fifty who viewed a very wide stage. Large images projected onto scrims were used as a layer of transparent screens stretched in front of theatrical scenery and museum objects. The show included voices, music, and sound effects delivered through multiple channels of digital audio, and it used a large mechanical turntable to add new scenic elements, as needed. The show was visually tied together by a theatrical lighting system which highlighted objects and exhibits settings. Theatrical show control and audio-visual technology were blended in this installation to tightly control a montage of short documentary stories that presented authors' notions about calling Minnesota home. A poem, written and read aloud by Garrison Keillor, anchored the end of the experience. As the first storytelling theater for MHS, the success of *Home Place Minnesota* sparked the development of many more immersive projects at the organization.

Documentary stories and a melange of technology devices have been woven into more than a dozen theatrical storytelling experiences at MHS that evolved from *Home Place Minnesota* in 1993, to *Everything Must Change in the Families* exhibit in 1995, to *Get to the Basement!* in 2001, to *This Must Be Hell* in 2009 — these projects were all installed in the exhibits of the Minnesota History Center. Large immersive storytelling theater projects were created for other MHS locations including Jeffers Petroglyphs, Historic Fort Snelling, and the Forest History Center. This group of larger projects also includes the most complex immersive storytelling theater created to date by the organization, the *Flour Tower* — the elevator ride with its eight vertical levels of immersive theater settings opened in 2003, at the Mill City Museum.

Similar techniques have been used for smaller, more focused documentary storytelling theater experiences completed by MHS staff in exhibitions including *Field to Table* in 1996, which used a hand painted children's book approach in its theater settings. The playful sets were unveiled through rotating turntables and used toy-sized props and a large video monitor with archival film footage of farm work and breakfast cereal manufacturing. The show was designed to help children understand how their food is produced. *Unpacking on the Prairie: Jewish Women in the Upper Midwest* opened in 1996 to include a sabbath setting contrasted in two Jewish homes, one wealthy and one less privileged. The dialog invented for the sabbath show was sequenced to work with the lighting cues. In 1998, *Our Gathering Places: African Americans in Minnesota* exhibition featured a full-scale barber shop and beauty salon setting. This allowed visitors sit in barber and salon chairs to experience object settings tied to stories from the community, revealed in large glass cases. These settings were lighted as the story progressed to illustrate powerful moments in 20th century African American history that were drawn from interviews recorded specifically for the exhibition. Both the movie theater and drug store installation in the *Minnesota's Greatest Generation* exhibit offered theatrical storytelling experiences when they opened in 2009. The movie theater used a Pepper's Ghost technique to create a grand 1930s theater experience inside a small exhibit space. It was designed to deliver stories with segments of vintage films from a generation who grew up watching movies as their main form of entertainment. The project team learned from interviewees that news about Pearl Harbor was heard when they traveled as teens to pick up the Sunday paper for their families at the drugstore. This setting became the physical metaphor in the exhibit for that fateful morning. The *1968* exhibit used video documentaries from the battlefields of Vietnam and gave them context by placing them inside an army helicopter, when it opened in 2011. In 2013, the *Minnesota and the Civil War* exhibit had two smaller immersive theater installations filled with short stories based on letters from men and women impacted by the war. Most of these installations use audio synchronized with lighting of objects and theatrical settings at the core of their storytelling technique. The light and sound show is the foundation of immersive storytelling experiences which are also called multimedia object theaters.

Large immersive shows offer opportunities to create compelling immersive experiences, but they often require a more complex team of museum staff and specialist vendors to create their intended experiences, along with a need for bigger budgets and a longer timeline for production.

Let's look at the *This Must Be Hell* as an example of how a larger immersive storytelling theater experience is developed by MHS staff. The project was part of the Minnesota's Greatest Generation initiative at the museum (see Figure 1). The initiative focused on gathering the stories of the generation born between 1911 and 1929

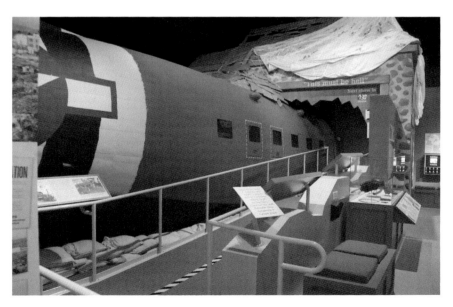

Figure 1.   *This Must Be Hell* exterior of WWII D-Day paratrooper plane immersive storytelling theater appears as a crash landed airplane in the gallery. Courtesy: Minnesota Historical Society.

who were children during the Depression, came of age in WWII, and looked to raise their families after the war. They made an impact worldwide through their work and careers, and now are in their golden years. A major exhibit was named after the initiative. The staff project team looked to find a centerpiece for the exhibit that would focus on WWII. The original idea was to create an immersive experience to take place in a glider that held troops and was pulled behind combat planes — the glider was let loose to land with troops in the battlefields of Europe. The plywood glider was manufactured in Minnesota.

Research did not turn up interviews or compelling stories of Minnesotans who were transported as troops to combat in these gliders during WWII. As other digital audio and video interviews were conducted, stories of Minnesotans who trained as paratroopers and then parachuted into France on D-Day began to appear. This is an example of research leading the direction of the visitor experience. After realizing the story needed to be refocused, the exhibit team proposed that a WWII paratrooper transport plane would make a powerful container for a theater installation about D-Day. The plan was to build a replica in the museum until a team member, and pilot, suggested a search for a fuselage from a C-47 paratrooper plane to install in the galleries. Staff traveled to an airplane junkyard and acquired the fuselage portion of the plane that would have flown paratroopers into battle. Dedicated volunteers worked hundreds of hours to bring the airplane interior back to its WWII era look and feel to allow visitors to sit in the paratrooper's small, steel seats — volunteers and staff also made certain the media and technology needed to tell the documentary's story was hidden and seamlessly installed.

MHS staff use a prototyping warehouse and workshop that allows them to mock up immersive theater shows out of cardboard to understand quickly, in full scale, if the story, settings, and proposed media and technology work together meaningfully. (If gallery space in the Minnesota History Center is available, this is also used for rapid prototyping). Production equipment includes high definition video, multi-channel and surround sound audio, theatrical lighting, and a show control system to tie all of the elements and special effects together. By keeping all aspects of the media digital and very flexible, early demonstrations of immersive installations move smoothly into production of the storytelling experience. For the final exhibition, the multiple computer stations used in the design and development of the project are replaced by equipment focused on delivering the show. In *This Must Be Hell*, the C-47 airplane fuselage was built as a prototype out of cardboard. Soon after, volunteers readied the actual fuselage to test stories samples and various technologies while it was still in the warehouse. After this phase and technology has been selected, the airplane fuselage and equipment were moved to the museum's galleries, where production on the show continued until the exhibit opening (see Figure 2).

There is an advantage to have the physical theater environment available for six months or more before an immersive storytelling

Figure 2. *This Must Be Hell* interior of WWII D-Day paratrooper plane with seats for visitors and cabin surface for video projections. Windows provide views to outdoor digital scenery. Courtesy: Minnesota Historical Society.

theater opens to the public — this is true whether you are producing work in a prototype or the final physical space. It takes time to work with full-scale settings and multiple technology platforms for audio, lighting, and video to hone stories for an immersive experience. The story editing process and timing of sequences of the disparate media elements of the show, as experienced in the immersive setting, leads to success.

This Must Be Hell had many facets that needed to be worked through to illustrate the story of paratrooper training, the D-Day flight into combat, and anxious loved ones waiting at home. The team decided to use airplane jump seats on one side of the fuselage for museum visitors, so they could look across at the other side of the interior and out through the plane's windows as they experienced the show. Objects and set pieces were tested inside the fuselage, but felt awkward. In the end, the use of special effects lighting, two small video projections inside the cabin interior, and large, blended video images viewed as digital scenery through the windows, all worked together to make the plane feel as if it flew through clouds into combat. Important to the experience was the audio that enveloped the audience with voices, sound effects, and music to let visitors suspend disbelief and feel they were part of the show. In this production, sixteen channels of sound were needed to carry a believable combat storytelling experience. All immersive storytelling experiences at MHS have quality audio delivery and sound design at the core of the production — audio is often overlooked, but it is an affordable and powerful aspect of this type of museum exhibit.

Overall, every immersive storytelling theater has unique factors that require custom work to create this type of museum experience. Starting with a good story and prototyping the media, technology, and physical aspects in several iterations will lead to a successful show. The impact of these shows on museumgoers is emotional, experiential and memorable. Immersive storytelling, with its power to deliver human stories in exhibits is best used to connect to visitors' emotions, rather than as a way to deliver didactic material.

Interactive Storytelling

After creating a number of successful immersive storytelling experiences, MHS staff wondered if the similar techniques could be applied to an exhibition — the idea was to make powerful, human stories available through free-choice learning and exploration by museumgoers. *Open House: If These Walls Could Talk* exhibition opened in 2006 at the Minnesota History Center and it applied a new layer of interaction design to the toolset developed from creating immersive projects. Through detailed research, a house in St. Paul was located which had evolved, in a century of use, from a single family dwelling built by German American immigrants to a triplex owned by Hmong American occupants today. In all, over fifty families lived in this one dwelling in the 118 years that encompassed the research — the interactive experiences focused on occupants' individual stories.

One of the trickiest aspects of the project was to have exhibit design recreate rooms in one dwelling that changed over a hundred year time span — the design needed to showcase stories from the house occupants, along with added contextual information from census records and archives. Through prototyping and testing, a plan was formed to use interactive media and technology tools to hold stories as digital files in media servers and provide instant responses to a variety of sensitive electronic sensors — sensors were triggered by visitors who explored the physical exhibit. Interactive media experiences were delivered in installations with technology that seemed appropriate to the era represented by each room. The German Americans who built the house in 1888 had stories from letters and written accounts delivered in a Victorian era parlor through the piano, a lantern slide interactive (with RFID tags hidden in the large slides), and cabinets and cupboards opened and explored by visitors to reveal audio, lighting surprises, and written text. Everyday objects from the time period became story containers. The boarding house era of the house in the early 20th century left no record of personal accounts from transient renters. Rather than make up or recreate stories, occupants were represented in a straightforward way by work clothes on hangers with minimal census record information — this section of the exhibit became a small hallway. The Italian Americans who occupied the home from the 1920s to the 1950s had living former occupants and owners, which allowed the team to do audio interviews. These rich stories were represented in the kitchen and dining room. Opening an oven door on a period metal stove offered stories centered around family life and cooking. The dining room showcased a more dramatic moment, as the plates on the table delivered the story of a railroad worker killed on the job on Thanksgiving Day. His family implored him not to leave the holiday gathering to go to work (see Figure 3). The narrative arc and drama of the stories contained in this exhibit were only revealed by visitors' curiosity and the desire to explore and learn more.

The more recent era of the house and its conversion to a triplex allowed audio interviews of the children and adult occupants who

Figure 3. *Open House: If These Walls Could Talk* dining room table installation with plates revealing occupants' images and stories. Courtesy: Michael Mouw.

lived in the apartments in the 1960s and 1970s. Along with audio, they supplied 35mm color slides and 8mm home movies. The bedroom became an opportunity to use a dresser and mirror to show home movies of family vacations hard-earned by saving silver dollars — touching a silver dollar on the dresser top activated this story. Sitting on the bed activated an event to drop the bed and visitor, as a story about the bed breaking down nightly was told. One of the doors in the entryway to the apartments was left slightly open to reveal a portable movie screen with slides and snippets of home movies along with audio stories of family parties and dancing. A look down into a basement window revealed another space with stories of occupants gathering to socialize. Finally, the Hmong American families and the current owners of the house were represented in a modern living room, as their picture window transitioned from a St. Paul street view to show a video documentary about an escape from war-torn Laos, the years in a Thai refugee camp, and arrival by airplane to Minnesota. The quick response to museumgoers' movements and touches by the media and technology show control system delivered short documentary story segments in immersive exhibit settings, yet in an interactive way.

Future of Documentaries

What seems to tie these diverse immersive and interactive storytelling theater projects together is the documentary approach used by MHS to create exhibit experiences, which are unique to a museum visit. Lively, social learning also started in 2007 with the *Minnesota 150 Challenge* eighteen player gallery game — players worked through the quiz show seated in a theater setting and selected their answers to four multiple choice questions on a button interface. Players gained knowledge through the short video documentaries used as feedback that explained the correct answer, as visitors competed for the highest score. The learning game experience proved popular with teens, often a difficult audience to reach in a museum. (Loud cheers in the gallery as youth played the game made their enjoyment of learning obvious.) This learning game project was followed by a four-player quiz show based on the same format called *The 1968 Music Trip*, which tested visitors' knowledge about pop music. With the playful, interactive youth-focused exhibit *Then Now Wow* which opened in 2012, with its *Play the Past* mobile learning game currently in development, MHS is weaving documentary stories into more interactive experiences.

Where will the experience with immersive and interactive documentary storytelling projects lead the Minnesota Historical Society and other institutions focused on a similar approach? We'll need to watch as opportunities appear that allow documentaries and future media and technology platforms create new, synergistic experiences for museumgoers.

7

THE MAKING OF BUDDHA TOOTH RELIC TEMPLE AND MUSEUM VIRTUAL TEMPLE

June Sung Sew and Eric Deleglise

The Buddha Tooth Relic Temple and Museum (BTRTM) was founded in 2002 by Venerable Shi Fa Zhao. This was after a period of collaboration with the Singapore Tourism Board.

In early 1997, Venerable Shi Fa Zhao — who had founded the Golden Pagoda Buddhist Temple in Tampines — was approached by the Singapore Tourism Board to develop a proposal for a temple at Sago Lane. Although a proposal was submitted, work was not carried out due to space constraint.

In early 1998, Venerable Shi Fa Zhao was again approached by the Singapore Tourism Board. This time, the Singapore Tourism Board was seeking to develop a traditional Chinese temple and opera stage for the entire vacant site at Sago Lane. A proposal to meet these new requirements was submitted and this became the basis for subsequent discussions that led to the construction of BTRTM which was officially opened on the eve of Vesak Day (May 30th, 2007).

Background

The mission of BTRTM is to promote and impart the Teaching of Lord Buddha. After its official opening, BTRTM was contemplating using a virtual temple on the web to meet this objective.

It was rather timely then, when Veldis Experience approached them offering to help them realize this idea in November 2010. By using the virtual Château de Richelieu in France as a proof of the concept, Veldis Experience demonstrated that the virtual temple could, indeed, forward the temple's objectives of promoting Buddhist Teachings and Values.

Further discussions followed with a detailed proposal submitted to BTRTM. After careful consideration, the Virtual Temple project started in March 2011. After six months of development, the virtual temple was completed and put online.

Why Virtual Temple

The design philosophy behind BTRTM is rooted in the Tang Dynasty and the Buddhist Mandala. A fair amount of effort was made to ensure that it is accurate and authentic. For example, the roof of the temple is structured according to the "Dou Gong" concept from traditional Chinese architecture. BTRTM's Dou Gong is Tang styled, characterized by its great size, heaviness and ability to withstand heavy loads. It is also exquisitely decorated with post-Tang carvings.

With such attention to detail, the temple provides a unique experience for local and overseas visitors and worshippers alike, to the extent that a single visit is insufficient for a full appreciation of what the temple has to offer. It is important therefore, that BTRTM to provide additional avenues for visitors. To this end, BTRTM created a website with information about its history, culture and heritage.

With the website in place, the next logical step was to evaluate how best to engage visitors to the website. One way of doing this is to go beyond the traditional layout of text and images of website.

While text and images are useful, the two mediums do not offer the spatial detail of a 3D object. Offering things in 3D also adds an additional level of interactivity to users. With users being able to examine objects up close which is not always physically possible in the temple. Such a service enriches the website visitor's experience and deepens the dialogue of the visitor when they visit the museum.

This deepening of the dialogue can be seen at two levels. These are the pre and post visit experiences.

By viewing the virtual temple before the actual visit, the viewer familiarizes themselves with the layout of the temple. This allows them to focus on the content of the temple during their visit. By also indicating specific points of interest in the virtual temple, together with a write up of the significance of the point of interest, visitors become more aware of the temple's background and will find greater meaning when they are moving around the temple during their actual visit.

After the physical visit to the temple, it is also important that visitors have a way of keeping the connection with the temple "alive." A virtual temple allows them to re-experience their visit. More importantly, it also affords them a way to share their experience with the people around them.

Impact of Virtual Temple

To date, the virtual temple receives about 4,000 hits per day. Feedback on the virtual temple has also been largely positive. The concept of virtualizing heritage sites has also begun to catch on and people are more receptive to the idea of an online virtual temple — viewing the temple before and after their physical visit.

The online experience will continue to improve as BTRTM receives feedback from the website's visitors.

Elements of Design

It was decided that the virtual temple had to be a faithful representation of the actual one. In addition, the virtual temple had to be friendly and intuitive to use. This had an impact on how interactivity was built into the website.

When the user first logs into the virtual temple, he is presented with an opening page where he has a choice of loading a low or high resolution version of the temple. With low resolution, the statues and artifacts in the temple and museum are shown as images while with a high resolution, they are shown in 3D. In the same page, basic guidelines for navigation are provided. The virtual temple loads when the user has made a choice between the high or low resolution.

By default, the temple is loaded with the "FREE CAMERA" navigation option. This allows the user to look at the external of the temple using a mouse. In the same interface, the user is presented with an option to enter the temple using the "ENTER COURTYARD" option or to have a preset fly-by of the temple with the "ANIMATE CAMERA" option. Figure 1 shows these options.

By selecting "ENTER COURTYARD", the user begins his virtual tour of the temple by choosing the floor that he wishes to view. At every floor, the user has the freedom to move in all directions.

In the course of implementation, four key considerations were taken into account. These are: Experience, Engagement, Education and E-Commerce.

(1) Experience: The user experience has to be a coherent one. This entails a faithful representation of the temple as well as ensuring that navigation feels natural. The first person perspective of viewing each floor also gives the user a sense of anticipation and preserves the sense of self-discovery when visiting a heritage site. Figures 2 and 3 show a close resemblance of the actual Maitreya Hall and Avalokitesvara Hall of BTRTM.

(2) Engagement: The virtual temple has to engage the user at different levels. Pop-ups are offered at many points of interest. Figure 4 displays pop-up information when clicked. In the near future, detailed views of statues and artifacts could also be offered to increase the number of points of engagement.

(3) Education: Content on the site has to be accurate and relevant. By collaborating with BTRTM closely, Veldis Experience ensures that what is being communicated in the virtual temple achieves BTRTM's mission of increasing the awareness of Buddhist teachings.

Figure 1. BTRTM virtual temple, navigation options.

(4) E-Commerce: The virtual temple has to facilitate the adoption process from visitors. There are two main benefits in making this a priority. First, the website gives BTRTM an additional avenue of growing the funds that go towards the operations and maintenance of the Temple and second, visitors are offered a convenient way of contributing towards BTRTM's.

Methodology and Production Process

Veldis Experience adopted the agile approach to deliver this project.

The agile approach has a strong focus on learning and this is achieved by breaking down the project deliverables into smaller

Figure 2.   Maitreya hall.

components that can be worked on in more discrete amounts of time. These discrete amounts of time with a specific goal is called a "sprint" and the learning effect comes into play when the experience from prior sprints allows Veldis Experience to adjust the goal and time frame for latter sprints.

The scope of work for the temple was broken down into a few stages. The first stage was the creation of the external of the temple and main hall on the ground floor. The second stage was the creation of the inner hall on the ground floor and the fourth floor. The third and final stage was the creation of the rest of the floors. With the Agile approach, Veldis Experience was able to learn from

Figure 3.   Avalokitesvara hall.

each development cycle and align the outcome with the expectation set by BTRTM.

At each stage, pictures of the temple were taken as reference. This was followed by the modeling and rendering process. The resultant models were then imported into the game engine where interactivity and pop-ups were created. At the end of each stage, a review meeting was carried out with BTRTM to validate what had been done.

Unfortunately, this project was not without its challenges. Specifically, a challenge that Veldis Experience faced was the process of digitizing the various statues of the Temple. These were of varying shape, size and detail and the initial use of scanning

Figure 4. Pop-up information.

technologies did not produce satisfactory results. It was decided at a later point that it was more efficient and economical to model each statue individually.

To support realistic visualization in real time, the ShiVa 3D engine from Stonetrip was utilized. This allows the 3D replica of the temple to be loaded on the website and the user is able to navigate in the virtual environment freely. The additional use of streaming technology improves the experience and reduces the delay experienced in the course of viewing the replica.

ShiVa 3D's ability to support multiple platforms was also instrumental in the decision made to adopt it as it gives BTRTM greater flexibility in extending the application to other platforms such as the iPhone and Android in future.

Veldis Experience assigned a dedicated team to this project. The project was led by a project manager. The project manager was in charge of communicating with BTRTM and setting the deliverables to meet the various milestones. In order to achieve this, the project manager planned, assigned and monitored the tasks that the team worked on. Veldis Experience made use of Google Drive as a workspace to make this possible and it allowed the team members to collaborate on the various tasks.

The 3D artist in the team was responsible for digitizing the various assets of the Temple. This included the building, rooms and statues of the Temple. Veldis Experience used various tools and aids to do this. For example, photos and 2D floor plans were used to recreate the various rooms in BTRTM, while 3Ds Max and ZBrush were used to model and render the Temple. In the course of creating the virtual environments, much attention was placed in the use of lighting to shape the atmosphere of the virtual temple.

The graphic designer in the team was responsible for creating the designs of the various interfaces of the virtual temple. He worked closely with the 3D artist to ensure that the textures of the various models were faithfully rendered.

The last member of the team, the 3D programmer was in charge of programming the various aspects of the virtual temple. Various algorithms were applied to stream the virtual Temple in an optimal manner. For example, rooms are loaded before artifacts to ensure that users always have a sense of space while they are using the site. The 3D programmer also worked closely with the 3D artist by importing the models incrementally.

Veldis Experience and BTRTM

The partnership between Veldis Experience and BTRTM is on a project basis and Veldis Experience will continue to help BTRTM to realize their vision and mission through innovative ideas and technologies. Valuable feedback from BTRTM continues to be instrumental in ensuring that the enhancement to the virtual temple is aligned to their goals.

In the course of the current relationship between BTRTM and Veldis Experience, via the provision of system maintenance services, Veldis Experience will continue to populate the virtual temple with new statues and objects as well as improve on the other qualitative aspects of the project.

Perspective

Veldis Experience is thankful for the opportunity to work with BTRTM and continues to be open to dialogue with BTRTM. Further work and enhancements that Veldis Experience would like to propose includes the provision of up close views of the various artifacts in the museum as well as upgrading the museum's mobile apps.

By extension, Veldis Experience is committed to playing a greater role in the community and will seek to work with other sites of heritage and culture.

Conclusion

To conclude, the digitization of BTRTM has certainly demonstrated itself to be a mutually beneficial relationship. On the one hand, the project has given BTRTM a new way of reaching out to its visitors — with pre and post visit experiences on top of the physical one.

On the other hand, the project was also an excellent opportunity for Veldis Experience to contribute by conserving the community's culture and heritage in digital form. Furthermore, the challenges faced in the process of executing the project have allowed the company's approach to such projects to mature.

Given the benefits, Veldis Experience certainly looks forward to continuing its relationship with BTRTM.

Acknowledgements

We would like to thank Mr EeTiangHwee, Deputy Director of BTRTM for taking his precious time off in reading our chapter and providing his most insightful comments and recommendations.

Besides, we also wish to extent our sincere gratitude to Mr Joseph Sia for his excellent work and skill in proofreading and editing.

8

DIGITAL MEDIA IN MUSEUMS: A PERSONAL HISTORY

Selma Thomas

While digital media is a relatively new medium, interactive technologies (originally based on a combination of analog and digital media) have been available to, and actively used by cultural institutions for many decades. Specifically, interactive technology has played a significant role in museum exhibitions, since the late 1980s. For this reason, the world of museums is a convenient microcosm in which to examine the transformative role of digital media on such essential factors as mission, operations and public programs. Furthermore, a brief summary of this history can provide some insights to contemporary practitioners and scholars on the development of both a strategy and an implementation policy in developing a digital heritage ecosystem.

Museums are civic and cultural institutions, created for the public good. They are physical manifestations of cultural aspirations, buildings filled with objects collected over time. Some of the objects are closely associated with famous individuals. In the US, for example, we have collected items from our most celebrated presidents, early portraits of George Washington, our first President; Thomas Jefferson, who wrote the Declaration of Independence; and, Abraham Lincoln, President during the American Civil War. History museums across the US, particularly the national museums of the Smithsonian Institution, hold objects and artifacts related to these most beloved leaders.

But our museum collections also reflect the lives of ordinary people, traditional clothing from earlier times, worn by farmers or fishermen. They might also include the tools of craftsmen, household furnishings, children's toys, or women's jewelry; those items that help us better understand the lives of our ancestors.

The reason for collecting, preserving and displaying is always the same: the public good. In the early days of museums, centuries ago, they were considered temples of knowledge, and they were constructed to house the treasures of a community. Beginning in the late 1980s, museums began to expand their role in society; they evolved into more open institutions. They became places of public learning, encouraging and supporting public discourse on both academic and popular culture. With the subsequent development of social media and smartphones, museums have continued to revise their role in the cultural sphere.

But the essential nature of museums remains: they are cultural institutions that collect, preserve, and display objects. All of these activities presume a physical structure, a collection and an audience. These three elements — building, objects, and public — will shape much of the intellectual and interpretive work done by staff and scholars. Museum programming traditionally takes place inside a dedicated public space. That space may reflect the architectural vocabulary of the museum building. A historic house, for example, will impose different restrictions on museum curators than a modern building with large, square rooms. Inside this public space, the staff will place collected or borrowed objects, selected to create a narrative experience, that is, to tell a story.

If the objects on display tell a story, it is the task of the visitor to listen to that story, and to reflect on it. Every institution knows the demographics of its visitors, their average age, where they live, what time of year they like to visit. A small site museum, for example, might welcome repeat visitors, neighbors who want to bring their children on repeat visits, to help them better understand their community. A large national museum will host both residents and tourists, introducing both groups to the cultural, social and historical dynamics of the country.

These factors help define the museum's role as an educational institution: all learning takes place inside a public space, animated by selected objects, in which visitors come and go at their own pace and at their own direction. But these factors also define the museum's role as a cultural institution: collecting and preserving a nation's cultural heritage, in the form of objects, and interpreting this heritage, in exhibitions, for the benefit of the public at large. This background is essential to understanding the role of digital media in today's museums, particularly today's museum exhibits.

When we discuss museum exhibits, we examine the essence of what museums promise to the public, we use words like "interpretation," "integrity," and "authority." We presume an object-based experience that takes place in a public space. The introduction of media into this experience is a challenge to all of these concepts. So it becomes an easy vehicle to look at how our ideas, about interpretation, authority and even audience, have changed (or not) since digital media was first introduced to museums, almost thirty years ago. At the same time, looking at digital media inside the microcosm of a museum system also helps us understand the role (real and potential) of digital media in a larger cultural ecosystem.

Early History

In the mid-20th century, many museums began to use 16mm and 35mm films to enhance their exhibitions. They created specially produced films that were screened in separate rooms, small theaters or auditoriums, and visitors were invited to supplement the exhibition experience and watch the films. Archeology museums, for example, might invite visitors to watch a short documentary film that introduced them to scholarly experts, or transported them to historic sites, in an effort to expand on exhibition themes. Art museums might have used such a film to discuss the biography of an artist featured in a special exhibition. Traditionally, museums set aside a dedicated space where films could be shown to visitors, and this gathering (small groups of people assembled for a shared purpose) was designed to enhance the exhibition promise of a collective experience.

The use of film, at this time, was seen as a special benefit, an opportunity to give visitors more background — on an artist, or a site history; but it was not considered a part of the exhibition. It was a separate experience, set aside in a room outside the exhibit galleries. Visitors could choose to walk past a theater showing such a film, and many did, since neither they nor the museum staff considered the film to be integral to the exhibition experience.

Film is not a digital medium. It is an old technology, first introduced in the 19th century, which became a vibrant and popular medium for audiences worldwide. Its use in museums was limited, but that early use of film, to remind visitors of background information (the lives of artists, or the history of archeological sites), was an attempt by museums to use more than just the traditional tools (of objects) to tell an exhibition story.

This use of film was based on a traditional idea of storytelling: the filmmaker (or storyteller) is in control of the story. Visitors can only watch and listen; they cannot change the terms of the story. They cannot interrupt it to follow a different narrative, or even to ask questions. There is great, and enduring, value in this technique, and museums used it in creative ways. Moreover, the nature of telling a story with a single voice reflected the museum's role as a cultural and educational institution. As experts, museums presented visitors with information and visitors welcomed this information.

In the early 1980s, this form of storytelling began to change; and it changed for several reasons. First, museum staff now had access to a new digital technology, controlled by computers. This allowed them to create "interactive" films, which invited visitors to select from a "menu" of choices. Visitors were invited to choose a selection from a pre-programmed menu and pursue a more in-depth relationship with an idea, an artifact or an individual. More significantly, these digital tools helped to establish a new relationship between visitors and museums. Designed with touch-screen computer controls, this new digital media supported a private experience. Visitors engaged the computer monitor individually, with perhaps a friend or two looking over their shoulders. This was not the group experience of the film theater and the grand moments of film gave way to the intimate experiences of digital media. The interactivity of computer-controlled media also gave visitors the means of controlling the narrative: they could pursue, for example, a set number of links to follow only a single aspect of a story.

By giving visitors the tools of their own exploration, museums in the 1980s altered the relationship between visitors and museums, inviting visitors to control their own experiences. In effect, by sharing the tools of exploration, museums were also sharing some of their cultural authority.

But museums were also placing these digital tools inside the exhibition, making them integral to the exhibition experience. Digital screens were placed beside cases of selected objects: they might be used to interpret the actual objects, or they might be used to help the visitor better understand the process by which the objects were selected. In either case, the digital screens contained information that engaged visitors directly. These digital programs were not set inside isolated theaters, like the documentary films of earlier generations. Instead, they were carefully designed to take their place alongside object cases and other significant artifacts.

With this placement, digital media seemed to challenge the authority of objects. If we want visitors to engage with museum objects, why are we asking them to watch a program on a digital screen? Why are we asking them to engage in pictures of other objects, when they are standing in a room full of carefully curated objects? This was, and remains, a critical question, for curators, educators and media producers.

There is no single answer to this question. Rather, it is a test that we, museum professionals, must use to evaluate our use of digital media. Sometimes we use digital media to introduce the significant resources of oral histories: we photograph elders talking about old craft traditions; or we ask them to sing old songs that we want to record. The best means of incorporating these stories into the exhibit is digital media. But, even as we are producing these programs, we are hoping to create "documents" that have the same integrity, the same significance, as our collections of objects.

Digital media allows us, as museum professionals, to create intimate experiences, to help visitors better relate to objects, or to exhibit themes. It helps us animate old and static objects; and it helps remind visitors that the past was once alive, with an uncertain future. All of these possibilities can enhance the exhibits that we are curating; and museums across the world have adopted digital tools to enrich their galleries.

Case Study

I began my career in museums as a historian and a filmmaker, in 1984, when I was invited to work on an exhibition at the National Museum of American History. The exhibit was about an aspect of American History that took place during WWII, and the museum staff wanted to incorporate digital media, which was then a new, and untried, tool.

We understood that this tool gave us the means of including oral histories, the testimonies of people who had been alive during the War. They could bring their untold stories into the museum gallery, to help visitors "read" the collected objects and to better understand that the United States of the 1940s was a complicated and modern world.

We recorded these histories with digital tools that allowed us to bring the face and voice of the informant into the museum. Again, using computer-controls, we let visitors choose which of the histories they wanted to access, helping to create an intimate relationship between visitor and informant, and (effectively) between visitor and the history that was being related.

But we also had to address the conceptual implications of using digital media. Specifically, we asked: "why are we using technology in a museum exhibition? When the museum experience promises a relationship to a real object, why are we asking visitors to look at a computer screen, especially a computer screen surrounded by real objects?" We asked that question and discussed with it on multiple terms, as curators, designers, media producers. That discussion led us to consider the relationship between museum and object — what was our responsibility to the artifact and how did our use of media effect the interpretation, or even the meaning, of the object? But we also questioned how the use of media effected the relationship between museum and visitor as well as the relationship between visitor and object — that is, how did our use of media enhance or diminish the visitor experience and, especially the visitor's trust in the museum.

Our discussion worried that the use of media undermined the "authenticity" of the visitor experience but, in the end, we agreed that media brought to the exhibit a sense of humanity and an emotional reality that was, in fact, a critical part of the historical record. This process of questioning our curatorial and scholarly intents helped us shape the digital media and also helped us integrate it into the exhibit. The digital tools allowed us to use a traditional historical source, oral histories, and to give it a new platform.

Almost ten years after our first experiments with digital media, the museum produced an online version of our WWII exhibit, under the direction of the original curator. I did not work on that version but, about the same time, I was working at the National Gallery of Art, in Washington, DC, helping to digitize their collection and creating the platform for several online programs. Both the curator and I talked about the design, and conceptual, problems inherent in translating a site-based experience into an online program. By then, ten years after the introduction of digital media into exhibits, both the visitor expectation of "interactivity" and the technology supporting that interactivity had Matured. By then, visitors no longer chose from a limited menu. Instead, they pursued a more open-ended search, adopting a protocol that had been established by the Web.

We, as museum professionals, also adapted to the new protocol: instead of creating a narrative defined by the size of an exhibit gallery, we used the parallel universe of the Internet, to address an audience of Web users. We paid more attention to things like interface design, navigation tools, and hot links. We also conferred with new colleagues; in addition to curators and educators, we also learned how to work with web designers.

The Internet

By the early 1990s, ten years after their initial use of digital media, museums had to address this new digital challenge. The Internet allowed virtual visitors to sit at a computer (whether at home or in a museum gallery) and pursue their own explorations. The early Internet allowed visitors more control over their own experiences, and it gave visitors the means to follow multiple links, even if this search took them away from the museum and its collections.

A visitor to an online exhibit on modern photography, for example, might choose to leave the museum site to visit a link to an individual photographer. A virtual visitor to the Louvre's website might search for an Renaissance painter, and then leave the Louvre site to learn more about that painter from multiple museum sites. This exploration, which takes place outside the museum's walls, allows the visitor to relate directly to the idea of collections (if not the actual collections); but it seems to undermine the visitor's actual relationship to the museum itself. Indeed, the Internet (more than any previous digital system) has transformed the relationship between museum and visitor, indeed, between collections and visitor.

At the same time, utilizing the technology of the Web, museums everywhere have been able to create a parallel universe for their audiences. Museum web sites now offer an interactive, visitor-controlled, exploration, sometimes based on exhibitions that might be found in the bricks-and-mortar museum, sometimes based on exhibitions designed exclusively for the Web. Unlike the social experience of the old museum films, these online programs address a single user at a time and allow each user to fashion a unique experience, navigating according to his, or her, own interest. This narrative experience generally takes place on a small screen, with the user (literally) an arm's length away from the screen.

With this second phase of digital media, we worried less about the notion of "authenticity"; we worried less about how the media would interfere with the visitor experience. Because, in fact, the medium was the primary experience, though it borrowed some of its authority from the traditional museum experience. More users trusted, and visited, those online sites developed by museums. More significantly, the most overt impact of the Web was to redefine the notion (and reality) of "public space". By the late 1990s, museums were forced to acknowledge, and address, the presence of two concurrent venues, the bricks-and-mortar museum (to use an old term) and the online museum.

Social Media and Mobile Apps

Today, the Internet is more than twenty years old, and it has changed so quickly that the experiences of the 1990s seem like ancient history. Now, with the growing significance of social media, smart phones and mobile apps, potential visitors have even more tools with which they can originate and manipulate museum programming. In one of the earliest examples of visitor-created programs, in the early years of the 21st centuries, students at Marymount Manhattan College, in New York, created their own audio programs, called *Art Mobs*, irreverent guides to the collections of the Museum of Modern Art, also in New York. These are available, free, on the Internet and they have become popular with visitors of all ages. The Smithsonian's American Art Museum has worked with schoolchildren to create podcasts, likewise, audio guides to their collections.

In the same time period, I taught two classes at the Johns Hopkins University Museum Studies Programs, in which students created digital media for the Textile Museum, in Washington, DC, and the Hillwood Estate Museum and Garden, also in Washington. Both museums posted these vodcasts, video guides, to their web sites, allowing visitors to explore their collections before, or after, a visit.

The general public now has the tools to create its own digital media and to share it with others, via social media, mobile apps or smartphones. These new tools give offsite "visitors" the means to create and maintain an autonomous venue for museum programs. The web is often a visitor's first encounter with a museum, giving directions to first-time visitors, sending updates and invitations to members. While this does not replace the act of walking into a building and visiting a gallery, the Web does create, and sustain, a solo experience, a long way from the group experience of visitors sitting in a theater watching a film, or walking through an exhibit.

These tools and experiences will not replace museums but they will alter the relationship between museums and their visitors. In some ways, they already have. One of the implicit lessons in museum exhibitions has always been the value of informal public education. We walk into the public space of an exhibit and we see other people. Some of them look like us, some look like "others," and for the duration of the program we are part of a group. The program addresses us with the plural "you."

The impact of digital media, starting with the earliest computer tools, has been to diminish the group experience. In its place, this media offers an intimate encounter between visitor and program and the degree of intimacy has grown at the expense of the big picture, as it relates to both collections and audience. At the same time that museums have opened their doors to a more and more diverse public, they have altered the "public" nature of their programs, leading visitors into more personal, less social, encounters; and they have used media to drive this development. What was once a general audience (people gathering in public spaces, like museums, to share a common cultural experience) has become an audience of niche markets, and media has been the driving force in this transformation?

Conclusion

I began my work in museums, as a documentary filmmaker, in the late 1980s, producing exhibit media. I made the transition with an academic interest in the kind of programming that museum media could support; and I enjoyed the degree of intimacy the medium afforded. Installed in small galleries, media could facilitate a conversation between visitor and museum, between visitor and text.

It was not the only source of information or interpretation, but it could enhance the relationship between visitor and object, to bring into the gallery an emotional reality that was not always obvious in more static installations. When the exhibit media worked, it could make the past more immediate, or a science more understandable. When it did not work, it was expensive wallpaper. Now, almost thirty years later, I see a landscape that has matured, for better and worse.

Could I predict the future, either long-term or short-term? No prudent professional working with digital media would make predictions. But I would not hesitate to say that media has transformed the museum: it has transformed the relationships between museum and visitor, between visitor and collection, and between museum and society. We can view this dynamic of transformation, of challenging long-held beliefs and even behaviors, inside the microcosm of museums as a means to examine how digital heritage will affect the cultural world at large.

Instead of predictions, I would offer some personal suggestions for evaluating the role of digital heritage. First, I would argue that it is important to know the history of digital media. An historical awareness helps us assess the impact of media, on our programs, our audiences, and our cultural infrastructure. I think this awareness also helps us shape effective digital media programs and effective relationships with both the public and potential partners.

At the same time, a knowledge of our professional history also helps to establish a professional community. It gives us an analytical vocabulary and a perspective that is critical to advance both the impact and the evolution of Digital Media. An awareness of professional history also helps us to understand digital media as its own discipline, albeit one with roots in multiple disciplines. In a very short time-span, digital media has become Digital Heritage. If we hope to nurture this new discipline, and create a supportive ecosystem, we must nurture the global community already at work on digital heritage. There are many diverse histories, similar to the museum experience that helped to shape the current landscape of digital heritage. If we can share that history, in professional conferences and publications, then we can begin to develop a stronger community and a stronger future for digital heritage.

9

USING NEW MEDIA FOR EXHIBIT INTERPRETATION: A CASE STUDY, YUAN MING YUAN QING EMPERORS' SPLENDID GARDENS

Herminia Din, Darrell L. Bailey and Fang-Yin Lin

Introduction

The rapid advancement of technology has transformed modern society. The development of animation, video games, interactive projection, augmented reality, mobile phones, and other new media applications has profoundly influenced contemporary lifestyle and social interaction. In the museum field, these advancements have had a significant impact on learning and experiencing cultural objects and the heritage associated with those objects.

Museums throughout the world have adopted various digital media strategies for exhibition design, spatial and floor planning, educational outreach, and social media interaction to take advantage of this shifting paradigm. Consequently, integrating new media interpretation into exhibition planning has become a standard practice for enhancing the museum experience.

This paper focuses on core concepts of digital storytelling in preserving cultural heritage. It describes the process of planning, developing, and organizing the *Yuan Ming Yuan — Qing Emperors'*

Splendid Gardens exhibit, as an example of a comprehensive approach in applying new media technology for interpretation. Although three dimensional computer simulation techniques have been used to visualize heritage sites, this exhibit goes further by using digital tools to represent archaeological artifacts and historical events in developing a "fully integrated" exhibit narrative.

This chapter will also explore and analyze the use of new media technology in exhibit interpretation to emphasize the appreciation of artistic beauty and meaning. The goal is for the visitor to both have an aesthetic experience and gain historical understanding.

Basic Interpretation and Appreciation of Asian Art and History

In exploring the use of new media for artistic interpretation, it is necessary to first gain a perspective of the Asian art culture. This is important in order to effectively implement appropriate technologies that will advance a better understanding of that art and its unique cultural elements.

Asian art covers a broad spectrum including calligraphy, painting, books, literature, bronzes, ceramics, jade, curios, furniture, religion, etc. The geographic region is vast incorporating China, Japan, Korea, Mongolia, Western Persia, South Asia, India, the Himalayas, and Southeast Asia. More than five thousand years of Asian art and history are in this domain from the arts and humanities to the affective realm of religious thought.

Developing an understanding and appreciation of Asian art and history without formal training is a challenge for the general museum audience. Empathizing with Asian art requires adjusting to a different time and space, and embracing one's own cultural background and poetic spirit. Cultivating an appreciation for Asian art and history is multifaceted. Observations of basic media features, historical backgrounds, life, genre, religion, culture, and geography begin this understanding. One then analyzes the formal structure (form, layout, techniques, etc.) to explore the meaning of the work including thoughts and feelings of the artist represented through the object.

Basic appreciation courses provide a insight by encouraging learners to: (1) develop a brief description of works in an intuitive way to describe one's impression, (2) analyze materials, techniques, layout, and characteristics of the genre, (3) interpret meaning from cultural, social, political and economic factors, artist's personality, thought processes, and outlook on art's relationship with the meaning to be explored, and (4) develop value judgments from multiple perspectives to draw conclusions (Anderson, 1988; Chapman, 1978; Feldman, 1967; Greer, 1987). All this is really a cognitive process of cultivating the audience's aesthetic sensibility and spiritual connection to art and history.

Essential questions must be asked. What role does new media technology play in this interpretive process? To what extent does media technology meet museum audience needs? How do narrative-based exhibit interpretations balance education and entertainment?

Essence of the Story and New Media Integration

As early as the 1960's, Molly Harrison (1956, pg. 18) observed that "whether intentionally or unintentionally, the museum has done everything educational." When digital media is used in a museum exhibition, it must have a clear purpose. It is necessary to first understand the cultural foundations of Asian art and history, and then apply new media tools to facilitate the process. Technology should remain in the background to allow viewers to authentically experience the object and/or the historical event.

However, the key lies in "content development" and that of the "story" rather than the technology itself. As the *New Century Museum* (AAM, 1984) stated: "If the heart of the museum was its collections, education was the museum's soul." This illustrates the importance of narrative-based interpretation. The museum's role is to inspire a desire to "know" and build the visitor's interest. How to use media technology to effectively convey the story and history of the cultural heritage becomes the real challenge.

To conceptualize the museum as an informal learning environment, one must have an environment that attracts visitors. Han (Han and

Lee, 1987) stated that the museum "requires a dedicated commitment to education and entertainment. This combination of continuous progress and improvement will be directly reflected in the visitor's impressions and attitudes." In later writings (Han, 2000), he pointed out that past successes of relics exhibitions needed to have at least two values: "first for beauty and second for the exotic." But today's exhibits often do not attract audiences to collections on their own merits, but rather for the design of new technology devices. Reflecting on Dewey's *Art as Experience* (1934), some may experience a pleasant first experience that might be lively and interesting, but eventually develop disinterest as it lacks coherence. These visitor experiences often are superficially built on "sound and light" entertainment. Chen (2004) mentioned, "Relationships between education and entertainment must be rethought.

Museums that offer a variety of diverse digital displays of interpretation, must ask whether this is merely grandstanding to meet audience expectations." Is the display content original or eclectic? How can one achieve an appropriate balance between entertainment and educational standards? How is the atmosphere of the museum exhibition space created to enhance the audience experience?

Keng (2006) writes that museum business strategies are shifting due to changes in the "heritage" based static display so that "people" become the center of participation. Many interactive display approaches emphasize that visual beauty should be restructured in the exhibition to provide elements such as creative lighting to enhance the visual field of focus. But she cautioned that the use of expedient, excessive digitization could create issues. Limitations exist and need to be recognized including using education and entertainment as "a show." Computer technology images and sound and lighting effects need to be assessed whether their purpose is mere entertainment. "Imaginary" (Imaging Technology) configurations, even skillfully decorated restoration, ecological landscaping, or virtual reality spaces cannot ultimately replace the "real" objects.

The use of new technology must be tempered based on the premise "for what purpose" is its use. Educational media should remain "faithful to the original" and the "faithful to the original" copy is not just dull presentation, but uses new technology to bring beauty, creativity, and inspiration (Din *et al.*, 2012). The intent is not to blindly follow outmoded audio-visual technology. Of most importance is to maintain high expectations in how to present the interpretation of results if one wants the audience to feel differently from past experiences with visual media. If the exhibition creates an interesting story, curatorial efforts will have succeeded. If the exhibition is a theater, curatorial efforts need to have roles and actors arranged in order to make dramatic impact (Huang, 2006). Also, stage (exhibition space), lighting design, and situational placement are equally important in creating the atmosphere.

The best investment in the exhibition is discovering how best to capture the beauty and meaning of the object and history itself. Providing viewers with collections containing authentic dialogue is the most important role of the museum. Liu (2007; 2010) believes that a museum can provide a theatrical experience to touch people's hearts and minds, and a place of interest to further lead the audience toward both the spirit and the heritage behind the story.

A Case Study: *Yuan Ming Yuan — Qing Emperor's Splendid Gardens* Exhibition

Background

The effective use of digital technology and understanding of Chinese art, history and culture have positioned Taiwan to transform traditional curatorial interpretation of asian art. Through international award-winning exhibits, participation in the Taiwan e-Learning and Digital Archive Program, museum projects with the National Palace Museum in Taiwan, Taiwan National Museum of Natural Science, Victoria and Albert Museum in London and many others, Bright Ideas Design's interpretations in the application of media arts, educational outreach efforts, creative solutions, and storytelling skills sets the tone for the creation of this exhibit. When the cross-strait cultural exchanges between the governments of Taiwan and China began, Bright Ideas Design's approach of using new media for exhibit interpretation gradually gained recognition.

In early 2010, the Beijing Yuan Ming Yuan Management Committee authorized Bright Ideas Design to develop a complete design and planning strategy for the cultural heritage site. It later signed a memo of understanding to be its future long-term partner. In 2011, Bright Ideas Design participated in the Beijing International Cultural and Creative Industry Expo, and officially presented the *Digital Yuan Ming Yuan* project. In 2012, the Beijing municipal government announced an important project, "Promoting the Development of the Haidian District Three Hills and Five Gardens Historical and Cultural Scenic Area," to create extended digital interpretations of lost cultural heritage sites. This will complement the Great Wall, the Forbidden City, and Temple of Heaven as another highly regarded cultural travel destination.

Exhibit Concept

Yuan Ming Yuan, also known as the "Gardens of Perfect Brightness" was first constructed in the year of 1709 during the reign of the Emperor Kangxi of the Qing dynasty (1644–1911). It is located in the "Three Hills and Five Gardens", an area in the northwestern suburbs of Beijing. The "Three Hills" refers to Xiangshan (Fragrant Hill), Yuquan (Jade Spring), and Wanshoushan (Longevity). The "Five Gardens" can refer to the Five Gardens of Yuanmingyuan, Changchunyuan, Xichunyuan, Chunxiyuan, and Qichunyuan, or the Five Gardens of the late Qing including Chaungchunyuan, Yuanmingyuan, Yiheyuan, Jiyiyuan, and Jingmingyuan.

In the early days these hills and gardens stood independent of one another yet were linked to form an integral whole. Expansion was continued for the next 150 years through six emperors that once comprised the imperial gardens of the Qing dynasty covering a total area of 350 hectares (over 864 acres).

Innovative by design, the *Yuan Ming Yuan — Qing Emperor's Splendid Gardens* exhibit is intended to reach both national and international audiences. The remains of the Yuan Ming Yuan are today only fragments, thus making it impossible to be completely restored to its former appearance. The artifacts of its gardens and buildings have been destroyed or scattered among various collections. Because their locations and intactness have long since changed, this has completely transformed the contemporary consciousness of the Yuan Ming Yuan.

Scholars in various fields have suggested not proceeding with an on-site reconstruction, which would destroy what precious little remains. Rather, they have suggested another form of reconstruction to preserve the historical appearance and meaning of the gardens and its history. This approach would combine the ideas of cultural creativity and heritage preservation that represents an important breakthrough to present more viscerally these historical remains and archaeological artifacts. With the interactive experiences of this exhibition, the unseen becomes visible again.

Using New Media for Creative Interpretation

In 2003, Bright Ideas Design began using animation to interpret the poetic soul and literary story of Chinese paintings. It first created a short animation — *Red Cliff* — and it was the quest of finding ancient memory and cultural link. Su Shi's poem *Red Cliff*, Zhao Meng's *Su Shi's Portrait*, and Kim Wu Yuan's painting *Red Cliff Map* form the blueprint to construct a 3D digital dynamic space. Recreated in ninety seconds of animation, it takes viewers into the traditional Chinese ink world by incorporating lute-like sounds that build an emotional connection with the mountain wrapping endlessly along the Yangtze River. Integrating the interpretation of the story between reality and imagination engages the audience with Chinese classical poetry and water-ink landscape painting (see Figure 1).

For the 2011 Taiwan International Cultural and Creative Technology Expo Culture Center, Bright Ideas Design launched the *Peach Blossom Spring* exhibition to interpret Chinese literati utopia. This was a fusion of digital technology and the performing arts in curatorial practices. Through this new media interactive installation, performance art and other cross-border performances engaged the audience's imagination of life and nature (Figure 2).

Within the *Peach Blossom Spring* section, the "Flow" presentation is most notable. "Flow" is cited from the *Tao Te Ching*, a Chinese classic text written around the 6th century BC by the sage Lao Tzu. It means "the highest excellence is like that of water" as it "benefits

Figure 1.   *Red Cliff*, Animation. Source: Bright Ideas Design.

Figure 2.   *Peach Blossom Spring/Painting Imagination*, Interactive Installation. Source: Bright Ideas.

Figure 3. *Peach Blossom Spring/Flow.* Source: Bright Ideas Design.

all things without struggle." This explores the Chinese literati highest level of good-deeded hearts. Integrating the *Paradise Dance Theatre* professional dancers and the koi-lotus multimedia interactive floor projection, this exhibit invites the audience to participate and experience the timeless aesthetics of life, and hopefully find utopia within their own hearts (see Figure 3).

About the Exhibit

In 2010, planning and research for the Yuan Ming Yuan — *Qing Emperor's Splendid Gardens* exhibit began. Yuan Ming Yuan is one of the grandest imperial gardens in Chinese history and one of the finest examples in the world's history of garden. It represents the essence of regional styles in China from north and south as well as east and west. After a clash with western powers in the middle of the 19th century, it was almost totally destroyed. One can only speculate how magnificent it must have appeared during its golden age. Scholars have continued to scour archival records and architectural history in an effort to reconstruct the original appearance.

The exhibit opened in Taipei, Taiwan on July 5th, 2013. It begins with a documentary of the tumultuous events of October 16th, 1860 when British and French invaders burned the Yuan Ming Yuan at the end of the Second Opium War (1856–1860). This overview enables audiences to understand how it was destroyed in a conflict between two different worlds. The exhibit is organized in six chapters to tell the story, and is created as a series of multi-dimensional experiences to explore the Yuan Ming Yuan from different viewpoints. Combining interactive installations, documentaries, animation, and digital displays, the exhibit takes audiences through time and space to one of the most beautiful reflections of the Qing dynasty.

Chapter 1: Scenes from Another Time presents the earliest glass-negative photography of the Yuan Ming Yuan by the German photographer Ernst Ohlmer (1847–1927), and fragments of imperial collections that made their way into foreign collections, medals of honor awarded to foreign officers, and accounts founds in diaries. Augmenting the historical objects, it uses a double-sided display combined with holographic projection technology for viewers to see one side of the building burning, and from another viewpoint see the building aligned with the garden landscape from the paintings of *Album of the Forty Views of the Garden of Perfect Brightness*. Separating the space-time framework for the exhibition into two different perspectives presents a unique visitor experience (see Figure 4).

Figure 4. *Burning of Yuan Ming Yuan,* Architectural Reconstruction, Exhibit Schematic. Source: Bright Ideas Design.

In *Chapter 4: Images of Jiangnan: Qianlong's Southern Design Journey,* animation techniques are used to depict the prosperous southern style of arts and design and its cultural impact on the north. Taken from several volumes from Qing court painter Xu Yang's *The Qianlong Emperor's Southern Inspection Tour* (1681), this large-scale interactive display uses sensory device to trigger descriptions of different sceneries, locations, shops, activities, and imitate daily conversations among people from the scroll. This adds amusing yet historically accurate aspects for audiences to become immersed in the story (see Figure 5).

The Qianlong Emperor's six tours of the south and his deep fascination for Jiangnan inspired a trend for imitating Jiangnan garden scenery in the north. In *Chapter 5: Reminiscing of Jiangnan,* interactive multimedia installation creates an immersive atmosphere to bring the audience into the emperor's garden home life. From rendering Qianlong's poetic paintings, audiences can experience enchanting manmade scenery where past and present intermingle in the four seasons at the Yuan Ming Yuan (see Figure 6).

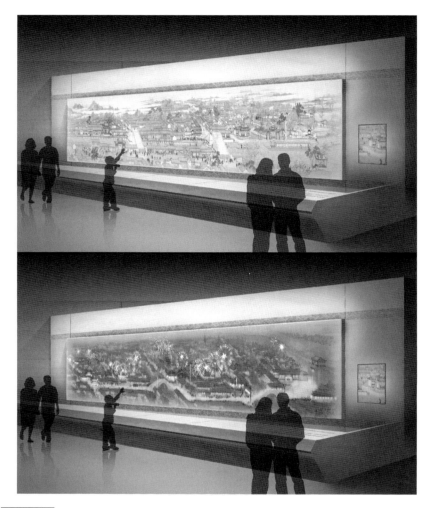

Figure 5. *The Qianlong Emperor's Southern Inspection Tour,* Interactive Multimedia Installation, Exhibit Schematic. Source: Bright Ideas Design.

The Qianlong Emperor had an enduring fascination with western culture. The western-style buildings complex at the Changchun Garden was once known as the *Versailles of the East.* It was the first large-scale imitation of western architecture and gardening at an imperial garden in China (see Figure 7). He was also quite fond of fountains and mechanical inventions, especially western

Figure 6. *Reminiscing of Jiangnan,* Interactive Multimedia Installation, Exhibit Schematic. Source: Bright Ideas Design.

Figure 7.   Haiyen Tang, Copperplate Print. Source: Bright Ideas Design.

methods of timekeeping. An interesting observation is that the first draft of the fountains at the Haiyen Tang by the famous Italian court artist, Giuseppe Castiglione (1688–1766), specified nude ladies. Instead, Qianlong had them changed to the twelve animals of the Chinese zodiac, which became the famous water clock with twelve animal heads and human body.

This section of the exhibit integrates modern forms of art and technology to reinterpret the action, providing a glimpse of imperial taste in the 18th century. The *Haiyen Tang Twelve Zodiac Animals Water Clock Fountain* is a multimedia installation using the latest clear transparent LCD flat screen technology (see Figure 8). Each of the animal heads spews water daily on a designated time schedule. The original display was destroyed during the war, but this new media interpretation provides an innovative way to tell the story.

Western art music, especially baroque music of the 18th century, played an important role in blending the east and west. During this period, the Italian emissary missionary Teodorico Pedrini (1671–1746) wrote select compositions for the Kangxi Emperor (see Figure 9).

Figure 8.   Haiyen Tang Twelve Zodiac Animals Water Clock Fountain, Multimedia
Installation. Source: Bright Ideas Design.

Figure 9. Pedrini's Portrait and Music Score. Source: Bright Ideas Design.

In order to provide to the audiences a 21st century experience to the glory past, Bright Ideas Design collaborated with a sound artist Santiago Latorre from Spain to recreate Pedrini's *Neipulidi Violin Sonata* — a historical archive retrieved from the University of San Francisco's Ricci Institute for Chinese-Western Cultural History. Through literature, crafts, music, performance, garden home life, and architectural design, visitors can more fully experience the Qing's royal lifestyle and pluralist outlook.

Conclusion

Technological innovations have forever changed people's lives. As part of this evolution, museums are facing constant innovation in digital technology. This presents both challenges and opportunities. If properly harnessed these can offer museums great potential but must be used wisely. Employing the vast array of interpretive media in the museum exhibit must be carefully and "thoughtfully" planned.

Designers should carefully assess their target audience and consider the use of only such technologies and practices appropriate for a given exhibit that is consistent with the purposes of the exhibition and core values. The selection of technology tools and the desired goals must be clearly defined. The quality of digital content is more important than technology — this should be a guiding principle. Sustaining the aesthetic is the core value that makes a museum exhibit what it truly is; yet balancing educational interpretation with entertainment in the application of new technologies is critical.

The purpose of this paper is to stimulate a more thoughtful conversation about the use of new media for exhibit interpretation. It seeks to be a starting point for thinking and reflection. Examples have been given that use a variety of interpretative technologies in museums. Considerations of the "story to be told" accompanied by academic research, place audience's needs and educational significance as the first priority. Planning how to effectively and coherently interpret an exhibit provides the blueprint for selecting the most appropriate media tools to achieve optimum results. Technology is a tool, and a beginning, not an end unto itself.

The "museum" is a very special place and uses its "exhibitions" as the interface to provide viewers with a direct face-to-face experience with an authentic collection to both educate and inspire. Reliving ancient civilizations through yellowed painting scrolls and artifacts in the 21st century under the guidance of new media technology, truly takes the arts and humanities to new levels. These goals are indeed lofty, but so is the human experience. The sense of "wonderment" is priceless, and that is the true legacy that museums can leave for generations to come.

References

AAM (1984). *Museums for a New Century: A Report of the Commission on Museums for a New Century.* Washington, DC: The American Alliance of Museums Press.

Anderson, T (1988). A Structure for Pedagogical Art Criticism. *Studies in Art Education*, 30(1), 28–38.

Chapman, L (1978). *Approaches to Art In Education.* New York: Harcourt College Pub.

Chen, SY (2004). Towards a New Pedagogy in Museum in a Global Risk Context. Taipei, Taiwan. *Museology Quarterly*, 18(1), 7–17.

Din, H, KC Chuang, TJ Tai, WC Huang, CY Wong and JP Lin (2012), Museum Media and Technology: Five Thought-Provoking Questions. *Journal of Museum and Culture*, (4), 169–196.

Dewey, J (1934). *Art as Experience*. New York: Minton, Balch & Company.

Feldman, EB (1967). *Art as Image and Idea*. New Jersey: Prentice-Hall.

Greer, WD (1987). A Structure of Discipline Concepts for Discipline-Based Art Education. *Studies in Art Education*, 28(4), 227–233.

Harrison, M (1956). Museums in Education. *Education Abstracts (Special Issue)*. UNESCO.

Han, PT and Lee, LC (1987). *Collection of Essays: Chinese Atheistic*. Taipei, Taiwan: Nan-Tien Publisher.

Han, PT (2000). *Museum Management*. Taipei, Taiwan: Garden City Publisher.

Huang, KN (2006). Museum Exhibit Design and Planning. Taipei, Taiwan, Taiwan University of the Arts Press.

Keng, FY (2006). The Real and the Virtual: Application of New Technological Media to Museum Exhibitions. *Museology Quarterly*, 20(1), 81–96.

Liu, YC (2007). *Museum is a Theater*. Taipei, Taiwan: Artist Publisher.

Liu, YC (2010). Needs and Wants: Museum Learning Resources. *Museology Quarterly*, 24(4), 19–35.

PART 3

Business and Partnership Models

10

THE VIRTUAL COLLECTION OF ASIAN MASTERPIECES: A UNIVERSAL ONLINE MUSEUM

Manus Brinkman

Introduction

Looking at the collections of Asian museums we see few "encyclopedic" collections, few collections that have objects from cultures other than those from the country or region where the museum is situated. Encyclopedic museums do exist in other parts of the world, especially in Europe and North America. Famous examples are the British Museum, the Louvre or the Metropolitan Museum. Those museums collected artifacts from all over the world, inspired by the Enlightenment and assisted by Colonialism. Especially because of that colonial past the encyclopedic museum has been challenged. European nations removed and transferred artifacts from other cultures. Nevertheless, having examples of the history and art from diverse cultures in one and the same collection enriches our understanding. Without forgetting the colonial history one could argue that these museums have kept their collections responsibly for the benefit of us, the public at large. Many objects of Asian origin ended up in the possession of museums in Europe and later the USA. Far fewer European objects came in the possession of Asian museums. Most countries in Asia do not lack art of their own cultures, but miss out on objects from others, often even close neighbors. An example: of the 2300 masterpieces of Asian origin in the Virtual Collection of Asian Masterpieces' (VCM)[1] database about 1000 are in the collections of European museums. When we look further we see that the masterpieces in the possession of participating museums in a specific Asian country mostly originate from the country itself. The fifteen Korean VCM-museums present a total of 276 masterpieces on the VCM of which 34 are non-Korean. The twelve Chinese museums including Hong Kong only present masterpieces from China and the eight museums from Mongolia only Mongolian masterpieces. The only Asian exception is Singapore, whose museums present a majority of masterpieces which are not of Singaporean origin.[2]

Basic Ideological Assumptions

The debate on who owns what, is already going on for some decades. Discussions on whether to return objects to the country that claims to represent the culture of origin are often front-page news. Whatever the arguments, one thing is clear: everybody has the right to learn from and enjoy works of art of all cultures. Therefore museums should make their collections available for mankind: they can do so by opening their doors, by lending the objects to others, by making travelling exhibitions, publish books and … by making images and information available on-line. It is true, on-line is not the same as the real object, but it is still much better than nothing at all.

Creation of the VCM

It was the asymmetry in collections that spurred the Asia-Europe Museum Network (ASEMUS) to create the VCM. ASEMUS is a network of Asian and European museums, set up to promote cooperation between them. VCM therefore was right from the start part of ASEMUS'

---

[1] VCM can be visited at: http://masterpieces.asemus.museum
[2] These numbers are of May 2013 and may change as more museums are added to the VCM.

goals: sharing of museum collections and professional competence through continued development and stimulation of cooperation between museums. For all of this the VCM would be a perfect tool.

Project Origin and Conception

At the beginning the project needed a specific focus. Bringing together all Asian and European art would simply be too wide a frame, as it would cover the vast majority of all art in the world. Therefore it was decided to focus on Asian art. But this also encompasses an enormous quantity of objects. We took masterpieces only: objects of the highest quality. A key question arose: what exactly is a masterpiece? There are many definitions to answer this. Ask any two curators, and you will have two different answers. Prof. Masatoshi Kubo of the Research Center for Cultural Resources at the National Museum of Ethnology in Osaka for instance stated "any invention that has drastically changed the life of ordinary people", and he designated the Sony-walkman a masterpiece. But a curator at the National Museum in Jakarta would point to the beautiful 13th century sculpture of Buddhist goddess Prajnaparamita.

Certain objects may be considered masterpieces not just for their beauty or sophistication, but because of some special association to a person, place, or time, because they are very rare, or they might be a splendid manifestation of the artist's techniques, world-view, philosophy, intentions or background. It could also be argued that most of the objects of the most famous museum in a country can all be considered as masterpieces and none of the objects in the collections of smaller museums. In the VCM every museum, however small, can participate and choose the masterpieces of its collection. What the VCM therefore shows is not a collection of all masterpieces of a certain culture, but the masterpieces of the participating museums.

Target Audience

The VCM is aimed at a global audience; hence the need to have all texts available in English. However out of respect for the multitude of languages, VCM requires all participants also to provide texts in their own language. It is of course impossible to have all texts available in many languages, but at least it will be possible for instance for Chinese people to read about the objects from museums in China in their own language.

Defining the Content

Because it would be impossible to find the final answer to the question "What is a Masterpiece?" it was decided to leave that open to the contributing museum. Each museum needed to indicate why its selected object was a masterpiece. Included in the texts of all VCM's objects is a text explaining why this specific object is considered a masterpiece. And the curators providing the texts come up with a surprising wide range of considerations and explanations.

Interesting examples are: A folding screen from the Nagasaki Museum of History and Culture is considered as a masterpiece, not because of its superior skill or beauty, but since 1614, the Tokugawa shogunate strictly prohibited the diffusion of the Christian religion and Western learning in general. By the middle of the century, all the missionaries had been expelled from Japan. As a precious example of the Christian relics, this folding screen should inevitably be called a masterpiece. Since it is most probable that they were drawn at the Jesuit seminary in Nagasaki from 1612–1614, they are especially valuable as one of the few examples which prove the first introduction of the Western art of painting to the "Christian century" Japan (1549–1650). The figures and the background in each panel display the use of Western perspective and shading technique, which could not be seen in the traditional Japanese painting method.[3]

And the Tropenmuseum in Amsterdam, the Netherlands has an even more peculiar example: an envelope from what in the colonial times was called the Dutch Indies: "Although not a masterpiece in

---

[3] VCM, Nagasaki Museum of History and Culture, Japan, retrieved from http://masterpieces.asemus.museum/masterpiece/detail.nhn?objectId=12040

the strict sense of the word, the Tropenmuseum considers this envelope to be of the utmost importance considering its relation to the collection and the information it conveys about communication. Not many have been saved from the ravages of time. Simple objects can appear to be of greater rarity and importance than those with more obvious masterpiece qualifications."[4]

Launch of the VCM

The VCM was conceptualized in 2005 and launched in 2007. For its development it received funding from the Asia Europe Foundation (ASEF) in Singapore. Other sponsors were the Gyeonggi Provincial Museum, Gyeonggi, Korea; Volkenkunde, National Museum of Ethnology, Leiden, the Netherlands; Musée du quai Branly, Paris, France and the National Museums of World Culture, Stockholm and Gothenburg, Sweden. Somewhat later the Museum für Völkerkunde, Munich, Germany also sponsored part of the development phase.

The VCM was registered under the top level domain .museum because it wanted to show its links to the museumworld clearly.

Cooperation Model

The basic idea behind the VCM is cooperation. Not only will having access to the heritage of other cultures enhance mutual understanding and respect, working together will also add a practical dimension to it. The project is not only about making images and knowledge available to the general public, it also aims to bring the museums together in a very practical way. Each museum has its own working space for its contribution, to which it has access at all time for updating or adding information. The site is like a company with several private workshops that all contribute to the final result.

---

[4]VCM, Tropenmuseum, Amsterdam, Netherlands, retrieved from http://master-pieces.asemus.museum/masterpiece/detail.nhn?objectId=11391

The VCM offers participation for all types of museums and of all sizes. It has art museums, ethnology museums and history museums. It includes world famous museums like the British Museum, the Tokyo National Museum or the National Museum of Korea, but also small local museums like the Traditional Arts and Ethnology Center in Luang Prabang, Laos or the Didrichsen Art Museum in Helsinki, Finland.

Museums are encouraged not only to present their masterpieces but also make cooperative educational or scientific projects available. There is for instance the travelling exhibition, *Posing Questions: Being and Image in Asia and Europe*, that looks skeptically at representations or surrogates of people, using examples from Asia and Europe. *Vietnamese Museums Share Collections with Colleagues in Asia* is another example. *The Hidden Base of the Borobudur* is a cooperative project between the National Museum of Ethnology in Leiden, the Netherlands and the National Museum of Indonesia in Jakarta. The Borobudur in Central Java is one of the most spectacular monuments of mankind. In 1885, an amazing discovery was made: the stones of the lowest terrace masked a set of 160 wonderful reliefs depicting the law of cause and effect, earth, heaven and hell. This series of reliefs, known as *The Hidden Base of Borobudur*, were photographed by Kasian Cephas in the 1890's before being covered again. These photographs constitute a unique and invaluable testimony. The VCM presents the whole series of relics from Borobudur's Hidden Base, on-line accompanied by a clickable map. There are many cooperative projects between museums with Asian art or heritage as its subject, but they remain often unknown outside of the museums directly involved. The VCM offers a space where they will be presented to the rest of the world and where they will also be able to lead a much longer life.

The VCM is in this respect as much a means, a tool as it is a product, a result. Yes, the masterpieces of asian art will be made available for the general public, but only by means of a cooperative effort. Museums provide the information for the VCM, but at the same time they "own" the project. They will be able to add, alter or remove their contribution at any time by themselves.

Administrative Structure

The VCM started as an ASEMUS project with financial support of the Asia Europe Foundation (ASEF). Later, a Board of Trustees was formed specifically for the VCM, the National Museum of Ethnology in the Netherlands and the Gyeonggi Provincial Museum in Korea being the Leading Members. The Leading Members provided considerably more support than the others.[5] The financial contribution of the trustees guarantees the basic functions for the VCM to sustain itself, like project- and content management, website hosting, maintenance, updating and some promotion.

Implementation Problems

We wanted the project to include a wide variety of museums. More sophisticated museums were relatively easy to target. They had digital images available and providing texts in English and their local language was not too hard. In smaller or less developed museums we encountered the following problems:

English language was a major barrier. Language skills were insufficient. This was especially the case in Asian museums. Participants struggled with understanding the web-procedures and with the texts for the images. Often the curators who needed to do the work did not have proficient English language skills and were forced to have the work done by a person who could communicate in English, but was much less specialized in the content of the object.

Quality of content differed. Excellent quality has been delivered by many museums, while others had difficulty with providing information because of lacking proper documentation and description of objects.

---

[5]As of May 2013, the Board of Trustees of the VCM consisted of: The National Museum of Ethnology (Volkenkunde), Leiden, the Netherlands and the National Museum of Korea in Seoul as Leading Members and further the Tropenmuseum in Amsterdam, the Netherlands; the Museums of World Culture in Sweden; and, the Chester Beatty Library in Dublin, Ireland.

Not all museums had digital images available. In some countries museums function under a central administrative body and permission to participate in the VCM could literally take years to achieve.

To create a robust database right from the beginning and gain momentum, the content editor of VCM has visited a few museums personally and assisted with making digital images, with the editing of texts and uploading of the masterpieces. Laos, Indonesia, Thailand and Vietnam were visited. During each visit museums were added to the VCM. Thanks to all the efforts at the start the VCM website could be launched in September 2007 with already 50 participating museums. After that two visits would follow, one to Myanmar and one to Mongolia where respectively four and eight museums were added. Personal assistance on the spot is costly, but the investment was worth the effort in the beginning to be able to offer a substantial and therewith attractive database of masterpieces. Later we let the expansion proceed on a slower pace.

Quality Issues

It would have been wonderful when all images would have been of the same (high) quality, but this, for the moment, is one step too far. "Google Art" guarantees the quality of the images in its database by being involved itself with high quality equipment and staff. VCM does not have these means and needs to rely upon what the participating museum has available and is willing to offer. The VCM owns no rights to the images provided because it functions from the principle that the participating museum owns its contribution, while Google Art asks some rights in return for its investment in producing high quality images.

Copyrights

There is often a conflict between the objectives of a museum (being a public institution with an educational objective) and the terms of (some) museums' policies with respect to copyrights. Museums must make their collections available to the public, but they often put restrictions in place that limit the access. And while most of the objects in their collections are already in the public domain and not covered by copyrights anymore, these museums nevertheless restrict the use of their images simply because they have control over access to the original. In most cases the copyrights are applied to photographs of the originals made by the museum itself. The copyright then covers the photographer who made the image and in most cases these rights have been taken over by the museum. In many cases the museums in their role as gatekeepers developed claims that may be overreaching.[6]

The contents of the VCM website are licensed under a Creative Commons "Some Rights Reserved" License. Creative Commons provides license models that let authors, scientists, artists, and educators easily mark their creative work with the freedoms they want it to carry. One can use CC to change the copyright terms from "All Rights Reserved" to "Some Rights Reserved."

The license model for the VCM website is the Creative Commons Attribution-NonCommercial-ShareAlike License. The text and images on the VCM website may be viewed and downloaded for general use, enjoyment, education purposes and reuse under the terms of this license.

Users are free to share, to copy, distribute and transmit the work and to adapt the work, however under some conditions such as the noncommercial use.

With respect to the Creative Commons Licences Agreement there is a lot of misunderstanding, because many contributors either do not know it or misinterpret it. Besides there is a continuing debate among museums about copyrights. The creative commons license agreement basically promotes free distribution within certain limits. This was the reason for a Greek museum with an Asian art collection not to participate. Some other museums do contribute to the VCM and agree with the Creative Commons License Agreement, but nevertheless provide watermarks on their images or mention other limitations of use.

---

[6] For a concise debate on this issue, see Crews (2012).

The VCM and Other Virtual Museums

Museums can publish their collections on their own website, which is of course necessary, but in this case a visitor has to search the websites of many museums to get an idea about the richness of a specific culture or to be able to compare. Encyclopedic on-line collections like Google Art,[7] Discover Islamic Art[8] and the VCM offer visitors the chance to look at, learn from and enjoy the rich variety of the masterpieces of mankind.

On the VCM you can with one click select all Asian masterpieces and with another click find in which museums they are. The VCM distinguishes itself especially because it offers not only images, but also detailed information about the artworks, their history and an explanation why the curator of the museum who owns them considers the objects masterpieces.

Recent Developments

The National Museum of Korea, VCM's leading partner in Asia and NHN Corp. established contacts in 2011 in order to establish a co-operation for mutual benefit. Part of this cooperation was an agreement to develop a new website for VCM. Designing a new website and back office system would not have been possible from the regular VCM-budget.

NHN Corporation is an important Korean Internet company, among others operating the nation's top search portal, Naver. It was Naver that took upon it the task of developing VCM's new website.[9] This new website was launched in May 2013.

The VCM was five years old in 2012 and it was surprising to see how fast a website becomes outdated. Many new features, which focus on a user-friendly approach, were not existent at the time. Besides, the design of the site was at the moment of creation rather

---

[7] See the official website: http://www.googleartproject.com

[8] See the official website: http://www.discoverislamicart.org

[9] Naver has its own art project: Available at: http://arts.search.naver.com which presents a wide range of art images and texts, but only in Korean.

trendy. For a website to live a long life the design should be somewhat timeless, what seems to have been achieved with the Naver design, but only time will tell. The current design is also image oriented instead of text oriented, an important element for a collection of art and museums. It also has more tools built in for networking and sharing knowledge and information. The VCM has added apps for mobile media and has opted for a better social media presence.

VCM's main focus will remain cooperation between museums and offering them a platform to show their content worldwide.

Reference

Crews, KD (2012). Museum Policies and Art Images: Conflicting Objectives and Copyright Overreaching. *Fordham Intellectual Property, Media & Entertainment Law Journal*, 22, 795–835.

11

A TALE ON A LEAF: PROMOTING INDONESIAN LITERATURE AND CULTURE THROUGH THE DEVELOPMENT OF THE LONTAR DIGITAL LIBRARY

Ruly Darmawan and Djembar Lembasono

The main theme of this chapter is the development and implementation of a digital library system for Lontar Foundation, an independent and non-profit organization, established in 1987. With its primary aims to promote Indonesian literature and culture through the publication of translations of Indonesian literary works, Lontar is ready to open its culturally-related contents to the wider public. In summary, after much planning and implementation work over a few years, Lontar has delivered a repository of its collections through the Lontar Digital Library (LDL).

Introduction

To be able to access information efficiently is crucial for a modern, productive lifestyle. In this respect, facilities like libraries play a prominent role in providing an abundance of well-organised information. Moreover, the transition of a conventional library to digital one provides an excellent opportunity for enabling ubiquitous information access. The benefits provided by a digital library are

163

certainly plentiful compared to a conventional library. The more significant among these are accessibility and connectivity. Besides enabling information gathering, accessibility and connectivity are also requisite for establishing a network of community/public information which can be evolved into a community/society of knowledge.

Opportunities to create digital libraries are welcomed by many parties, especially those that are information-rich and have a lot of support from community networks, such as Lontar Foundation. The Foundation is engaged in cultural literacy and obtains a lot of support in its activities. Few institutions like Lontar presently exist in Indonesia. The needs and interests of special interest groups, especially of the cultural researchers, are far better addressed as compared with the cultural content provided for public users. Based on this consideration the Lontar Foundation aims to open its content for public access by pursuing the implementation of a digital library system. In 2001, the foundation joined a forum of Indonesian digital libraries and began to look for possible implementation of an adequate digital libraries system.

This chapter will share the accomplishments of the LDL project from initiation to recent multi-party developments. As a brief summary of the project report, it is hoped that this chapter can provide inputs for further development programs and provide ideas to others who are embarking on similar systems.

IndonesiaDLN at a Glance

The Indonesian Digital Library Network (IndonesiaDLN) is the first of its kind in Indonesia. The development was pioneered and driven by the Knowledge Management Research Group (KMRG) at Institut Teknologi Bandung (ITB) Indonesia, together with other librarians and information engineers. This work was carried out with the aid of a grant from the International Development Research Center (IDRC) Canada and the Indonesian Foundation for Telecommunication and Information Research (YLTI) for the period 2000–2002. Other organization that support this work are Asian Internet Interconnection

Initiative (AI3) ITB, ITB Central Library, and Computer Network Research Group (CNRG) ITB.

The mission of IndonesiaDLN is to unlock the knowledge of Indonesian people, especially the local content, and share it nationally. It means to distribute widely information about Indonesia such as final project reports, theses, dissertation, research report, heritage, regional potency, and history in an easy, user-friendly way, and invite contributions from Indonesian people from across the nation. Such information will be very useful to increase the number of information literates and collaboration among them, and to promote Indonesian scholarly works to international readers. Indonesia DLN is to be positioned as a mother network of digital library networks in Indonesia. It is because there will be many networks connected to IndonesiaDLN. All of these networks can be integrated under IndonesiaDLN easily as long as they use IndonesiaDLN Interoperability Metadata Standard for data exchange.

IndonesiaDLN has a wide network of partners from research, education, business, NGO, government, etc. This network will create a big national knowledgebase that should be maintained and can be repurposed to be become a useful information resource. For example, the existence of the knowledgebase makes it possible to produce documentary series for children education, theses and dissertation, national heritage, human rights and democratic developments.

Lontar Digital Library Project Overview

The Lontar Foundation is a non-profit institution established in 1987 and has a special attention on culture. The main vision of this foundation is to promote Indonesian knowledge through literature translation. Over time, the foundation has broadened the scope of its activities, including the organization of international seminars and exhibitions. The Foundation has a variety of collections. In general there are four types of collections, which are printed materials, films and videos, images (such as slides, transparencies), and Audio Recordings. All these collections are targeted at scholars who have an interest in discovering the knowledge of Indonesia.

In the context of providing as well as obtaining access for potential users to the collections, Lontar aims to deliver the solution by implementing a digital library system. It is hoped that such a system will also help other organizations to join and integrate their collections under a digital library system, namely the Lontar Digital Library (LDL).

In 2003, Lontar Foundation and Knowledge Management Research Group (KMRG) from Bandung Institute of Technology or ITB, began to initiate a cooperation to establish the LDL. The cooperation covered several activities which are software installation and modification, training on digitalization and digital library operation, and consultancy on information management. LDL is developed using Ganesha Digital Library (GDL), an open-source software developed by KMRG ITB, as a platform engine. This first establishment project was successfully delivered in 2004. After the accomplishment of this first project, the cooperation between Lontar Foundation and KMRG ITB was continued in 2011. This time the cooperation is headed for further improvement of LDL system, especially on its connectivity and accessibility capabilities.

With this goal, the Lontar Digital Library will automatically be connected with other heritage networks, as shown in Figure 1 below:

Although LDL uses the GDL standard application, it is possible for the Lontar to customize the content, including the interface in order to accommodate the specific needs of any organization.

Network Infrastructures of LDL

To optimise the operation of LDL, two Local Area Network (LAN) infrastructures should be provided. The first is the office LAN which supports the daily activities for the whole body of organizations and supports the production LAN, and the second is the production LAN, which supports the digitalization processes. The topology of office LAN is illustrated in Figure 2:

Between the two LANs, a cable connects the switch hubs. There are also two servers, namely Mail server and File server. Mail server is recognized by Internet, so it is connected to the first hub. The File

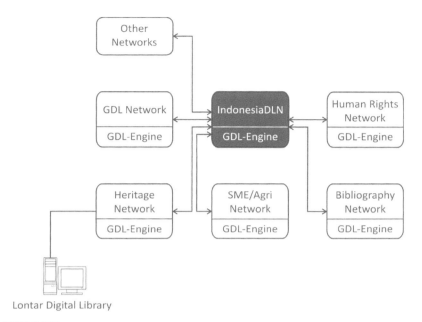

Figure 1.   Topology of Lontar Digital Library connected to Indonesia DLN.

server is required to manage all files related to Lontar administrative works and other files that are not related to the production. Within the office LAN, there is a workstation for display of Lontar digital library. Visitors of Lontar office can use the workstation for searching, browsing, and viewing the digital collections. They also can play the multimedia presentations of the collections.

Meanwhile, the production LAN is required to support the digitalization process. Digitalization of document, image, audio, and video will be done at this LAN. It is actually the important infrastructure because its importance in providing excellent qualities of each collection. The topology of this network is shown in Figure 3:

There are at least six components in the production LAN. The six components are:

1. Internet Servers that contain servers and routers that can be accessed from the Internet. For example: Lontar digital library server, web server, email server, and router. GDL Server is the

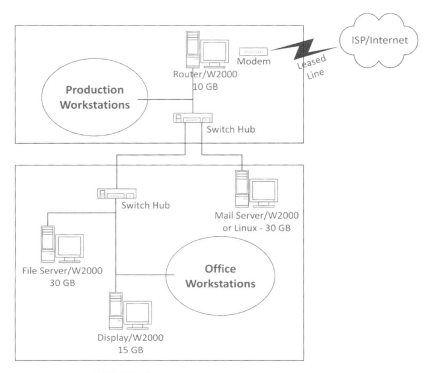

Figure 2.   Topology of Lontar's office LAN.

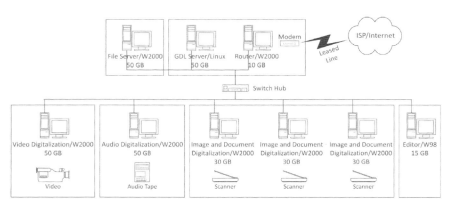

Figure 3.   Topology of Lontar's production LAN.

Lontar digital library server that acts as the show room of the digital collections,

2. File Server as a repository server of Lontar's digital collections,

3. Video Digitalization Workstation which functions in converting the collections from analog into digital format. Before the final format is uploaded into digital library server, the video files will be processed and edited here,

4. Audio Digitalization Workstation,

5. Image and Document Digitalization, and

6. Editor Workstation which is used by editor or knowledge officer to check the digitalization result (document, image, audio, and video) and then upload the accepted result into digital library server.

LDL Implementation

The LDL implementation was undertaken in two phases: the initial and the development phase. In the initial phase, the LDL was prepared by completing basic requirement, such as network infrastructure, hardware and software of computer graphics, and collection preparation for digitalization. Besides, human resources were also prepared through workshop and training sessions. The development phase is a continuation from the previous phase with some additional technical enhancements, such as adopting linked data technology for better information connectivity and integrated repository.

In 2011, the Lontar Foundation initiated the development phase of Lontar Digital Library (LDL) and placed an emphasis on adopting the latest technology. The development was focused on building linked data based on available information through networked information such as Wikipedia, Freebase, Open Library, VIAF (Virtual International Authority File), and other networked information providers. Since the beginning of this development phase, LDL tried to share information with the South East Asia Digital Library (SEADL), an initiative by Northern Illinois University. However, they were not ready to exchange information over digital library exchange protocol such as OAI. The metadata were also different. LDL uses Dublin Core metadata while SEADL is using VRA Core. LDL creates metadata crosswalk to comply with SEADL's system. Unfortunately, these systems were not connected with each other.

Data Issues and Directions

In implementing the two phases, the issues in data creation, data harvesting, and linked data are significant. These issues are discussed below.

Data Creation

Digitalization is a crucial element in any development and implementation of a digital library system. It is because that the quality of digitalized collections may affect the progress in other stages. And this may eventually affect the success of project as a whole. Digitalization is not considered to be a process that will produce genuine collections. It means that the existing analog collections are still important. Digital collections so created will only be like "complementary" collections. Therefore, the success of digitalization process depends on the proper preparation of the analog collections.

All digitalized images are recorded and classified based on a specific metadata standard. Although GDL adopts Dublin Core metadata, Lontar's existing metadata for collections were not be neglected. The metadata was just synchronized with the Dublin Core's. However, if necessary, this metadata can be re-structured and redefined in the future.

LDL has more than 70 metadata elements set which is adopted from 15 Dublin core element set. In fact, Lontar Digital Library's metadata is deliberately extended to accommodate a wide range of metadata standards, like: VRA Core, World Digital Library, Freebase, Open Library, and Library of Congress.

Data Harvesting

Data harvesting is advantageous for time-saving, especially when the information matches the users' needs. Some information has actually been provided by a superset "networked information," which may not be complete.

Several harvesting target sites were defined from the beginning. Because Lontar has submitted data to Wikipedia, Open Library, and Freebase, the development is then focused on how data can be harvested. The first attempt was the establishment of communication with the Library of Congress (LOC) and National Library of Australia (NLA) database that has different exchange protocol. LOC uses Z39.50 as exchange protocol. Information harvested from LOC is the LCCN (Library of Congress Control Number). This control number will be used to harvest information from other information providers' sites. It is because all information on the aforementioned sites supports LCCN data.

ISBN is used for harvesting data from LOC and NLA. These databases also provide detailed information about people (such as creators and contributors). Information about people can be harvested from Wikipedia. LDL uses the harvested information and augments it to create complete records. Information about the author(s) can be harvested from VIAF web site as well. This web site provided a names authority service for people, organization and conferences names based on the names authority files of over 18 major national libraries and organizations around the world. VIAF also provides information in xml format, which is easy to reuse for any purpose.

Linked Data

The semantic web is networked data that require standard metadata format, accessed and managed using a web tool. Semantic web usually stored in common formats such as RDF. Linked data contains semantic information, which are interconnected with one another, and connected by an identifier of information. Figure 4 shows a sample of linked data from LDL.

Linked data is used with the aim to make it easier for users to get related information from other information provider. Linked data is usually formed with identifier or permalink; data can be harvested

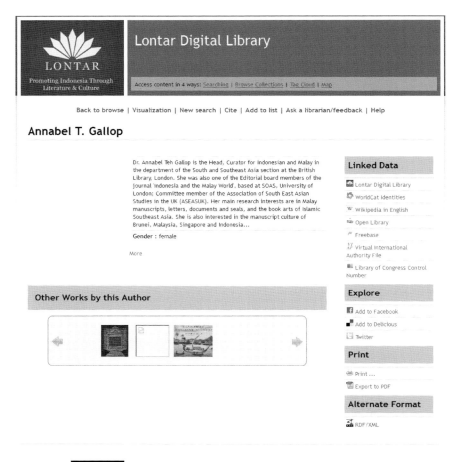

Figure 4.   Linked data sample from Lontar Digital Library.

from web service as discussed before above, or even filled in manually if we already know the identifier or permalink.

Linked data visualization can also be developed. It is interesting because it can help users to see the overall map and/or affinity of any information they search. Data visualization is made by mapping data from the LDL system, and generating a data visualization of related subject and author and their relationships as circles with connection lines. The data visualization module is still under development for enhanced relations between the data. Figure 5 shows a snapshot of a data visualization output.

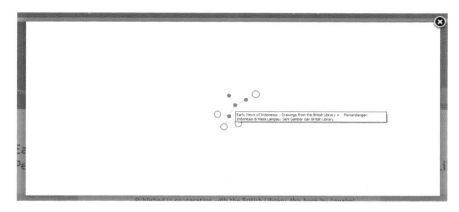

Figure 5.   Data visualization on LDL.

The final linked data with its visualized connection may also be significant in connecting people and/or institutions that have relevant collection with Lontar's. In this sense, the LDL may become a host where people and information meet. Through this host, it is expected that the Indonesian literary and culture can be fostered in alignment with the mission of Lontar Foundation.

Future Development

Digital libraries still have a bright future for further development.[1] The opportunities exist through the possibility of systemic mechanism of a digital library application. Furthermore, the rapid development of media technology with its attention to user convenience becomes one of many opportunities in developing digital libraries. With efforts similar to those discussed in this chapter, the digital library can also be developed for mobile access. By employing a Virtual Reality (VR) application, digital libraries can be modified into a

---

[1] Clifford Lynch (2005) writes that the development of digital libraries can be directed to the effort of connectivity building and integration with users, either individually or in group. In this context, Lynch pays more attention to the next step after the implementation of digital library system. He is concerned not only with the users' information accessibility, but also on how information can inspire the users to be connected with each other as well.

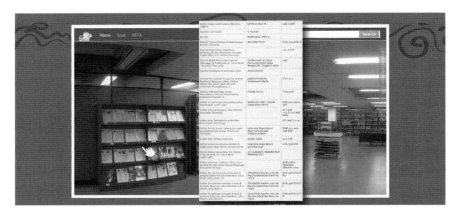

Figure 6.   VR library of ITB.

more attractive interface where users can seek information through spatial exploration. One example is the VR library of ITB as shown in Figure 6.

Through this application, users are allowed to use their spatial experience when seeking information. This VR application was developed for the internal users of ITB such as lecturers and students. The VR panoramic landscape helps them to seek information based on actual experience obtained when visiting the real facility. Based on some unstructured observation, people may forget some of critical attributes of information they seek (like title of book, author, keyword, etc.). However, they are assisted by the visual attributes (such as color of book) and the location where they found it before.

We believed that seeking information is not a mere technical matter with rigid mechanisms. Seeking information in the digital world is also accompanied by the experience of seeking information in the real world. Although the site is different and hosted in a region that may never have been visited, users may actualize the site and bring it together with their experience in a specific context of space.

The future development and implementation of digital libraries is still unclear. There are many technology alternatives that can be used as a reference and platform towards more human-oriented digital libraries. Digital libraries are not merely about coding, data synchronizing, and other technical matters. It is also about the users' information search habits and approach. Although the VR Library of ITB is still far from perfect, the overall result is satisfactory. Moreover, this application is expected to be a compact VR library that is continuously developing to be adequate for users' needs while retaining the value of library.[2]

Conclusion

The Lontar Digital Library (LDL) development makes the promotion of Indonesian culture and literature possible. It also provides wider accessibility for potential users in obtaining specific information with various formats. The future implementation of the VR library will be a challenge for LDL in providing a service that addresses the preferences of users in the digital era.

Acknowledgement

We would like to thank Tanya R. Torres for her support in writing this chapter.

References

Besser, H (2008). The Past, Present, and Future of Digital Libraries. In S Screibman, R Siemens and J Unsworth (eds.) *A Companion to Digital Humanities*. London: Blackwell Publishing. Available online at: http://www.digitalhumanities.org/companion/

Lynch, C (2005). Where Do We Go From Here? The Next Decade of Digital Libraries. *D-Lib Magazine*, 11(7/8). Available online at: http://www.dlib.org/dlib/july05/lynch/07lynch.html [Last accessed on May 27th, 2013].

---

[2] Howard Besser (2008) writes about the importance of digital library to humanity and issues to be resolved to avoid ending up with just a collection of works.

12

THE FUTURE OF HISTORY IS MOBILE: EXPERIENCING HERITAGE ON PERSONAL DEVICES

Christopher Jones

The use of personal devices for mobile tours in museums and heritage sites, which began with audio tours decades ago, is experiencing a renaissance in the age of the smart phone. Visitors to museums and heritage buildings or ruins spend a large percentage of their time on site using their smart phones or tablets for finding information, texting or taking pictures to send to friends and families. For heritage professionals, the logical progression was to find ways to turn these personal devices into next-generation guides that tell stories and convey contextual information. With the onset of apps, there has been a surge of creative energy as organizations use advanced mobile technologies to transform the experience of visitors to museums and to historical and archaeological sites, with the potential not yet fully realized. Mobile technology can now bring inanimate artifacts to life, provide virtual windows to the past and add layers of knowledge and information to give users deeper insights. More and more heritage organizations are testing the waters by creating their own mobile media and native apps, and while the results have sometimes been ineffective or gimmicky, some early adopters have already gotten it right. The successes so far are driving a paradigm shift of how heritage organizations relate to their collections, to the public and even to the world at large.

The Birth of the "Mobile Guide" — Audio Tours

One word often associated with heritage sites and museums within the digital native generation is "boring." The traditional piles of ruins, discretely labelled artifacts, not to mention the unofficial quiet policy of many museums to ensure a tranquil atmosphere are becoming less appealing to a public constantly engrossed with personalized interactive media on their smartphones, tablets and computers. Nothing is less appealing to young digital natives than going into an old building and having to turn off their smart phones and quietly walk around pondering the objects they know little or nothing about. Indeed museum artefacts and some historical sites can be next to meaningless if the visitor is not exposed to contextual or background information about their significance. Traditionally, before their visit, people have read guidebooks or websites to gain this information; and, once on site, read brochures, signage and placards. But normally there is not enough space on site for heritage professionals to place all the contextual information would ideally like to provide, leading initially to the widespread adoption of audio-guides on dedicated devices provided by the organization to augment interpretation.

The use of mobile devices to provide interpretation at heritage attractions is not new. Audio guides have been a common part of museum and heritage site interpretive strategies since 1952, when perhaps history's first audio tour was introduced at the Stedelijk Museum in Amsterdam using radio broadcast technology (Tallon, 2009). In the seventies and eighties, audio guides on dedicated devices proliferated world-wide, including the famous tongue-in-cheek audio tour of the Forbidden City in Beijing narrated by the James Bond actor Roger Moore. More recently there has been limited success in engaging the public with podcasts, downloadable, themed audio tours that museums such as the National Gallery in London have, and still are, implementing (Laugoudi and Sexton, 2010).

However the audio tour has never gained the status of an essential part of the heritage site or museum experience. Despite having been introduced so long ago, the traditional audio tour reaches a sobering minority of on-site audiences, with less than ten percent of visitors typically opting in for permanent collections. In fact, the usage rate for the Louvre's traditional audio guide dropped to four percent of its 8.9 million visitors in 2012 (Iverson, 2012). Perhaps part of this lack of uptake is partly due to the anti-social nature of audio — the necessity of earphones can block out whispered conversation between friends and family about their shared experience.

From Audio Tours to Mobile Media

Because of the public's general lack of enthusiasm for the audio tour model, museums and heritage organizations have tried to improve on this experience in recent years by leveraging the powerful personal computers that users bring in their pockets and bags: smart phones, tablet and "phablets" (iPad Mini, Galaxy Tab, etc.). This approach is sometimes referred to as the BYOD (Bring Your Own Device) model. Mobile media downloaded from the internet can add extra layers of interpretation: stories that give context, themed tours, archival photos and enlightening videos, quizzes or even games.

One cost-effective and often effective approach of delivering this media is through the mobile web app, which repurposes website content for delivery on mobile web browsers. More easily designed for use on the full range of smart phones than dedicated "native" apps like iPhone or Android apps, web apps serve mobile media free to the end user wherever wireless or data connectivity is available. Because browsers are accessible on all smart phone models, this is an effective way to reach the largest number of visitors. Mobile media increases access to the content not only for on-site visitors, but also for non-visitors, who can virtually tour collections and exhibitions independently of the physical site. The BMA (Baltimore Museum of Art) *Go Mobile* web app[1] is an example of a simple and

---

[1] Official website: http://gomobileartbma.org/

elegant mobile app guide to visiting a museum. Users can select galleries and works via gallery maps which give the user access not only to additional audio and video media, but to an intriguing "Connections" feature which encourages visitors to look at objects in a new ways, hear perspectives from a range community voices, and see links between the works. Visitors can also share any object with friends on Facebook, Twitter or by e-mail or even leave comments for the community.

Producing mobile web apps designed for the BYOD model comes with challenges and potential pitfalls. For example, web apps rely on files accessed on remote servers through the internet; so when the connection is interrupted, the application is no longer usable. To make matters worse, internet connectivity is often limited inside the old buildings with thick walls which often house museums, or on rural heritage sites that lack mobile data coverage. Even if mobile data coverage is robust, tourists may not to wish to download data due to expensive mobile roaming rates. Therefore it is essential that the institution make wireless connectivity available in the building or site. In addition, batteries are often drained by mobile media downloads, so ideally institutions ideally should also provide opportunities for visitors to charge their phones, and, if there is an audio component, extra sets of headphones. In addition, rental devices should be offered for visitors who not bring or are unwilling to use their own. This can be problematic, however, as institutions that choose to keep a small inventory of devices on-site for permanent collection tours may be overwhelmed by demand during special temporary exhibitions. Because of the above challenges, implementing a BYOD mobile web app media guide is far from straightforward.

QR Codes — The New Information Board?

Even if all the challenges with connectivity and hardware are overcome while launching a mobile web app guide, visitors are still sometimes frustrated at having to navigate through sometimes complicated user interfaces and content layers to find media related to a specific gallery, object or place. Many museums and heritage sites have tackled this problem via QR codes. QR stands for Quick Response and the codes are best defined as mobile-readable URLs, a way of simply and inexpensively directing users to specific web app content on mobile phones. The code itself is a square grid of black and white blocks and can occupy minimal space when applied as a sticker on existing signs and labels. QR codes can even remove the need for signage, an unobtrusive alternative to the traditional information board. A quick optical scan of these codes with a smart phone application can launch specific content within a web app.

Another intriguing application of QR codes is instant translation via websites like QRpedia which creates QR codes that link to Wikipedia articles. The Fundació Joan Miró in Barcelona used QRpedia codes to augment interpretation for their *Joan Miró — The Ladder of Escape* exhibition (Hinojo, 2012). These QRpedia codes detected the language of the device and presented the Wikipedia article in the user's preferred language, substantially improving the experience of international visitors. However this model requires considerable effort and coordination, as the institution must start a Wikiproject and recruit experts to create these articles in different languages.

The QR codes solution, though cost-effective, comes with real implementation difficulties. Printing and displaying QR codes takes considerable trial and error, as shadows, reflections and poor lighting can make the codes too difficult to scan. Another common mistake is producing and displaying codes that do not send users to a native app or site that is optimized for mobile. Trying to navigate a traditional website on a mobile device will quickly deter users. Visitors also sometimes complain about a lack of messaging on just what QR codes do or how to scan them. They need simple instructions for guidance and an explanation of how scanning codes will heighten their experience. This information can be printed on signage, palm cards or even on the back of tickets. In addition, some museums have even provided labels next to QR codes that describe what the visitor will gain in return for the effort of scanning the code, such as a small screen cap with duration in the case of videos, to encourage engagement.

Heritage on the Go

With the launch of the iPhone in 2008 and other smart phones featuring Google's Android operating system, heritage organizations quickly began to grasp the considerable potential of platform and device-specific dedicated applications with embedded functionality and content, otherwise known as "native mobile apps." Native apps are a more complex than web apps. They are also more expensive to develop, almost always requiring the involvement of an external development company. Unlike one-size-fits-all web apps, native apps require a separate version for not only each operating system (iOS, Android), but also for each mobile device. So why, despite these complexities, are we seeing a profusion of native apps developed by museums and heritage organizations? Native apps offer many advantages over web apps: because they are built for a particular device and its operating system they have the ability to use device-specific hardware and software such as a global positioning system (GPS), the graphics chip and the camera. Another key advantage of the native app for heritage organizations is that, depending on the nature of the native app, data can be stored in the app, so internet connectivity is not required and the app can be used "offline" (although the app must be downloaded initially — usually via wireless connectivity in the lobby or visitor center).

One example of the added functionality that a native app can utilize to benefit heritage awareness is the geo-location app, which uses GPS location-based services to track the users and offer up heritage content that pertains to their current location, straight from their device. Some geo-location heritage apps, such as the State Library of Victoria's *Historypin,* give the user to ability to search and select archival photographs, paintings and audio files and pin them directly on Google Street View.[2] This provides a great comparison between the present and the past and is a way for heritage organizations to breathe life into their archived collections, by creating a sort of museum without walls in authentic context.

---

[2] Official website: http://www.historypin.com/app/

Mobile Heritage Games

Another effective implementation of the native app is the heritage mobile game. Games can be effective vehicles for education and help break down the perception of museums as boring, elite institutions, by encouraging them to play and interact — not just for children but also for adults. There are two types of heritage mobile games — those meant to be played during a visit and those meant to be played at home or on the go and are focused on furthering institutional missions, awareness and educational goals.

An overly complicated or demanding mobile game as part of tour app can actually be counterproductive as it focuses attention on the screen for extended periods of time and distracts visitors away from the real artifacts or environments the visitor came to experience. Games meant to be played on site should therefore be "mini-games" — very simple, quick and focused on a particular artifact or message. The Asian Civilization Museum's (ACM) *Terracotta Warriors* exhibition app provided a good example of how to integrate mobile games into an on-site experience. The app featured a trail of in-gallery artifact markers which launched a variety of experiences, including two mini-games, each of which was aimed at augmenting the understanding of an artifact. The first game, "Battle Tactics" (triggered at the chariot artifact) demonstrated how Qin dynasty chariots were commanded on the battlefield (Figure 1). Users were prompted to sound the drum to advance the troops, and ring the bell to signal retreat (with sound effects). The second mini-game taught users how to learn to write the word "Emperor" with correct stroke order in Qin Dynasty seal script — the first standardized writing script in China. Each mini-game took no more than a couple minutes to experience, and could be played at home after the visit for long-term engagement.

An example of a mobile game meant to be played off-site is the Tate Gallery's *Race Against Time*, although the game also has features to encourage players to go to the gallery. Users play as a chameleon that must save colors from being removed from modern art history by the game's villain. The art in each progressive level in the game reflects a consecutive era in modern art history. The app also

Figure 1.   Battle Tactics mini-game from the ACM Terracotta Warriors App.

encourages players to go to the actual museum: opening the game inside the Tate (detected by smart phone Geo-positioning Service or GPS) unlocks special content.

A well-planned and developed game has the players learning something new and meaningful, sometimes without even realizing it. However, amongst more traditional visitors and indeed curators and professionals, there is still a fear that games run the risk of cheapening the perception of the institution and its message. Yet the emerging consensus is that heritage related mobile gaming as is an overlooked area of learning that has considerable potential.

Mobile Augmented Reality

In the last few years, mobile augmented reality (Mobile AR) has gone from being seen as a novel gimmick to draw attention, to a tool with serious potential for audience engagement and education. Mobile AR allows the user to see contextually relevant information or virtual objects superimposed on their view of reality via a personal device's camera. Often confused with virtual reality, which is about creating a completely simulated world, AR overlays augmented virtual content into the real world view, so it appears to co-exist with the real, as if the device has uncovered it by magic. This mixed-reality aspect of AR is what is so exciting for heritage organizations; it can free objects from the confines of their displays and put them back into their original context, reveal windows in time to the past, or magically restore ruins to what they looked like in their heyday.

The advantage of mobile AR is that it does not take attention away from real objects and landscapes; if done properly it will help visitors understand what they are seeing in real time. By holding up a mobile device and looking through the camera view, the visitor keeps their focus on the real object or landscape, rather than down and away, as is normally the case with museum interactives. In this sense mobile AR can be thought of as a modern, visual counterpart to audio guides, as it helps visitors understand what they are observing rather than distracting them from it. Unlike audio, however, mobile AR is not limited to didactic interpretation; the sense of genuine delight augmented reality can foster can help make the difference between an ordinary visit and a lasting memory.

Museums Without Walls

Mobile AR technology can open up possibilities to exhibit collections outdoors, without needing white walls on which to hang photographs and paintings, or glass cases to display objects. The first dedicated AR apps produced by heritage organizations and museums aimed at returning archival materials to the streets in an attempt to give them context, by placing them where they were originally produced or at the places, buildings and scenes that they depict. This type of app is essentially an AR-enhanced version of the heritage geo-location tag app, with the main difference being that the AR version seems to magically suspend paintings and photographs in-situ, instead of just displaying them on-screen. Technically these apps use a combination of an electronic devices' accelerometer, compass and location data to determine not only the users' position in the physical world, but also which way the device is pointing and on which axis the device is operating. This data can then be compared to a database to determine what the device is looking at, and thus allows the device to spawn paintings or photographs which appear to be floating in mid-air, framed in a precisely chosen manner by the surrounding real world environment. This gives the viewer what seems to be a "window through time."

One benchmark case study for the great potential of this type urban augmented reality app was the Museum of London's *Streetmuseum* app.[3] This popular app let pedestrians in London feel like they were holding a time machine in their hands, adding delight and a sense of interactive wonder to heritage discovery. By directly juxtaposing the past and the present, the *Streetmuseum* app offered a trail a moments of reflection on history, modernization and change. The success of this app and large number of downloads was exponentially more than initially planned for or expected by the museum. This model has since been mimicked by heritage institutions in other parts of the world, including Saint Louis, Missouri in the USA. The full potential of "mobile museums without walls" is yet to be realized in a digital heritage context.

Augmenting Galleries

The geo-location AR heritage app, though a groundbreaking model for engaging the public outdoors, typically cannot function indoors, as GPS positioning is inaccurate (though new indoor positioning system technology is on the horizon). So what is the current potential of mobile apps in an indoor gallery or exhibition context? The solution many museums have come up with recently is what is known as marker-triggered or vision-based AR, which uses the device camera to recognize an arbitrary image marker and superimpose 3D graphic or other virtual content into the camera feed. The virtual content is spawned by the markers rather than the user's location. One of the earliest successful applications of this type of indoor

---

[3] Official website: http://www.museumoflondon.org.uk/Resources/app/you-are-here-app/home.html

mobile AR was the British Museum's *Passport to the Afterlife* exhibition app launched in November 2011 (Mannion, 2012). Attendees used smart phones provided by the museum to scan markers that displayed 3D models of ancient Egyptian objects. They were then tasked to use these 3D models to solve clues about the ancient Egyptian Book of the Dead.

These AR markers do not have to be black and white squares like QR Codes. The latest AR technology can recognize almost any image as a marker, such as interpretive panels and labels in existing displays, and can even recognize planes in a 3D space as a reference point. This means the markers are less obtrusive and more consistency can be achieved with the exhibition design as a whole.

Though undoubtedly awe-inspiring and attention-grabbing, what allows a mobile AR gallery or exhibition experience to go beyond the mere gimmick and become truly educational? Some successful apps have demonstrated augmenting learning occurs when AR helps the visitor gain a deeper understanding of the object it is applied to, or conversely helps users understand an objects' context spatially or historically. For example, the ACM: *Terracotta Warriors* exhibition app by the Asian Civilizations Museum of Singapore placed a marker next to many Qin dynasty artifacts, including a bronze crossbow trigger (Thian, 2012). Viewing the crossbow marker through the free app spawned overlaid ranks of 3D archers that appeared marching on top of the glass display case that contained the trigger artifact (Figure 2). Observing the archers showed the viewer how the tactic of alternating ranks of fire contributed to the Qin army's superiority, and achieved this pedagogical goal in a highly entertaining and memorable fashion. In addition, closing the camera view launched a video of a 3D animation showing how the trigger worked mechanically inside the crossbow. Thus, the AR experience augmented the understanding of the real artifact in a memorable manner.

In another example from the same app, the museum placed a marker on the glass case containing a Zhou Dynasty bronze bell artifact. The bell of course could not be rung for conservation reasons, but with the app, visitors could spawn an 3D AR copy of the

Figure 2.   Educational augmented reality at the ACM.

bell right beside the real one, and "ring" the bell by swiping the screen (triggering an audio recording of the actual bell being rung) thus hearing the deep resonating tone that the bell was originally cast to produce and perhaps something the feeling it was meant to evoke. Because these AR gallery experiences are so engaging, many visitors are moved to take photos with the app and via social networks with an embedded link or hashtag that promotes the site or exhibition. This can have a positive viral marketing effect to spread awareness of the both the app and the exhibition to the public.

Virtual content generated by mobile AR can be 2D informational layers, dynamic and interactive 3D models, or even real costumed actors, as the *New Sukiennice* app from the Museum of Krakow, Poland demonstrated in spectacular fashion. The museum wanted a novel way to combine two mediums so they came up with the idea to film costumed actors against green screen, reciting dialogue that would tell the backstory or shed light on the theme of the painting.

When users launched the free app and viewed the paintings through their device cameras, the actors seemed to emerge from the paintings and recite their lines. The exhibition was hugely successful, with a waiting list for tickets. Another reason for the success of the app is that it was part of an integrated marketing campaign, including billboards in the city.

For every cutting-edge mobile heritage app, however, there is a dissatisfied group traditional patrons who feel it is a waste of effort and funding. Institutions must consider how increased excitement and engagement of mobile users is balanced towards a different kind of patron who is interested in the more traditional, quieter and contemplative gallery experience. In some cases there has even been pushback from curators, who fear of diluting the heritage by popularizing the experience with blockbuster visual media as a way to bring in a non-academic audience. This is indeed possible if mobile apps are done in such a way to take attention away from real objects, ruins, etc. But if done right, mobile heritage apps can blend history, art, and culture with technology to keep heritage relevant to new generation of digital natives.

Business Models

Though the considerable interpretive potential for mobile in a heritage context is now widely accepted, coming up with sound business strategies for said mobile projects is still a topic mired in confusion. Although profit is not normally the main goal of heritage initiatives, revenue to recover costs and even to fund further initiatives and programming is often at the forefront of mobile project planning. Questions abound, such as: do revenues compensate for the loss of users when mobile apps carry a download price? Conversely, does the drop in users for "paid apps" compromise the institution's educational mission?

One thing is certain — developing and implementing a mobile project carries considerable expense — not just for development but also for implementation (for example, setting up a free Wi-Fi service). Sponsorship by private industry and foundations can potentially cover these costs but usually heritage professionals must find funding from within their institution. Return of investment (ROI), whether in revenue or fulfilment of mission goals, therefore becomes of paramount concern. The metrics of a successful ROI can range from number of downloads or web app visits, to the return of investment indirectly through an increase in ticket sales driven by social and marketing features in the app, or directly through app store purchases (which can potentially result in profit above and beyond the development and implementation costs).

Advertising displayed in the app is another way to generate revenue. Integrating this system can be outsourced to the developer or done through an ad provider. But the most straightforward way to monetize mobile is to sell digital images of collections packed into a native app (though this usually results in a very large download). There are many positives to this approach, especially in the digital heritage preservation domain, as monetizing archives can cause organizations to value and ramp up their digitization process. The Louvre and the Uffizi Gallery amongst others have released this type of app for purchase — each marketed as the "museum in your pocket." The depth of content in these apps — hundreds of paintings in high resolution — ostensibly justifies the comparatively steep up-front price. However, the potential negatives of this model are the loss of goodwill that results from a publically funded institution charging for content that the public may complain should be free. Another concern is that mobile access to a large percentage of an institution's collection may decrease the public's perceived need to visit the actual physical museum (this can be countered by making some content unlockable only by attending the museum or visiting the heritage site via GPS tracking and/or marker recognition). In addition, case studies have made clear that apps that are free of charge are downloaded at least four times more than those that must be purchased from app stores. For example, the National Gallery of London's *Love Art* app experienced a significant decrease in the number of downloads after an up-front cost was implemented.

In many cases the ideal business model would be to combine heritage mobile educational and revenue imperatives by balancing the app with some amount of free content (analogous to a permanent collection with free entrance), and the possibility via in-app purchases to access premium content (analogous to a special museum exhibition within an otherwise free museum which requires a ticket purchase). This approach constitutes the "freemium" model: where an app is provided free of charge, but money is charged for advanced features, functionality, or virtual goods via an in-app purchase (IAP). Premium content can be anything from additional archival material, augmented reality experiences and features such as themed tours. The app of National Constitution Center of the United States, for example, offers basic concierge features, a digital copy of the constitution, and a news feed for free. On top of this, the app offers IAP of themed tours within the app for US$0.99 each.[4] The purchasing process is performed directly with the app and is seamless to the user in most cases, with the mobile platform provider facilitating the purchase and taking a share of the money spent (around 30 percent), with the rest going to the app developer. A key question heritage institutions must ask themselves when selecting the freemium business model is can they offer enough depth and breadth of premium content. In the same way charging for a book is acceptable but charging for a pamphlet is not, purchased content must be robust and perceived as valuable.

Conclusion

It is now clear that mobile media and applications hold huge promise for the heritage sector, but the technology is still experimental, user experiences are unsatisfactory in many cases and proper implementation is still problematic. There is still much to be learned and many challenges going forward as mobile technologies evolve. For example, studies predict that the public will soon be exposed to a new wave of augmented reality applications in the near future, driven mainly by the business sector (ABIresearch, 2011). Commercial drivers are pushing mobile AR technical

---

[4] Price (as of June 15, 2013) for the iOS app obtained from the Apple iTunes store: https://itunes.apple.com/us/app/national-constitution-center/id399722048?mt=8

capability towards marker-less recognition of objects and landscapes, as well as server-based content that can be downloaded on demand. Moreover, this functionality will not be exclusive to smart phones, as Google and other companies are working on wearable computing products such as AR glasses, which could turn out to be a hugely disruptive mobile technology that will change the way people see and interact with the world.

No matter how mobile technology evolves, it is evident that if heritage professionals wish to reposition their institutions as modern, connected organizations with the public's interest at heart, producing mobile projects cannot be shied away from or ignored. Mastering the potential of mobile to promote heritage is essential in capturing new, digitally savvy younger audiences who will value and preserve heritage institutions moving in the future.

References

ABIresearch (2011). *Mobile Augmented Reality.* [Online] March 2011. Available online at: https://www.abiresearch.com/research/product/1006117-mobile-augmented-reality/ [Last accessed on May 11, 2012].

Bahl, S (2011). Sukiennice "Secrets Behind Paintings." *Ramble* [blog] October 13th, 2011. Available online at: http://www.ramble.sunmatrix.com/2011/10/sukiennice-secrets-behind-paintings/ [Last accessed on May 29th, 2013].

Hinojo, A (2012). QRpedia use at Fundació Miró. Case Study. *The Glamwiki Experience* [blog] April 26th, 2012. Available online at: http://theglamwikiexperience.blogspot.com/2012/04/qrpedia-use-at-fundacio-miro-case-study.html [Last accessed on May 28th, 2013].

Iverson, J (2012). Un-Stuffy Museum: The Louvre Goes High-Tech with Video-Console Guides. *TIME magazine,* [online] May 29th, 2012. Available online at: http://www.time.com/time/world/article/0,8599,2115750,00.html#ixzz2YMRfBzsR [Last accessed on May 26th, 2013].

Laugoudi, E and C Sexton (2010). The New Black, Museum Apps and Audiences on the Go. In G Chamberlain (ed.) *Interactive Galleries: Digital Technology, Handheld Interpretation and New Media.* London: Museum Identity, pp. 1–4.

Mannion, S (2012). Beyond Cool: Making Mobile Augmented Reality Work For Museum Education. *Museums and the Web 2012 Conference*. Available online at: http://www.museumsandtheweb.com/mw2012/papers/beyond_cool_making_mobile_augmented_reality_wo [Last accessed on May 6th, 2013].

Tallon, L (2009). About that 1952 Sedelijk Museum Audio Guide, and a Certain Willem Sandburg. *Musematic*, [online] May 19th, 2009. Available online at: http://musematic.net/2009/05/19/about-that-1952-sedelijk-museum-audio-guide-and-a-certain-willem-sandburg/ [Last accessed on May 22nd, 2013].

Thian, C (2012). Augmented Reality — What Reality Can We Learn From It? *Museum and the Web 2012 Conference*. Available online at: http://www.museumsandtheweb.com/mw2012/papers/augmented_reality_what_reality_can_we_learn_fr [Last accessed on May 9th, 2013].

PART 4
Technology and Other Issues

13

A CULTURAL HERITAGE PANORAMA: TRAJECTORIES IN EMBODIED MUSEOGRAPHY

Sarah Kenderdine and Jeffrey Shaw

The six installations described in this chapter contribute to the reframing of cultural heritage interpretation and the reformulation of somatic, kinesthetic and embodied experiences in immersive digital environments. These installations have been articulated through a series of trans-disciplinary experiments in large-scale, interactive cinematic display systems and are designed for major exhibitions in the public domain. The immersive display systems and their associated visual, sonic and algorithmic techniques offer compelling means for mapping and remediating cultural heritage landscapes and are based on significant tangible and intangible world heritage from India, Hong Kong and China.

PLACE-Hampi (2006) is focused on the world heritage site located at the former Kingdom of Vijayanagara in Karnataka, South India (Figure 1). *iJiao* (2011) represents significant Jiao Festivals held in Hong Kong (Figure 2) while the two Pacifying the South China Sea Pirates projects (2013) are based on an iconic handscroll painting from the Hong Kong Maritime Museum (Figures 3 and 4). The *Pure Land* projects (2012) are focused on the Mogao Grottoes at Dunhuang, Gansu Province, China (Figures 5 and 6).

These installations encompass four central ways of seeing: panoramic (360° × 50° screen configurations) exploited for the display systems PLACE and the Advanced Visualization and Interaction Environment known as AVIE; hemispheric (360° × 180° screen configurations) utilized in the iDome; linear spatial navigation (where a viewing window moves horizontally or vertically through space to reveal pictorial narrative sequences) as designed for the Linear Navigator; and augmentation (where screens with real time computer graphic overlays are used to navigate the real and virtual worlds simultaneously) such adopted in the Augmented Reality Edition display.

These uniquely configured display systems are primary research platforms that exploit innovative strategies of new media and narrative; they drive aesthetic change, stimulate cognitive understanding, expand cinematic theory, and enhance interactive, multimodal and hypermedia design. Each work involves a complex of software and algorithmic design, spatial acoustic arrangements and customized hardware engineering. Table 1 organizes each of the specific display systems described in this chapter with their respective installation, primary viewing modality, visual depth (monoscopic or 2D; stereoscopic or 3D), together with the average number of participants and spectators who can be part of an experience in a single installation at any one time.

When dealing with the representation of cultural heritage in these installations, we do not intend to overtly assert translation of real-world phenomena in the implementation of the digital or virtual. Nor do we assume that a mapping of phenomenological attributes of material forms in the virtual are possible or even desirable. We do not equate historical forms of representation (for example, rock art) with the potential of the digital transcription. However, we do believe that a wide cross-referencing to preceding strategies of representation and interpretation better enables us to articulate new forms of engagement and embodiment to produce new experiential interfaces for cultural heritage that must, if we are to do our work well, have their own intrinsic aura.

Table 1. Display system, respective installation, configuration and viewing modality, visual depth (2D or 3D) and average number of participants.

Display System	Installation	Modality of Viewing	2D or 3D	Number of Participants
PLACE	*PLACE-Hampi*	panoramic	stereoscopic	1 primary user, 25 spectators
iDome	*iJiao*	hemispheric	monoscopic	1 primary user, 8 spectators
Periview[SK]	*We are like the Vapors*	panoramic	monoscopic	25–30 spectators
Linear Navigator	*Scroll Navigator*	linear spatial	monoscopic	1 primary user, 4 spectators
AVIE	*Pure Land: Inside the Mogao Grottoes at Dunhuang*	panoramic	stereoscopic	1 primary user, 25–30 spectators
Augmented Reality Edition	*Pure Land Augmented Reality Edition*	augmented	stereoscopic	2 primary users, 25–30 spectators

The term "scopic regime" follows Martin Jay's (1988) identification of the "scopic regimes of modernity" (such as "baroque" and "Cartesian perspectivalism"). Scopic regimes are culturally specific ways of seeing. Identifying the scopic regimes specific to cultural groups replaces the traditional definition of "vision" as a universal phenomenon. It also supersedes the traditional discussion between technological determinism and social construction, allowing culture and technology to interact. These ideas underlie the methodology of the research presented in this chapter, as the installations often deal with a multiplicity of culturally informed ways of seeing that cannot be ignored. For example, the "reading" of handscroll as a process of revealing the narrative sequentially or, the immersive setting of a meditation or devotional cave with its specific spatially defined iconographic renderings.

Selected Works

Presented here, for the reader's further reference, is a brief description of each installation while corresponding website reference to videos, additional images and other related materials can be found in the References. Key reference texts are cited for further study. The remainder of this chapter is then dedicated to philosophical reflections on these installations encompassing embodiment, immersion, performance and narrative.

PLACE-Hampi (2006)

Display system: PLACE

PLACE-Hampi is an embodied theatre of participation in the drama of Hindu mythology focused at the most significant archaeological, historical and sacred locations of the World Heritage site Vijayanagara (Hampi), South India. It is an interactive installation that projects 3D panoramas onto a nine-meters in diameter 360° panoramic screen from a motorized platform that is controlled by one of the visitors (Figure 1). The user stands on the platform and with the

Figure 1. The rotation field of view of the PLACE 360° screen 3D screen showing *PLACE-Hampi* (2006).

handles mounted either side of an LCD screen, is able to steer the platform in 360°, simultaneously rotating a 120° field of view across the panoramic screen.

Enfolded in this interactive installation, visitors explore a virtual landscape of panoramic locations enlivened by animated mythological events that reveal the folkloric imagination of contemporary pilgrims active at the temple complex. Comprised of high resolution augmented stereoscopic panoramas and surrounded by a rich acoustic field composed from ambisonic recordings *PLACE-Hampi* articulates an unprecedented level of viewer co-presence in a narrative re-discovery of a cultural landscape (Kenderdine, 2013b).

iJiao (2011)

Display system: iDome

iJiao incorporates 360° videos sequences from a series of Taiping Qingjiao (also known as *dajiao* or Jiao Festival) into the interactive hemispherical projection system, iDome (Figure 2). The Jiao Festivals displayed in *iJiao*, are held throughout Hong Kong, appease the ghosts and give thanks to the deities for their protection. They take place every year or every five, eight, or ten years, depending on local customs. The religious rituals involved are meant to purge a community and prepare it for a new beginning. The display system is configured with a high-resolution projector, a spherical mirror as reflection surface, reflecting the image back in the fiberglass dome which as the surface for 180°.

The size and shape of this projection set-up covers the peripheral vision of the user, who stands directly in front of it. Typically, an iDome measures three-meters in diameter but it can be up to five-meters in diameter. A track ball allows the user to rotate the 360° projected image — freely. *iJiao* encapsulates a unique record of these auspicious events and allows the visitor to interactively navigate and control the point of view inside these experiences of rich cultural activities that surround *dajiao*.

Figure 2. The 360° spherical video of a thanksgiving performances of shen-gongxi performed during the Jiao Festival in the hemispheric viewing system iDome, *iJiao* (2011).

We are Like the Vapors (2013)

Display system: Periview^{SK}

A digital re-presentation of the 180cm by 55cm Pacifying the South China Sea Pirates handscroll is staged in a monoscopic 360° display system (Periview^{SK}), 10m in diameter and 4.5m high (Figure 3). The scroll is the icon object of the Hong Kong Maritime Museum collection. Inside this cylindrical enclosure, the high-resolution scroll slowly rotates, although the painting itself is largely obscured from viewers by digitally generated sea mists that drift over its surface. Inspired by the "vapors" described in the pirate Zhang Bao's records (in scroll painting, the concept of mist and clouds are often used to delineate one scene from the next), these mists thin and part to reveal the key situations, characters and events in the painting, which are then brought to life as animated vignettes.

Figure 3. The 360° panorama screen showing *We are like the Vapors* (2013), Pacifying the South China Sea Pirates, Hong Kong Maritime Museum © Applied Laboratory for Interactive Visualization and Embodiment.

These 55 animations are revealed in a sequence around the screen so that the viewer makes a complete 360° turn inside the display system during the 15 minute experience. When the mists open, each animation zooms out from the scroll background and is strongly magnified within a circular window. The level of magnification was only possible because of an ultra-high-resolution scan at 1200 DPI (Kenderdine, 2013c).

Scroll Navigator (2013)

Display system: Linear Navigator

The *Scroll Navigator* (Figure 4) explores another interactive modality for revealing the narrative sequences of handscroll painting Pacifying the South China Sea Pirates. A reduced-scale photograph of the entire scroll is presented in a five-meter-long light-box. Above this, a motorized 4000 pixel resolution, 42in LCD monitor is

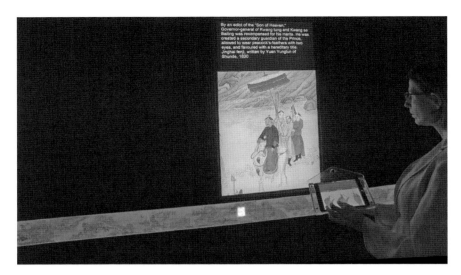

Figure 4. The linear spatial navigation system used for the handscroll painting narrative *Pacifying the South China Sea Pirates* installation Scroll Navigator (2013).

mounted on a track that is able to move freely above the entire length of the light box photograph. Any given section of the scroll that is seen on the monitor is simultaneously illuminated in the corresponding section of the light box. The visitor uses a small handheld digital tablet to control the movement of the LCD screen from one narrative zone to the next. Within the entire scroll image, the viewer can pan and zoom into minute details of the painting — a capability afforded by the aforementioned 1200 DPI ultra-high-resolution scan. Every notable element in the painting has also been described. The textual descriptions appear dynamically on the LCD screen above the scroll image as the visitor navigates (Kenderdine, 2013c).

Pure Land: Inside the Mogao Grottoes at Dunhuang (2012)

Display system: AVIE

Exploiting the high-resolution photography and laser scanning data recorded by the Dunhuang Academy at Cave 220, *Pure Land: Inside*

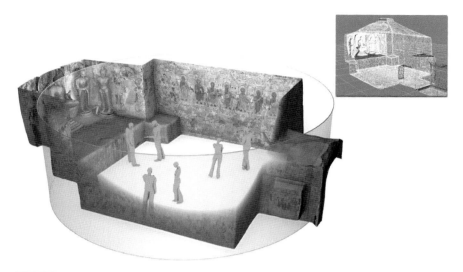

Figure 5.   The 360° 3D panorama screen Advanced Visualization and Interaction Environment (AVIE) showing *Pure Land: Inside the Mogao Grottoes at Dunhuang* (2012).

the Mogao Grottoes at Dunhuang (Figure 5) reframes and reconstitutes the extraordinary wealth of paintings found in the caves at Dunhuang inside an immersive 3D, 360° visualization system, the AVIE. Inside its panoramic enclosure (10m in diameter by 4m in height), visitors interactively engage in a surrogate true-to-life experience of being inside this cave temple and seeing its magnificent Buddhist wall paintings at one-to-one scale. As well as offering a powerful space of embodied representation, *Pure Land* uses various digital image processing techniques, 2D and 3D animation, and 3D cinematography to further develop its experiential and interpretative capabilities (Kenderdine, 2013a).

Pure Land Augmented Reality Edition (2012)

Display system: Augmented Reality Edition

Pure Land AR uses mobile media technology to create a complementary "augmented reality" rendition of the data from Cave 220 at

Figure 6. The augmented reality system used in the *Pure Land Augmented Edition* (2012).

Dunhuang (Figure 6). Walking around inside the exhibition space with tablet screens in hand, visitors are able to view the architecture of the cave and to explore its sculptures and wall paintings, as they appear on viewers "mobile" windows' — a kinesthetic revealing of the painted architectonic space. In this installation, the walls of the exhibition room (which share the same scale as the real cave) are covered with one-to-one scale prints of Cave 220's "wireframe" polygonal mesh derived from the laser scan — which provides visitors with visual cues as to what they are to exploring (Kenderdine, 2013a).

Frameworks

Experiencing and embodying

In the installations described in this chapter, narrative content and immersive "architectures" (displays) combine to provide a context for multisensory mediation between humans, machine agents and virtual environments. Modalities of interaction can be described as forms of prosthetic vision, acoustic immersion, kinesthetic activation, telepresence, inhabitation and dwelling, travelling, driving and walking. In the cultural imaginary activated by the installations, the sensory world of participant visitors is tuned for encounter and emergent narratives become possible. The sensory experience has been placed at the forefront of cultural analysis, overturning linguistic and textual analysis and supporting phenomenological and experiential enquiry.

Similarly, in the post-processual frameworks for interpretive archaeology, practitioner Christopher Tilley advances a phenomenological understanding of the experience of landscape. His arguments emphasize approaches to archaeological assemblages that go beyond their material manifestation. In his book, *Body and Image: Explorations in Landscape Phenomenology* (2008), Tilley usefully contrasts iconographic approaches to the study of representation with those of kinesthetic enquiry. Tilley's line of reasoning provides grounding for the research presented here into large-scale, immersive and kinesthetically provocative environments that designed specifically for the experience and embodiment of cultural and heritage. By suggesting that landscape studies are transformed by re-focusing on the kinesthetic, Tilley stresses the autonomy of images to convey meaning. Imagery has a "direct agency" (Tilley, 2008, pg. 46) that acts as one inhabits and moves through the landscape. In this context it is useful to quote his discussion of the interpretation of rock art:

> "The potential of kinesthetic approaches tell us something different (...). Iconographic approaches are usually primarily cognitive in nature. They grant the primacy to the human mind as a producer of the meaning of the images through sensory perception. It is the mind that responds in a disembodied way (...). Kinesthetic approaches, by contrast, stress the role of the carnal human body. The general claim is that the manner in which we perceive, and therefore relate to visual imagery, is fundamentally related to the kinds of bodies we have. The body both limits and constrains and enables us to perceive and react to imagery in specific embodied ways" (Tilley, 2008, pg. 18).

The installations described here encapsulate the understanding of the body in motion, in both real and digital spaces. In museums, we see how these installations reflect the increasing trend to merge architecture form with media. The museum itself is an immersive architecture that increasingly promotes interactive activities and has been analyzed for its sensorial attributes, not just in terms of vision but also acoustics, tactility and somatic impacts (e.g., Classen and Howes, 2006). Western culture generally describes architecture to be a visual experience; other senses play a role in how we experience both natural and built environments. The importance of aural or acoustic architecture to the cognitive map is indisputable (e.g., Blesser and Salter, 2006).

In many of the installations, the design of the immersive systems demands that people ambulate and circumambulate, continuously re-orienting themselves in relation to real-world scale imagery of augmented virtual landscapes. In *PLACE-Hampi* for example, by putting the viewer on a rotating platform, it forces them to abandon their bodily relation to the surrounding real space and kinesthetically enter the imaginary space that the work offers. The acoustic cues in the systems are dynamic in relation to the positioning of visitors and their movements further reinforcing this sense of "being there". In *Pure Land AR*, the tablet screen shifts from being considered as an object in and of itself to functioning as a mobile framing device for the staging of a "virtual" rendering of the real cave that relies on an intricate spatial tracking system. This is not a passive televisual environment, but an interactive performance where Cave 220 is being exactly mapped between real space, and digital model. In this instance, *Pure Land AR* is activated in the twists and turns of the hand-held screen. By moving the monitor around the space, the viewer can walk along and examine three walls of the cave and by holding the tablet aloft one can also see the magnificent ceiling painting. Thus the tablet reveals the cave as something that is apparently located in the real space, and as visitor/user/participant entertains the various possibilities of moving through the space with the tablet, the changing views of the cave are fluidly and accurately shown on the screen. In this way, the classic trope in art of a "window on to the world" is virtually enacted.

Looking Around and Being Inside

In virtual reality, the panoramic view is joined by sensorimotor exploration of an image space that gives the impression of a "living" environment (Grau, 2003, pg. 7).

Four of the installations described in this chapter — *PLACE-Hampi*, *iJiao*, *We are like the Vapors* and, *Pure Land: Inside the Mogao Grottoes at Dunhuang*— involve panoramic modalities of experience and, strategies of display. The relationship between new forms of cultural heritage exhibitions and the history of panoramic immersion has been extensively described in previous media-archaeology reflection (e.g., Kenderdine, 2007; 2010). The mass public screen entertainment of the panorama is also the subject of a number of extensive analytical histories (e.g., Oettermann, 1997; Comment, 2000; Altick, 1978; Huhtamo, 2013) and this led Stephen Oettermann to claim the panorama as "the first true mass medium..." (Oettermann, 1997, pg. 7). The oeuvre of the panorama as a strategy of immersion can be traced from prehistoric period of cave painting through to the 19th century history of exhibition complexes, and it continues to hold fascination for contemporary audiences.

The installations described in this essay amalgamate traditional panoramic forms with new media and virtual reality technologies. Extrapolating from the 360° immersive panorama has been a basis for developing new ways of representation, embodiment, inhabitation, navigation and narration. These paradigms have also been the focus of much new media art practice (e.g., Shaw, 1997; Shaw and Weibel, 2003). Indeed, the re-emergence of the panoramic scheme in current media practices as "the new image vogue" (Parente and Velho, 2008, pg. 79) is based on the desire to design virtual spaces and places that can be inhabited by the viewer, maximizing a sense of immersion and ultimately "presence." The panorama thus reveals itself as a navigable space, persistent throughout media history, which is charged with socio-cultural implications (for further discussion, see Kenderdine, 2007; Flynn, 2013). By defining strategies for embodiment, the installations reactivate the history of the immersive view for museums and reinvigorate archeology with aliveness, extending the role of digital facsimiles for new levels of aesthetic and interpretative experience.

Performing

In immersive installations participants interact and perform with both the imagery of the virtual world and with the other people who co-inhabit the space. The issues of inhabiting these multimodal, hybrid spaces are fundamental to understanding how the installations function as participatory, socializing experiences within museum spaces (e.g., Kenderdine *et al.*, 2009).

The theoretical discussion of performative qualities of interactive installations often neglects the primary communication that occurs between all people as they either perform the act of spectatorship or user participation. The aesthetics of interaction is 'rooted in the user's experience of herself performing her perception' (Dalsgaard and Koefoed-Hansen, 2008, pg. 1). Both performance theory and sociology, when considering how computer-human interaction (HCI) works, suggest that the user is simultaneously the "operator" of the system, the "performer" of the system and the "spectator." In multi-participatory installations, which embody a single-operator/ user and multiple spectators, numerous bonds exist between the user and the spectators and, the user and the system.

As already highlighted in the preceding, the concept of embodiment between the user and the system is of primary concern. Embodiment is a "participatory" status and a foundation for exploring interaction in context (Dourish, 2001). In terms of the trichotomy of the system-user-spectators, embodiment implies a reciprocal relationship with the context, encompassing users, interactive systems, spectators, co-users, physical surroundings, and the meanings ascribed to these entities (Dalsgaard and Koefoed-Hansen, 2008, pg. 5 cited in Dourish, 2001). Researchers of HCI, Reeves, Benford, O'Malley and Fraser, address the issue of how a spectator should experience a user's interaction with the computer (Reeves *et al.*, 2005, pg. 748). Borrowing from performance theory, the user is the inter-actor with the system, and the interaction between the user and the system is the performance. While this relationship is what is mostly described in media art and HCI, it is the spectators' relation to and experience of the performance that is also of interest here, that is its participatory and socialization affordances. In *Pure Land AR*, which has an area (24sq m) equal to the actual Cave 220, two mobile tablets allow two users and, typically, groups of three to 10 people to follow the tablets around. *Pure Land AR* thus demonstrates the dynamics of a single-user, multi-spectator interface that is important to the notion of museums as places of socialization. A group of people will always surround the user, and will follow, direct, gesture, prompt, and photograph the user's view of the world. These relationships are integral to the interpretation, and to the performance of the work. The view that everyone should have his or her own tablet interface would deny the dynamic of this interchange and only advantage more isolated journeys of discovery. Indeed, the ideas of performing the work are at the core of socialization in museum spaces. As Dalsgaard and Koefoed-Hansen describe:

> "It is the ways in which the user perceives and experiences the act of interacting with the system under the potential scrutiny of spectators that greatly influences the interaction as a whole … it is precisely this awareness of the (potentiality of a) spectator that transforms the user into a performer" (Dalsgaard and Koefoed-Hansen, 2008, pg. 6).

The investigative framework of performance also addresses a complex mix of HCI issues that arise during the hermeneutic, phenomenological and epistemological encounters with digital archaeological and cultural heritage landscapes. The methodology of the research described here recognizes that the past is constantly re-created in learning experiences, a never-ending process of "making sense". This supports the notion that interpretation is always in flux, and never final, because more can always be said or learned in recurrent acts of making meaning. This concept is fundamental for two reasons: firstly, it reinforces the experiential real-time encounter with interactive systems, wherein no participant will experience the same thing twice, even after recurring visits to the system. Secondly, it strengthens the personalized cognitive and kinesthetic encounter as a valid form of interpretation — particularly important in new forms of digital cultural heritage, which is supported by interactive narrative agency.

Navigating and Narrating

The key to the success of hybrid cinematic forms such as those described in this chapter, is the notion of navigation of virtual spaces. As Jeffrey Shaw describes: "By creating virtual extensions to the image space that the viewer must explore in order to discover its narrative subjects, the navigable artwork allows the visitor to assume the role of both cameraperson and editor" (2003, pg. 23). In the context of the display systems described in this chapter, specific narrative formulations emerge from the interactive and immersive affordances of these systems. Researchers at the iCinema Research Center for Interactive Cinema (Del Favero *et al.*, 2002) have defined three narrative formulations for new media interactive installations:

> Polychronic — a synthesis of multi-branched and algorithmically determined navigable systems (e.g., *PLACE-Hampi, iJiao,* e.g., Kenderdine 2010);
>
> Transcriptive — beholder-initiated, editorial actions involving the manipulation of duration and movement in the reassignment of eventfulness to episodic media content (for example, *T_Visionarium* (2008) not discussed in this chapter: see Bennett, 2008);
>
> Co-evolutionary — intelligent agents acting autonomously in response to emergent situations in consultation with their own scripted beliefs (see *Hampi-LIVE*, as described in Kenderdine, 2013a).

To compliment these modalities and ascribe a narrative form to the remainder of installations in this chapter we could add scenographic spatial narrative — the practice of design that unites the visual, auditory image and environment into a single, artistic form of communication (e.g., *We are like the Vapors*; *Pure Land*). In *We are like the Vapours* for example, the temporal dramaturgy of mists parting to reveal magnified animated details of the painting is an effective way to communicate to visitors the scroll's twenty narrative sequences. The visual experience is accompanied by an evocative surround sound audio design, and the animated events are synchronized with vivid sound effects. The overall scenography is punctuated by narrated scene titles (derived from the painting itself) that further help to elucidate the meaning of each phase of the scroll's unfolding drama. The visitors follow the animations around the screen so that by the time the entire story is told, they have turned physically in 360°.

Augmented reality could be described as a mixed reality narrative. The conjunction between the "actual" and the overlay of the virtual as demonstrated in *Pure Land AR*, operates in the borderline between the indexically real and the phantasmally virtual — between re-embodiment and dis-embodiment. *Pure Land AR* weaves a set of subtle paradoxes into its web of virtualization and actualization, and these paradoxes feed the kinesthetic excitement that is clearly evident in all visitors' astonished enjoyment of this installation. It thus aligns with the technologies of telepresence that virtually transport the viewer between the present location and another place — in this case, from the exhibition space to the site of Dunhuang.

As Peter Greenaway prompted "maybe we should re-invent cinema as a scroll" (cited in Bruno, 2002, pg. 138). Typically the narrative of a scroll resembles the unfolding strips of a film and this narrative literally unravels as the scroll is transported or the viewer moves along its horizontal and sequential visual plane. The *Scroll Navigator* with its partial field of view simulates this movement along the scroll, transporting the physical presence and viewers' gaze through the narrative of the painting. This linear panning through time (of the scroll's narrative) and space (the length of the scroll and the exhibition space) as one walks the length of the digital version could be called spatial located narrative, that is narrative that unfolds at a particular location. Spatial located narrative is

Table 2. Six installations mapped to their respective interactive narrative paradigm.

Installation	Interaction Design	Narrative Paradigm
PLACE-Hampi	custom navigation (rotating platform, and custom interface tools)	polychronic
iJiao	reconfigured trackball	polychronic
Pure Land: Inside the Mogao Grottoes at Dunhuang	reconfigured joystick	scenographic spatial
Pure Land Augmented Reality Edition	tablet interface	mixed reality
We are like the Vapors	contemplation	scenographic spatial
Scroll Navigator	reconfigured tablet interface	spatially located

appropriate to all forms of story-telling using locative media. In *Scroll Navigator*, when "zoomed in" (the digital scroll is twenty times greater in length than the actual object) specifically prepared texts augment the visitors journey and thus parallel narratives unfold in real-time; those of the visual and spatial imagery of the scroll being revealed and, those of the dynamic textual descriptions associated with zooming and panning "inside" the painting itself. In the hands of the user, the interface is a prosthetic device unfolding this temporal spatial narrative.

By way of summary, Table 2 tabulates each installation correlated to its respective interactive narrative paradigm.

Conclusion

The installations described in this chapter, and the frameworks considered in their analysis, offer ways of thinking about cultural heritage presentation in the digital domain, and in the museum setting. *Pure Land: Inside the Mogao Grottoes at Dunhuang* (2012) that has been described as "the exhibition experience of the future" by Julian Raby, director of the Smithsonian's Freer and Sacker galleries (Smithsonian Press Release, 2012). Philip Kennicott for the Washington

Post (November 30th, 2012) wrote, "... at last we have a virtual reality system that is worthy of inclusion in a museum devoted to the real stuff of art." The installations described here contribute to the development of new strategies for the rendering of cultural content and heritage landscapes, demonstrating the potential for "presence" and "co-presence" with the past, as theatres of embodied experience from a cultural imaginary located in the here and now. These experiences are not concerned with the didactic learning requirements often associated with the rhetoric of heritage nor the desire to transport the participants back through time using virtual technologies. In a celebration of the landscape as "alive," post-colonial cultural theorist Homi K. Bhabha describes well the spirit of our endeavors:

> The borderline work of culture demands an encounter with "newness" that is not part of the continuum of the past and present. It creates a sense of the new as an insurgent act of cultural translation. Such art does not merely recall the past as social cause or aesthetic precedent: it renews the past, refiguring it as a contingent "in-between" space, that innovates and interrupts the performance of the present. The "past-present" becomes part of the necessity, not the nostalgia, of living (Bhaba, 1994, p. 12).

The installations offer fresh visualization and audification strategies, directed towards artistic rendering of cultural heritage. The discussion broadly spans themes such as embodiment, immersion, performance and narrative, describing a new wave of digital cultural heritage.

References

Advanced Interaction and Visualization Environment (AVIE) (2004). Available online at: http://www.icinema.unsw.edu.au/technologies/avie/project-overview/ [Last accessed on May 30th, 2013].

Altick, R (1978). *The Shows of London*. London: Cambridge University Press.

Applied Laboratory for Interactive Visualization and Embodiment (ALiVE) (2012). Available online at: http://alive.scm.cityu.edu.hk/ [Last accessed on May 30th, 2013].

Bennett, J (2008). *T_Visionarium: A Users Manual.* Sydney: University of New South Wales Press.

Bhabha, H (1994). *The Location of Culture.* London: Routledge.

Blesser, B and LR Salter (2006). *Spaces Speak, Are You Listening? Experiencing Aural Architecture.* Cambridge, MA: MIT Press.

Classen, C and D Howes (2006). The Sensescape of the Museum: Western Sensibilities and Indigenous Artifacts. In E Edwards, C Gosden and R Phillips (eds.) *Sensible Objects: Colonialism, Museums and Material Culture,* pp. 199–244. Oxford: Bloomsbury Academic.

Comment, B (2000). *The Painted Panorama.* New York: Harry N. Abrams Inc.

Dalsgaard, P and L Koefoed-Hansen (2008). Performing Perception: Staging aesthetics of interaction. *Transactions on Computer-Human Interaction (TOCHI),* 15 (3). New York: ACM.

Del Favero, D, I Howard, J Shaw and R Gibson (2002). The Reformulation of Narrative within Digital Cinema as the Integration of Three Models of Interactivity. *ARC Discovery Project.* Canberra: Australian Research Council.

Dourish, P (2001). Seeking a Foundation for Context-aware Computing. *Human-Computer Interaction,* 16 (2), 229–41.

Flynn, B (2013). Spaces of Mnajdra. Available online at: http://spacesofmnajdra.com. [Last accessed on May 30th, 2013].

Grau, O (2003). *Virtual Art: From Illusion to Immersion.* Cambridge, MA: MIT Press.

Huhtamo, E (2013). *Illusions in Motion: Media Archaeology of the Moving Panorama and Related Spectacles.* Cambridge, MA: MIT Press.

iDome (2009). Available online at: http://www.icinema.unsw.edu.au/technologies/idome/project-overview/ [Last accessed on June 30th, 2012].

iJiao (2011). Available online at: http://alive.scm.cityu.edu.hk/projects/alive/ijiao-2011/ [Last accessed on May 30th, 2013].

Jay, M (1988). Scopic Regimes of Modernity. In H Foster (ed.) *Vision and Visuality,* pp. 3–23. Seattle, WA: Bay Press.

Kenderdine, S (2007). Speaking in Rama: Panoramic Vision in Cultural Heritage Visualization. In F Cameron and S Kenderdine (eds.) *Digital Cultural Heritage: A Critical Discourse,* pp. 301–32. Cambridge, MA: MIT Press.

Kenderdine, S (2010). *In situ: Immersive Architectures for the Embodiment of Culture and Heritage*, PhD thesis, RMIT University of Melbourne.

Kenderdine, S (2013a). *Pure Land: Inhabiting the Mogao Caves at Dunhuang. Curator: The Museum Journal*, 56(2), 199–118.

Kenderdine, S (2013b). *PLACE-Hampi: Inhabiting the Panoramic Imaginary of Vijayanagara.* Heidelberg: Kehrer Verlag.

Kenderdine, S (2013c). Pacifying the South China Sea: A Digital Narrative of Annihilation and Appeasement. *Orientations*, 44(3), 79–84.

Kenderdine, S, J Shaw and A Kocsis (2009). Dramaturgies of PLACE: Evaluation, Embodiment and Performance in PLACE-Hampi. In *Proceedings of the International Conference on Advances in Computer Entertainment Technology (ACE '09)*, 249–56, November 2008, Athens, Greece. New York: ACM.

Kennicott, P (2012). "Pure Land" Tour: For Visitors Virtually Exploring Buddhist Cave, it's Pure Fun. *The Washington Post*, [online] November 29th, 2012. Available online at: http://www.washingtonpost.com/entertainment/museums/pure-land-tour-for-visitors-virtually-exploring-buddhist-cave-its-pure-fun/2012/11/29/3d30c13c-3a62-11e2-8a97-363b0f9a0ab3_story.html [Last accessed on May 30th, 2013].

Oettermann, S (1997). *Panorama: History of a Mass Medium* (trans. Deborah Lucas Schneider). New York: Zone Books.

Parente, A and L Velho (2008). A Cybernetic Observatory Based on Panoramic Vision. *Technoetic Arts: A Journal of Speculative Research*, 6(1), 79–98.

PLACE-Hampi (2006). Available online at: http://place-hampi.museum [Last accessed May 30th, 2013].

Pure Land Augmented Reality Edition (2012). Available online at: http://alive.scm.cityu.edu.hk/projects/alive/pure-land-ii-2012/ [Last accessed May 30th, 2013].

Pure Land: Inhabiting the Mogao Caves at Dunhuang (2012). Available online at: http://alive.scm.cityu.edu.hk/projects/alive/pure-land-inside-the-mogao-grottoes-at-dunhuang-2012/ [Last accessed May 30th, 2013].

Reeves, S, S Benford, C O'Malley and M Fraser (2005). Designing the spectator experience. In *Proceedings of the SIGCHI Conference on Human Factors in Computing Systems (CHI'05)*. New York: ACM, pp. 741–750.

Scroll Navigator (2013). Available online at: http://alive.scm.cityu.edu.hk/projects/alive/the-scroll-navigator-2013/ [Last accessed May 30th, 2013].

Shaw, J (1997). *PLACE: A User's Manual*. Karlsruhe: ZKM (Center for Art and Media Karlsruhe).

Shaw, J (2003). Introduction. In J Shaw and P Weibel (eds.) *Future Cinema: The Cinematic Imaginary after Film*, pp. 19–27. Cambridge, MA: MIT Press.

Shaw, J and P Weibel (eds.) (2003). *Future Cinema: The Cinematic Imaginary after Film*. Cambridge, MA: MIT Press.

Smithsonian Press Release (2012). New Technology Resurrects Ancient Chinese Cave at Smithsonian's Sackler Gallery: "Pure Land" Digital Installation Brings Buddhist Treasures to Washington, D.C., [online] November 26th, 2012. Available online at: http://newsdesk.si.edu/releases/new-technology-resurrects-ancient-chinese-cave-smithsonian-s-sackler-gallery. See also video documentation, available online at: http://www.youtube.com/watch?v=rrTKARGeUfQ [Last accessed May 30th, 2013].

T_Visionarium (2008). Available online at: http://alive.scm.cityu.edu.hk/projects/related/t_visionarium/ [Last accessed May 30th, 2013].

Tilley, C (2008). *Body and Image: Explorations in Landscape Phenomenology*. Walnut Creek, CA: Left Coast Press.

We are Like the Vapors (2013). Available online at: http://alive.scm.cityu.edu.hk/projects/alive/the-360-scroll-experience-we-are-like-vapours-2013/ [Last accessed May 30th, 2013].

14

FROM PRODUCT TO PROCESS: NEW DIRECTIONS IN DIGITAL HERITAGE

Eugene Ch'ng, Henry Chapman and Vince Gaffney

From Product to Process

The comparison between illustrations created by a gifted artist and those created by a technical illustrator without such skill provides significant contrasts. Illustration is traditionally associated with the final communication of a lengthy research process, demonstrating the summative work of an academic enquiry. Illustration therefore, is an end product, produced by a contracted few. The results are clearly seen in countless publications, such as Tim Taylor's impression of a Mesolithic village (Wymer, 1991), and the numerous illustrations by archaeological illustrators such as Alan Sorrell (Sorrell, 1976) and, more recently, Victor Ambrus (Ambrus and Aston, 2009; Ambrus, 2006). These should, of course, also be compared with the requirements for technical illustration which may provide relatively realistic reconstruction of artefacts or structures for interpretative purposes and which might lead to physical reconstruction (Barker, 1982, pg. 233–247, pg. 254–267).

In a typical archaeological process, layers of fieldwork and subsequent analysis take place prior to the ultimate interpretation and, in these cases, reconstructive illustration is commissioned as a final product to fulfil the requirements of dissemination, within reports and publications for public outreach. Factors influencing the final product will include archaeological accuracy, interpretation, limitations of knowledge and, of course, aesthetics. Whilst this description is a generalization of a highly variable process, the notion of illustration as an end product is in itself curious. In particular two primary, though related, factors emerge. Firstly, the process of illustration will normally highlight areas of uncertainty in the archaeological record and its interpretation. For example, for prehistoric buildings, it will require educated guesses to be made regarding elements such as roofing which are not normally preserved. The second factor is the position from which illustrations are drawn. Commonly, a distant view is chosen which limits the need for detail and hence for certainty in interpretation (Wymer, 1991). From a distance, figures can be represented in a way that limits the requirement for detailed information about their clothing, for example.

These challenges to archaeological illustration are largely centered on the limitations of the archaeological record. However, from an alternate perspective, this might be considered to be one of the great strengths of the process. Illustration effectively combines archaeological 'reality' with supposition to create something that seamlessly brings the two together, but it also provides an extremely critical eye to the archaeological process itself. In text, the interpretation of an archaeological site can be focused on known factors, whereas an illustrative reconstruction is forced to consider less well-known or understood elements. An example of such an interpretation can be seen in Figure 1. Here a structure dating from the late Neolithic period has been recreated to illustrate a circular ditch surrounding a ring of 24 internal pits up to one meter in diameter and designed to allow posts to support a free-standing structure. The circle's estimated date of 2,500 to 2,200 BC suggests that it was operating when Stonehenge was in its final and most dramatic form. However, the heights of the posts and how the structure actually looked are both unknown. The blending of a series of features — such as the internal mound is almost certainly incorrect as this was likely to have been a later feature — although

Figure 1.   Virtual reconstruction of the wooden hengiform structure located
approximately 600 m from Stonehenge (http://archpro.lbg.ac.at/).

the absolute dates for the individual parts of the monument are unknown. Visualization at this site also combines real data acquired from Ground Penetrating Radar (GPR, inset of Figure 1) to provide an impression of realistic visualization.

Consequently, the ability of visualization to highlight the "unknowns" of the archaeological interpretation should present a positive challenge for archaeologists. Rather than disguising these "unknowns" through artful illustration, illustration itself can be seen as a process whereby hypotheses are created, many of which could be tested through further fieldwork and enquiry.

The overarching theme of this chapter describes the changing role of visualization. The chapter begins, in the introduction, with a narrative of how visualization has indeed become a process within the archaeological and heritage research framework. This is followed by the transformation of the interpretive process as a result of technological development in the next section. Subsequent sections illustrate the process of visualization in research, and provided guidelines for visualization in digital heritage before a summary conclusion is given on the topics discussed in the article.

Contributions of Technological Development to the Interpretive Process

The effort and skill required to produce high quality illustration has always been a restriction (Hills, 1993, pg. 217–222). Our predecessors had limited access to illustrators, and that may be one of the reasons that illustrations are an end product of their research. This has changed significantly in the last decade when programmers begin to capture and reproduce skills of artists in a mechanical way using computer algorithms, this has inadvertently paved the way for the "now everyone can do it!" paradigm (Frischer and Dakouri-Hild, 2008). Image processing and manipulation software such as Adobe Photoshop and Illustrator, with various filters and toolkits, is enabling a wide range of users to create professional quality images. Furthermore, video editing software with transition effects, audio and special effects libraries empowers users armed with cheap HD video cameras to create their own videos, as is evident in the explosion of videos in online video streaming services such as YouTube, etc. 3D content generation software now with professional tools were previously accessible only to the entertainment industry, but have now made their way into platforms used by students to create high quality 3D animations (e.g., Autodesk 3ds Max, Blender 3D, etc.). Games engines and Integrated Development Environments (IDE) and a library of assets provide a new way for non-specialists to create games with high quality computer graphics and interactivity (e.g., Unreal SDK, CryEngine, Unity3D, etc.). Agent-Based Modelling (ABM) (Bonabeau, 2002) and visualization packages such as Netlogo (Tisue and Wilensky, 2004), created for teaching high school students with simple English language-like programming languages, allow a wide range of users to generate new data for their studies. Many of these computer applications have their origin as Open-Source products, providing free distribution of source codes accessed by programmers, and end products consumed by non-programmers. These developments naturally open up new ways of working with and presenting data, and somewhere along the line, it has transformed the way academic research is being conducted.

It is widely accepted that non-linear laws of technological development are speeding up academic research. The information revolution has contributed to our research in many ways, as is evident in our ability to accurately process large amounts of data, the speedy access of scientific communications and the emergence of online collaborative research and authorship. This has been beneficial in many respects, and will probably continue to support intellectual development. This, in many ways, is the product of three primary laws. The better known of the three, Moore's law (Moore, 1998) demonstrates that the processing power of a microchip doubles every 18 months and, effectively, the price of a given level of computing power halves over a similar period. This has great implications, for it affects not only the processing speed of machines but also the capacity of information storage devices (Walter, 2005) and imaging devices that deal with pixel data (Myhrvold, 2006). Gilders' law (Gilder, 2000) states that the bandwidth of telecommunications systems triples every 12 months, and Metcalfe's law (Metcalfe, 1995) asserts that the value of a network is proportional to the number of connected nodes or users in a network. This means that the increase of nodes or users in a telecommunications or social network increases the value or usefulness of that network in terms of the ability to communicate and disseminate information. These exponential growths in computing power are not only contributing to our ability to collect and store large amounts of heritage-related data, but have also provided the research community with the capability to process these data into structured information. A major advantage is the ability to visualize data and, as a result, produce meaningful content for the interpretation of the past within the framework of heritage research. Meaningful content can be packaged by combining elementary and advanced digital formats for research investigation and public consumption:

- 2D pixels forming an image (images, maps, etc.).
- 3D pixels (voxels) in volumetric rendering (internal investigation of objects using CT and MRI scanning equipment and landscapes using remote sensing technology).
- 3D vectors as points, connected as lines, with triangles forming polygons (virtual objects and environments).
- Static and dynamic datasets with time as an added element (progression of objects, monuments and landscape changes).
- Interactivity, where content can be manipulated by users.
- Navigation, where virtual environments can be explored.
- Adaptive content where a measure of intelligence in Artificial Intelligence (AI) is applied to allow content to respond to the environment the content resides in.
- Evolvable content where Darwinian theories, particularly evolutionary algorithms selects the next generation of content.
- Physical 3D prints reproduced from 3D scans of physical objects and environments.

These digital illustration formats have, in the last decade, become part of the process of research. While traditional illustration is an end product of a research, digital visualization has become a fundamental part of the research itself.

Visualization as a Process Rather than a Product

Visualization is an integral part of our lives. We learn about the world we live in through our visual observations and this naturally transfers to our work and how we communicate and disseminate knowledge in the wider context. These processes, which are driven by external demands (e.g., the entertainment industry), are advancing technological developments. These are displays with larger pixel resolutions or faster refresh rates, along with the hardware and computer graphics algorithms that drive the rendering process pipeline. As a result, the industry has become relatively mature for large scale heritage and archaeological inquests. The need for immersion in visualization drives the size of displays — they become larger with back projection as well as massive plasma screens. On the other hand, the need for ubiquity reduces the size of displays and the processing power required to run interactive graphics on smaller digital devices. Furthermore, research in Human-Computer Interaction (HCI) improves interactivity and adds greater utility to these displays so much so that it actually transforms how users access information and, in the academic arena, the workflow of researchers. The relatively recent inclusion of gestural multiuser-multitouch capability further enhances the intuitiveness of interactive displays. Heritage objects, text, behaviors and environments, once accessible only to a select few in the academic community, can now made available to a wide range of users. In the past decade, an explosion of content is witnessed in the Virtual Heritage conference tracks of the International Society of Virtual Systems and Multimedia (VSMM), since 1999, the International Symposium on Virtual Reality, Archaeology and Intelligent Cultural Heritage (VAST) since 2006, and the more recent EuroMed conference (International Conference on Cultural Heritage 2012). These activities indicate not only that the public has a growing appetite in digital heritage, but that there is an ever increasing need for digital visualization within the process of research. Visualization, a means of communicating research not two decades ago has now become an integral part of the interpretive research process (Figure 2.1–2.5).

Figure 2 is a roadmap of data flow in heritage research and illustrates how visualization plays a role in the major phases of a project. It is evident from the figure that visualization is used in every phase of larger research-focused projects, such as the Stonehenge Landscapes and North Sea visualization projects (Ch'ng *et al.*, 2011; Gaffney *et al.*, 2007).

Data Acquisition

The setting up of a research inquest leads to the first phase where data is gathered from the environment using remote sensing

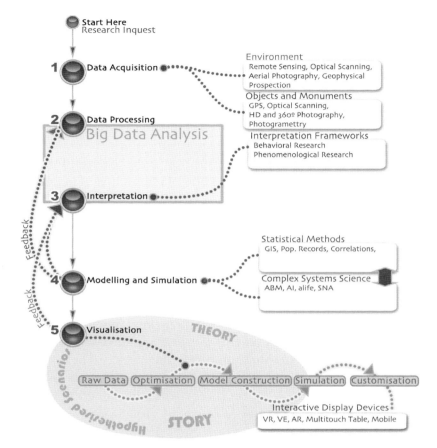

Figure 2. Data flow in archaeological research and how visualization plays a role in the major phases of a project. Figure 2.1 depicts the process of data acquisition. 2.2 and 2.3 are cohesive segments of work on the processing and interpretation of data. Work in 2.4 uses statistical methods and complex systems science to bridge gaps in the interpretation of data and Figure 2.5 visualizes the interpreted reconstructions via phenomenological research as both product and process.

technologies and geophysical prospection. These technologies include airborne (LIDAR and hyperspectral remote sensing) and satellite remote sensing (CORONA declassified intelligence satellite imagery) which captures and reconstructs landscape level information about the earth's surface for archaeologists, geomorphologists and environmental managers.

Objects and monuments are also increasingly being digitized using a variety of technologies, such as laser scanning, for a variety of purposes which include accessibility for both researchers and for broader public consumption such as through virtual museums (e.g., Chapman *et al.*, 2010), through to the generation of digital reference collections (e.g., Niven *et al.*, 2009). Furthermore, there have also been studies that have used digitized objects for direct analyses, such as the calculation of ceramic metrics (Karasik and Smilansky, 2008) or of lithics (Grosman *et al.*, 2008). However, the digital reconstruction of degraded or broken objects to highlight their envisioned 'complete' forms remains an element of communication rather than research.

Data Processing

Computer-generated data processing and visualization has a relatively long history within archaeological research. There has been a considerable legacy through the use of Geographical Information Systems (GIS) and image processing applications to process, map, model and visualize abstract data, such as patterns of visibility (Exon *et al.*, 2000; Gearey and Chapman, 2006; Lake *et al.*, 1998; Llobera, 2001; Wheatley and Gillings, 2000; Wheatley, 1995), route-ways through the landscape (e.g., De Silva and Pizziolo, 2001) or site location analysis and predictive modelling (e.g., Westcott and Brandon, 1999).

The data processing phase requires visualization and involves viewing and analyzing datasets that have been combined and processed into human-readable formats using appropriate software (coupled with intensive compute power (e.g., high-end workstations) and High Performance Computing (HPC), at the University of Birmingham's BEAR (Birmingham Environment for Academic Research). Core workstation facilities are needed to provide access to a suite of software tools, including GIS and image processing applications such as Erdas Imagine, Idrisi, and Avizo for mapping, manipulating and visualizing 2D and 3D datasets (Ch'ng *et al.*, 2004).

The processed datasets from raw remote sensing formats lays the foundation for proper interpretation. The datasets that flow from Figure 2.2–2.3 and 2.4 are human readable maps integrated from GIS and image processing applications with levels of information overlays depicting patterns, route-ways and site locations. The phase 2.4 in particular requires greyscale images as height maps for generating polygon terrains so that software agents acting as ancient inhabitants may be used for hypotheses testing, such as their navigation through the route-ways of the landscape being investigated.

Interpretation

Interpretation (Figure 2.3) is partly realized through visualization in the first two phases, and involves behavioral research and phenomenological research. With regards to phenomenology, there has been considerable research into the use of digital technologies for the 'experiential' visualization of archaeological sites and landscapes using 3D modelling software and gaming technologies. For example, the use of 3D reconstruction and the application of virtual engagement with landscape have been explored since the 1990s (e.g., Barceló *et al.*, 2000; Forte, 1995; Reilly, 1990). Oddly, the drive for generating virtual archaeological worlds has been similar to that from more traditional archaeological illustration, as an end product, albeit with the increased function of interactivity. As such, virtual environments can be found on the Internet (e.g., Murgatroyd, 2008), within the online journals such as "Internet Archaeology," within museum interactive displays, and in published form through established monograph series such as Computer Applications in Archaeology (CAA). More recently, there have been some attempts to integrate reconstruction with archaeological research in a more fundamental way. For example, the use of virtual reality has been linked with experiments to explore themes such as the application of phenomenological theory to the interpretation of archaeological landscapes (Ch'ng, 2009a; Gillings, 1999; Winterbottom and Long, 2006). Thus, whilst the majority of virtual reality approaches remain effectively as end-products of the archaeological process, there have been developments in the application of digital reconstruction as part of the interpretation process. However, this remains focused on the re-interpretation of archive data rather than a part of the data acquisition phase (Figure 2.2).

Modeling and Simulation

Phase four delves into Agent-Based Modelling (ABM), Artificial Intelligence (AI), Artificial Life (ALife), and Social Network Analysis (SNA) as a means of connecting data in the first three phases. Whilst data is being assembled and interpreted, it is inevitable that the data captured may not be sufficient to fill the information space. Therefore, statistical and complex systems approaches are needed to fill gaps in the interpretation where traditional frameworks are lacking. This necessarily involves autonomous agents. Agents are individual software units that have Beliefs, Desires and Intentions (BDI), they are created to carry out tasks as individuals or as collective units for a common purpose. Agents in the ABM, ALife and AI process may depict flora, fauna and ancient humans (Ch'ng and Gaffney, 2013; Ch'ng and Stone, 2006a; Ch'ng, 2009b; 2011). The ALife methodology populates the landscape datasets from Figure 2.2 with plants and animals, and AI and ABM models and simulates human agents and their navigation and settlement strategies based on the resolution of the environment reconstructed from remote sensing data, such as the macro-micro link in environmental changes (Ch'ng, 2012). Statistical methods become necessary when the population of agents in the simulation exceeds a threshold. In such cases, statistical analysis was found to be a very good complement to ABM and SNA for making sense of the simulated datasets. Visualisation is an integral part of phase four to the graphical nature of ABM simulations; it also provides feedbacks to phases two and three, contributing to behaviour research in the interpretation framework. The datasets that are generally transferred between Figure 2.4 and 2.2 and 2.3 are statistical regression as a correlation between factors affecting agent population, charts depicting agent population, and network graphs showing communities. Geo-positional information of agents within the 3D terrain is useful for reconstructing the virtual environments for phenomenological research.

Visualization

During the final stages of a project (Figure 2.5), when research has become mature and when hypothesized scenarios are clear, visualization then becomes a product. At this stage, multiple scenarios of a site may be presented using interactive virtual environments as a feedback to phenomenological research. At the conclusion of a project, the knowledge gained is disseminated to a wider audience via interactive display devices.

Despite the growth in the use of digital technologies for the creation of reconstructive illustrations in archaeology, for sites, landscapes and objects, the majority of applications have remained focused on the end-product, synthesizing data to provide a representation of the "best guess" of what might have been. Where there have been explorations into the use of reconstruction for archaeological research purposes, these have mostly remained focused on the re-analysis of archival data rather than on informing the process of archaeological data collection.

Productions of Visualization

The final output of a research should include imagery to both illustrate outputs and to support the dissemination of the research to a wider audience. In the field of high-end interactive computer graphics, this requires a production process and, as high quality standards are expected from 21st century digital heritage projects, the production process can be quite similar. This section outlines such a process using a pipeline of entertainment industry-oriented tools and procedures (see Figure 2.5, visualization process chart), including possible features of visualization, learning from over a decade of experience from research at the IBM Visual and Spatial Technology Centre.

For academic publications, TV and online media, it is generally sufficient to have either pre-rendered images or videos of the research outcome. However, the advancement of computing technology means that different audiences may be provided with an enhanced access to heritage objects, monuments, and landscapes in a digital format (Ch'ng, 2007; 2009a; 2013a). Newly discovered treasures such as the Staffordshire Hoard and the 52,500 Roman coins found in Somerset (BBC, 2010), United Kingdom can be captured via high-resolution 3D imaging devices, reproduced digitally and viewed interactively on handheld or desktop computing devices. Monuments such as Stonehenge, where public access has been limited may benefit from English Heritage's decision to capture a 3D high resolution digital version providing the public with the opportunity to "walk" amongst the digital stones and experience the different textures and features of each stone in the 3D reproduction. Submerged landscapes populated by ancient inhabitants prior to flooding as a consequence of climate change can now be repopulated with flora, fauna, and people, and explored by audiences using a standard desktop computer (Ch'ng and Stone, 2006a; 2006b; Ch'ng, 2007; Gaffney *et al.*, 2007). Accessibility is increasingly the key motivation for developing real-time computer graphics and virtual environments and therefore is becoming important to the academic community who may benefit intellectually from high resolution images and digital objects demanded by an informed visitor population.

A good example of the issues relating to digital reproductions rather than illustrations is provide by the digital model of a Greek Wild Goat style cup (Figure 3) created from an original in the museum of the Institute of Archaeology and Antiquity at Birmingham. The cup itself is a relatively simple stemmed vessel and of interest mainly because of the suggestion that the painted design might indicate that the vessel was a skeuomorph whose metal prototype possessed incised angular designs that were repeated in paint on the clay copy. Some time ago, this cup was scanned and rendered with an image of the surface design. This model was used, with the surface of the design raised, to create a casting in metal but the digital model

Figure 3.   Wild Goat-style cup. The image is the physical cast of a digital model
that was also rendered with haptics interaction.

was also rendered with haptics interaction to permit the user to view
the digital model either as metal or clay. Aside from the apparent
veracity of the scanned surface the significance of the exercise was
not so much the ingenuity of permitting visitors to touch, virtually, an
object that would otherwise have only been experienced through the
glass of a museum case: Rather it was the fact that the visitor
experienced an enhanced act of interpretation. It may be that there
never was a metal original of the stemmed cup and its representation
(digital or physical), remains an act of subtle imagination. The
experience of interpretation is therefore a central role of visualization
rather than the simple representation of any particular reality.

**Visualization for the Interpretive Research
and Exploratory Learning**

If the main purpose of interactive visualization is to provide
informed access to multiple audiences, it is worth exploring the
nature of these groups and how data is generated for their
consumption. This effectively includes two primary audience groups.
The first is composed of researchers and students, who may use the
virtual environments for the process of investigating the data and to
generate further questions and test hypotheses. The second type of
audience is the public(s), those who are curious to explore the

Table 1.	Feature comparisons for two main audiences of interactive and navigable virtual heritage reconstruction.

Interpretive Research — Researchers	Exploratory Learning — Public Access
Layered Information: Turning on/off hypothesised scenarios	
Interactive Note Taking	Crowd-Sourced Content
Networked Multiuser Access	
Phases Through Time: Ability to travel between archaeological periods for comparison	
Recorded Routes of Researchers as Inhabitants: Mapping routes of researchers for phenomenological interpretation	Recorded Routes of Visitors: Crowd-sourced virtual visitor interests and popularity 'heat maps'

outcome of a particular heritage research project. Therefore, the information presented must be equally accurate as the second group may have a tendency to accept the digital reconstruction as factual because of the apparently realistic visualizations provided. Table 1 shows the partitioning of the two groups of users.

The process to provide visualization for these groups begins with collating information from the captured and analyzed object. It is inevitable that the data may not be complete, and that there remain gaps within the interpretive framework. In such cases, developers of the system must provide a clear statement, either visually or textually distinguishing between confirmed facts and acceptable hypotheses. However, for aesthetic purposes, textual communication is preferred over a virtual world that has dummy artefacts (objects representing hypothesized scenarios). On the other hand, the layer data structure, where 3D objects are partitioned in the virtual scene, could also be used to turn on or off these artefacts so that users can choose between investigative (researchers and students) and exploratory mode (public audiences). With regards to time, it is possible to reconstruct different periods of a site so that users can 'time-travel' between them, standing at the same location for comparisons. This method of comparative study is being developed from the Flag Fen reconstruction project (Figure 4), a wooden causeway some 3,500 years old that was developed by the IBM VISTA Centre for

Figure 4. The screenshots show the Flag Fen Bronze Age virtual reconstruction
at Peterborough, UK. Flag Fen is a wooden causeway some 3,500 years
old that was developed by IBM VISTA for Peterborough Vivacity. One
of the features of the virtual reconstruction that users could explore
was an Xbox 360 controller that allows the users to not only navigate
the landscape, but also teleport between preset locations.

Peterborough Vivacity. One of the features of the virtual
reconstruction that users could explore was an Xbox 360 controller
that allows the users to not only navigate the landscape, but also
teleport between preset locations.

Other modes of interacting with the digital reconstruction may
include collaborative virtual note taking from researchers but also as
crowd-sourced content. Attaching notes and markers to objects in a
site is a useful way for recording thoughts and also as a way of filling
gaps in the interpretation. On the other hand, crowd sourced
comments may be useful for determining visitor interest and
impressions of the digital object. Multiple users may be able to access
a site simultaneously through the Internet. Routes of researchers
"living" within the virtual site and acting as inhabitants for
phenomenological interpretation can be mapped for later evaluations.

Figure 5. Screenshots of a part-hypothetical model of Georgetown World Heritage Site located in Penang, Malaysia. Algorithms for mapping the routes of visitors through a heritage site (connecting nodes and lines). Nodes (as masks at top right) records the height of the visitor, time spent on a location and objects viewed. Connecting lines between the nodes records the routes of visitors through the site.

On the other hand, routes of virtual visitors may be recorded as a heat map as they explore the virtual world, attracting other visitors to follow in the same route (Figure 5). These statistical maps may also generate useful visitor-interest information for researchers for tourism management purposes. Table 1 lists these features.

The Reconstruction Process: From Research Finding to Visualization

A good example of a developmental process flow (Figure 2.5) can be illustrated with the Flag Fen project (Figure 4). The credibility of represented objects, monument and environment is important as the virtual environment is exhibited at the center of the archaeological site. The digital display and Xbox 360 controller is strategically positioned on top of the 3,500 year-old platform for access by visitors. Prior to the digital development, the ancient platform had paintings on all four walls to depict the site's past environment. The virtual environment was commissioned to allow users to stand on site whilst exploring a virtual version of the excavation results. This mixed-reality system enables users to time-travel to the Iron Age site, to the period when the ancient monument was originally constructed. To ensure that the model was as accurate as possible, the reconstruction of the landscape, Iron Age houses (Figure 4 inset), the wooden structures and platform around Flag Fen was informed by a number of sources and specialists.

As well as information from excavation, environmental sampling, photographs and previous artists' reconstructions, GIS data such as topographic information and modern maps of the area were used to create the landscape and background within which the model of the monument would sit. There is a boundary to the Flag Fen landscape after which virtual reconstruction stops. This ensures that the virtual reconstruction will eventually be accessible to a wider range of computers via Internet browsers whilst recreating a background that was as factually correct as the model would allow.

The reconstruction of the monument is tedious process. As the recovery of a complete timber pole for 3D laser scanning is impossible, a diverse set of timber poles were reconstructed in Autodesk 3ds Max and Blender from 3D polygons with different wood material textures mapped to the surfaces (each and every piece of texture is created and modified in Adobe Photoshop). These are then positioned across the lake and rotated to add variation to the apparently orderly image. The base of the monument uses textures that are blended to create a timber pile. The houses are similarly created from 3D polygons and textured based on the life-sized model at the Flag Fen site. Boats are created using a similar approach. Subsequently, the models were assembled within the Unity 3D development environment. As part of the ancient environment, special effects were added for realism. These are water reflections, the swaying of vegetation to simulate mild wind conditions and birds and insects 3D sound effects, which were placed at strategic locations to create an atmosphere. Sun shafts simulate radial light scattering when the virtual sun is partly obscured by objects such as the timber poles, and lens flares. Aerial perspective effects were also added to add a depth of field camera effects to distance objects. All virtual objects are light-mapped for an appropriate contrast between light and shadows after virtual light sources are positioned. As there are thousands of 3D objects in the virtual reconstruction, Occlusion Culling, a technique to optimize a 3D scene for faster and smoother real-time exploration, is applied. These effects enhance the phenomenology of the landscape (Tilley, 1994), giving users a sense of time and space through the sensory experience of sight and hearing by being in a landscape.

The C# programming language was used to script the interactivity of the system, such as for the Xbox 360 Controller. Computer algorithms were created to enable "virtual teleportation" — visitors are able to transport themselves from one location to the other within the boundaries of the landscape using buttons from the controller. The aim of such a virtual reconstruction is to allow users a means of exploring the landscape through virtual "time travel" (Ch'ng, 2009a).

Other modes of visualization are also possible for heritage projects. Although the interaction styles, display technologies and process of delivering real-time computer graphics to the different devices are different, the process of digital heritage reconstruction is largely similar. Figure 5 depicts the different interaction and display devices that have been explored to meet different heritage project requirements. The image and inset on the left shows an Augmented Reality system used for merging the real world with the virtual, such as the virtual campfire on the ground viewed through the head-mounted display. The images on the left of Figure 6 depict a multitouch table

Figure 6. Modes of interaction and display devices. An AR system, and multiuser-multitouch tables with digital heritage applications.

with two heritage applications (Ch'ng, 2013a). The first (middle and inset) allows the manipulation of objects using multitouch gestures such as the zoom and drag. The image on the right is a virtual environment that contains autonomous agent-based trilobites, each with different behaviors that competes for food dropped off by users.

Conclusion

It should be clear that there has been a "secondary digital products revolution" in the last few years. The move from static illustration to rich media was important and has been well documented (Frischer and Dakouri-Hild, 2008). Recently, however, there has been a more fundamental movement. Digital products such as remotely sensed data or Agent-Based Modelling, may be self-referential, having no prior existence in reality but may fundamentally impact upon received knowledge. Objects which are recreated digitally may now also have a significant other life in which the responses (e.g., shared comments, Facebook "likes," and Tweets) of academic and interested public may be attached and used in wholly novel ways to understand how objects are understood academically but also as unique digital products. The requirement of media and the informed public may drive intellectual capacity to a new level. It is however, important to note that it is doubtful whether museums themselves could have driven the development of digital environments which will be increasingly used to display archival materials. "Edutainment" has actually led development and actually stimulated demands for increasingly rich digital environments — a process which is likely to continue and perhaps even deepen as other commercial interests see value in creating immersive environments (Thomson, 2012). The world of heritage visualization as both a product, and as part of the process of research is therefore likely to become increasingly complex as a reflection of such developments, but the value of the availability of technology that reproduces and engenders heritage objects with additional attributes and linkages with a broader world is also one that will benefit academics — although they will have to ensure that the contents that are to be made public are both accurate and ethically appropriate.

In this chapter, we outline the transformation of visualization as a new direction of archaeological research with the overarching theme "From Product to Process," presenting two decades of experience in digital heritage research. Illustration was traditionally associated with the final communication of a lengthy research process. It was meant to demonstrate to a certain level of accuracy, the collected data, interpretation, limitations of knowledge and aesthetics that is associated with an archaeological research. Illustration was mainly an end product to fulfil the requirements of academic dissemination within reports and publications for public outreach. In the last few decades however, as the restrictions associated with computing resources and the accessibility of automated software needed to produce high-quality digital visualizations were gradually lifted, researchers begin to discover an entirely new approach for working with, and interpreting datasets. The exponential growth of technological development has opened a new direction for archaeological research using interactive visualization. The advent of the Big Data (Ch'ng *et al.*, 2011) era in remote sensing and modelling and simulation (Ch'ng, 2013a) also meant that acquired data can no longer be laid out on a physical work desk without filling up the entire room. In such an era, interactive visualization, managed by efficient computing interfaces, that presents massive amounts of information on digital displays becomes a necessity. At this juncture, researchers naturally discovered new ways of interpreting data that were presented to them. This novelty in visualization has created new research directions that were unheard of a decade ago.

In our narrative, we have demonstrated that visualization has now become a process rather than merely a final product of the research process. Looking into the future, as our inquisitiveness grows together with technological revolutions, and as the volume, velocity and variety of data that researchers in the digital heritage domain deal with becomes larger, visualizations will become an even more integrated component within the interpretive framework of research.

References

Ambrus, V (2006). *Drawing on Archaeology*. Stroud: Tempus.

Ambrus, VG, and Aston, M (2009). *Recreating the Past*. Stroud, UK: History Press.

Barceló, JA, M Forte and DH Sanders (2000). *Virtual Reality in Archaeology*. Oxford: Archaeopress.

Barker, P (1982). *Techniques of Archaeological Excavation*. London: Routledge.

BBC (2010). Coroner Decides Somerset Roman Coin Hoard is Treasure. *BBC* [online] July 22, 2010. Available online at: http://www.bbc.co.uk/news/uk-england-somerset-10722715 [Last accessed on May 14th, 2013].

Bonabeau, E (2002). Agent-based Modeling: Methods and Techniques for Simulating Human Systems. *Proceedings of the National Academy of Sciences of the United States of America*, 99(Suppl 3), 7280–7287.

Chapman, HP, VL Gaftney and the HL Moulden (2010). The Eton Myers collection Virtual Museum. *International Journal of Humanities and Arts Computing*, 4(1–2), 81–93.

Ch'ng, E (2007). Using Games Engines for Archaeological Visualisation: Recreating Lost Worlds. *11th International Conference on Computer Games: AI, Animation, Mobile, Educational and Serious Games, CGames '07*, 26–30.

Ch'ng, E (2009a). Experiential Archaeology: Is Virtual Time Travel Possible? *Journal of Cultural Heritage*, 10(4), 458–470.

Ch'ng, E (2009b). An Artificial Life-Based Vegetation Modelling Approach for Biodiversity Research. In R Chiong (ed.) *Nature-Inspired informatics for Intelligent Applications and Knowledge Discovery: Implications in Business, Science and Engineering*. Hershey, PA: IGI Global.

Ch'ng, E (2011). Spatially Realistic Positioning of Plants for Virtual Environments: Simple Biotic and Abiotic Interaction for Populating Terrains. *IEEE Computer Graphics and Applications*, 99. IEEE.

Ch'ng, E (2012). Macro and Micro Environment for Diversity of Behaviour in Artificial Life Simulation. *Soft Computing and Intelligent Systems (SCIS) and 13th International Symposium on Advanced Intelligent Systems (ISIS), 2012 Joint 6th International Conference*, 883–889. November 20–24, 2012. Kobe, Japan.

Ch'ng, E (2013a). The Mirror Between Two Worlds: 3D Surface Computing Interaction for Digital Objects and Environments. In D Harrison (ed.). *Digital Media and Technologies for Virtual Artistic Spaces*. Hershey, PA: IGI Global.

Ch'ng, E (2013b). Model Resolution in Complex Systems Simulation: Agent Preferences, Behavior, Dynamics and *n*-tiered Networks. *SIMULATION,* 89(5), 635–659.

Ch'ng, E, H Chapman, C Gaffney, V Gaffney, P Murgatroyd and W Neubauer (2011). Landscapes Without Figures: Big data, Long Waves and the Formative Role of Archaeological Computing. *IEEE Computer: Special Issue on Computational Archaeology,* 44(7), 40–46.

Ch'ng, E and RJ Stone (2006a). Enhancing Virtual Reality with Artificial Life: Reconstructing a Flooded European Mesolithic Landscape. *Presence: Teleoperators and Virtual Environments,* 15(3), 341–352.

Ch'ng, E and RJ Stone (2006b). 3D Archaeological Reconstruction and Visualization: An Artificial Life Model for Determining Vegetation Dispersal Patterns in Ancient Landscapes. *Computer Graphics, Imaging and Visualization (CGiV),* 112–118. Sydney, Australia: IEEE Computer Society.

Ch'ng, E, RJ Stone and TN Arvanitis (2004). The Shotton River and Mesolithic Dwellings: Recreating the Past from Geo-Seismic Data Sources. In K Cain, Y Chrysanthou, F Niccolucci and NA Silberman (eds), *The 5th International Symposium on Virtual Reality, Archaeology and Cultural Heritage, VAST04: Interdisciplinarity or "The Best of Both Worlds": The Grand Challenge for Cultural Heritage Informatics in the 21st Century,* 125–134. Brussels, Belgium: The Eurographics Association.

Ch'ng, E and VL Gaffney (2013). Simulation and Visualisation of Agent Survival and Settlement Behaviours in the Hunter-Gatherer Colonisation of Mesolithic Landscapes. In E Ch'ng, VL Gaffney and H Chapman (eds.) *Visual Heritage in the Digital Age.* New York: Springer.

De Silva, M and G Pizziolo (2001). Setting up a "Human Calibrated" Anisotropic Cost Surface for Archaeological Landscape Investigation. In Z Stančič and T Veljanovski (eds.) *Computing Archaeology for Understanding the Past. CAA 2000. Computer Applications and Quantitative Methods in Archaeology. Proceedings of the 28th Conference, Ljubljana,* April 2000, 279–287. Oxford: Archaeopress.

Exon, S, VL Gaffney, A Woodward and R Yorston (2000). Stonehenge Landscapes: Journeys Through Real-and-Imagined Worlds. Oxford: Archaeopress.

Forte, M (1995). Scientific Visualization and Archaeological Landscape: The Case Study of a Terramara, Italy. In G Lock and Z Stancic (eds.) *Archaeology and Geographical Information Systems,* 231–238. London: Taylor & Francis.

Frischer, B and A Dakouri-Hild (2008). *Beyond Illustration. 2D and 3D Digital Technologies as Tools for Discovery in Archaeology*. Oxford: Archaeopress.

Gaffney, VL, K Thomson and S Fitch (2007). *Mapping Doggerland: The Mesolithic Landscapes of the Southern North Sea*. Oxford: Archaeopress.

Gearey, BR and HP Chapman (2006). Digital Gardening: An Approach to Simulating Elements of Palaeovegetation and Some Implications for the Interpretation of Prehistoric Sites and Landscapes. In TL Evans and P Daly (eds.) *Digital Archaeology: Bridging Method and Theory*, 171–190. London: Routledge.

Gilder, G (2000). *TELECOSM: How Infinite Bandwidth will Revolutionize our World*. New York: Free Press.

Gillings, M (1999). Engaging Place: A Framework for the Integration and Realisation of Virtual-reality Approaches in Archaeology. In LS Dingwall, S Exon, V Gaffney, S Laflin and M van Leusen (eds.) *Archaeology in the Age of the Internet. CAA97. Computer Applications and Quantitative Methods in Archaeology. Proceedings of the 25th Anniversary Conference, University of Birmingham*, April 1997, 247–254. Oxford: Archaeopress.

Grosman, L, O Smikt and U Smilansky (2008). On the Application of 3D Scanning Technology for the Documentation and Typology of Lithic Artifacts. *Journal of Archaeological Science*, 35(12), 3101–3110.

Hills, C (1993). The Dissemination of Information. In J Hunter and I Ralston (eds.) *Archaeological Resource Management in the UK: An Introduction*, 215–224. Sutton: Stround.

Karasik, A and U Smilansky (2008). 3D Scanning Technology as a Standard Archaeological Tool for Pottery Analysis: Practice and Theory. *Journal of Archaeological Science*, 35(5), 1148–1168.

Lake, MW, PE Woodman and SJ Mithen (1998). Tailoring GIS Software for Archaeological Applications: An Example Concerning Viewshed Analysis. *Journal of Archaeological Science*, 25(1), 27–38.

Llobera, M (2001). Building Past Landscape Perception with GIS: Understanding Topographic Prominence. *Journal of Archaeological Science*, 28(9), 1005–1014.

Metcalfe, B (1995). Metcalfe's Law: A Network Becomes More Valuable as it Reaches More Users. *Infoworld*, 17(40), 53–54.

Moore, GE (1998). Cramming More Components onto Integrated Circuits. *Proceedings of the IEEE*, 86(1), 82–85.

Murgatroyd, P (2008). Appropriate Levels of Detail in 3D Visualization: The House of the Surgeon, Pompeii. *Internet Archaeology* 23.

Myhrvold, N (2006). Moore's Law Corollary: Pixel Power. *New York Times*, [online] June 7th, 2006. Available online at: http://www.nytimes.com/2006/06/07/technology/circuits/07essay.html?_r=0 [Last accessed on May 14th, 2013].

Niven, L, TE Steele, H Finke, T Gernat and JJ Hublin (2009). Virtual Skeletons: Using a Structured Light Scanner to Create a 3D Faunal Comparative Collection. *Journal of Archaeological Science*, 36(9), 2018–2023.

Reilly, P (1990). Towards a Virtual Archaeology. In K Lockyear and S Rahtz (eds.) *Computer Applications and Quantitative Methods in Archaeology 1990*, 133–139. Oxford: Archaeopress.

Sorrell, A (1976). *Reconstructing the Past.* London: Batsford Academic.

Thomson, I (2012). Google Shows off Project Glass Augmented Reality Specs. The Register, [online] April 4, 2012. Available online at: http://www.theregister.co.uk/2012/04/04/google_project_glass/[Last accessed on May 15th, 2013].

Tisue, S and U Wilensky (2004). NetLogo: A simple Environment for Modeling Complexity. *International Conference on Complex Systems*, 16–21.

Walter, C (2005). Kryder's Law. *Scientific American,* [online] July 25, 2005. Available online at: http://www.scientificamerican.com/article.cfm?id=kryders-law [Last accessed on May 14th, 2013].

Westcott, KL and RJ Brandon (eds.) (1999). Practical Applications of GIS for Archaelogists: A Predictive Modeling Kit. Taylor & Francis.

Wheatley, D (1995). Cumulative Viewshed Analysis: A GIS-based Method for Investigating Intervisibility, and its Archaeological Application. In G Lock and Z Stancic (eds.) *Archaeology and GIS: A European Perspective*, 171–186. London: Routlege.

Wheatley, DW and M Gillings (2000). Visual Perception and GIS: Developing Enriched Approaches to the Study of Archaeological Visibility. In G Lock (ed.) *Beyond the Map: Archaeology and Spatial Technologies.* Amsterdam: IOS Press.

Winterbottom, SJ and D Long (2006). From Abstract Digital Models to Rich Virtual Environments: Landscape Contexts in Kilmartin Glen, Scotland. *Journal of archaeological science*, 33(10), 1356–1367.

Wymer, J (1991). *Mesolithic Britain.* Colchester: Shire Publications.

15

I SHO U: AN INNOVATIVE METHOD FOR MUSEUM VISITOR EVALUATION

Anita Kocsis and Sarah Kenderdine

This chapter proposes innovations in evaluation techniques that will help us understand visitor cognition in large-scale interactive immersive visualization environments (IIVEs). I Sho U (literally "I Show You") is a design-led method for encouraging visitors to engage with the evaluation directly inside the space of experience. This research enhances current visitor evaluation methodologies by developing visitor agency. It is applicable for large and diverse visitor communities, in a range of museum contexts. I Sho U compiles quantitative data about a qualitative experience and this data is visible in real-time to participants and to stakeholders (such as curatorial staff and exhibition developers). This ongoing research is being undertaken by the Laboratory for Innovation Galleries, Labraries, Archive and Museums (iGLAM), College of Fine Arts, University of New South West (UNSW) in collaboration with design research at Swinburne University, Australia. The case study introduced in this chapter used five I Sho U interfaces at the Hong Kong Maritime Museum, deployed for visitors engaged with two IIVEs (see the two Pacifying the South China Sea Pirates projects (2013) in Chapter 13). While the methods discussed here are using IIVEs for prototyping purposes, the application is easily reconfigured for any situation or museum context. I Sho U is ultimately applicable

245

to the entire situated experience of going to a museum irrespective of the nature of the content on display.

Evolution of Visitor Research

The evolution of visitor research in museums since the 1900's reflects an array of diverse evaluation typologies, pedagogy, collections and curatorial trends. The museums' emphasis on quality of their collections and scholarly frameworks has evolved to include visitors framed by these qualities (Trevelyan, 1991; Black, 2005; MacLeod, 2005; Parry *et al.*, 2010; Macleod *et al.*, 2012). "Experience economy" discourse (Pine and Gilmore, 1999; Mastai, 2007; Klingman, 2007) has, through the lens of marketing, evolved the visitor experience to consumer and thereby acknowledging the demographic that does not visit, the non-visitor. The evaluation of the non-visitor or visitor-as-consumer experience pervades museum culture, particularly where cultural organizations compete for attendees in a complex landscape where alternative venues are constantly on offer (Kotler and Kotler, 2001). The evaluation of the non-visitor or visitor-as-consumer experience pervades museum culture, particularly where cultural organizations compete for attendees in a complex landscape where alternative venues are constantly on offer (Kotler and Kotler, 2001). The contribution of visitor studies is acknowledged as a vital museum service yet identifies a significant resistance to the voice of the visitor (Hein, 2000; Simon, 2010). This situation has created a disjuncture between those with assumed knowledge (the museum) and those who do not know (visitors) (Weil, 2002).

However, constructivist learning, pluralist and participatory thinking have influenced an evolution towards visitor agency in the museum (Macleod *et al.*, 2012). Exhibition evaluation procedures are now broadening with a spectra of visitor analysis ranging from for example, learning capacity, knowledge retention, fatigue, comprehension, modes of navigation, length of stay and, enjoyment (Screven, 1990; Weil, 2002). Syntax specific to museum visitors derived from unobtrusive evaluation methods has developed descriptors such as "hot" and "cold" spots, "attracting power," and "holding power" (Falk *et al.*, 1985). Retelling the museum experience through visitors drawing has also been applied to elicit subjective visitor experience (ibid.). The inclusion of non-museum experts in marketing, design, education and other social sciences has also brought new methods for quantification of visitor types via focus group analysis, visitor demographic analysis, personas and scenario building. Methods also derived from anthropology and ethnomethodologies are used during stages of exhibition evaluation (Macdonald and Basu, 2007; vom Lehn, 2001).

In museums, formative and summative evaluation in exhibition cycles extrapolate the efficacy of the mission, function and pedagogy. The planning, development and design phase of an exhibition is predominantly content focused with groups of experts contributing to the overall exhibition. Visitor research has also become part of this cycle. During the summative phase or occupation stage, once the exhibition is opened, visitors are consulted, observed and studies take place (Dean, 1996). The final stage, normally towards the end of the exhibition cycle, engages focus groups and visitor analysis occurs (Frechtling, 2002). At this point common methods include structured observations, formal "testing" with visitors or groups, in-depth interviews, critical appraisal, media reviews, and demographics. Media such as guest books, online forms and forums, promotional workshops and traditional interviews are common tools, garnering visitor interest. Data from the evaluation provides a gauge for the institution including: its messaging; how people use it; what they learn from it; or, how they are changed. The information is usually disseminated as reports, helping planning for future projects, suggesting new research avenues, identifying visitor usage problems, interest levels and learning outcomes. Crucially, this data provides strategic direction for museum stakeholders, driving rationalization.

Meanwhile, social media technologies, smart phones and the internet has bought new levels of mediation for people in public, private, social and civic spaces including retail, transport, galleries and museums, and once novel social behaviors and activities are integrated as the norm. Social media activities adopted by museums as interactive learning aids have also facilitated new modes of learning consumption. People contribute to content through Web 2.0 media and crowdsourcing activities (Armstrong and Stojmirovic, 2011) and in the case of interactive exhibitions they are able to make decisions about "what" content, "when" they want it and, furthermore are encouraged "touch" the (digital) objects. Knowledge consumption and learning modes have "flattened." Free-choice learning for example and informal learning practices (Falk *et al.*, 2006) through the web and TV in conjunction with formal learning traditionally applied at universities, museums and schools have democratized access and made redundant traditional structures of sender (knowing) and receiver (less knowing) (Falk *et al.*, 2006; Weil, 2002) to non-linear non-hierarchical nodal structures. Today it is acknowledged that what museum visitors value and bring in terms of their own learning styles, makes contributions to how the museum shapes its content thus driving curatorial mandates. An adjunct to this thinking requires that the museum and its stakeholders are equally responsible for learning about their visitors. If the new museum intends to reach "beyond its walls" (Marstine, 2006; Friman, 2006) then visitors must be considered as part of the expert group who contribute to the content, design and architecture of the exhibition (Kocsis *et al.*, 2010).

Efforts by the museum in education and community engagement programs now are engaging new modes of co-creative activity to attract visitor participation (Simon, 2010). The inclusion of design and technology (Henning, 2006) to attract public consumption of sophisticated experiences, requires content that fulfill people's sense of pleasure and raises the level of user engagement (Blythe *et al.*, 2003). The adoption of user-centered thinking (Sanders, 2002; Sanders and Stappers, 2008; Parry *et al.*, 2010; Wright and McCarthy, 2010) has pervaded museum activities repositioning visitor participation as central in efforts to be relevant and reflect a multi-vocal, dynamic, responsive, community (Kelly, 2004; Simon, 2010). For museum stakeholders, the challenge of these participatory paradigms (often involving new technologies) is in understanding the contribution the technology makes and, how these technologies affect the dynamics of visitor experience in relation to the content.

This chapter focuses on the analysis of IIVE, increasingly incorporated in museum exhibitions (see chapter 13 for examples; Kenderdine, 2010a; Kenderdine, 2010b). These environments can be framed as spatial-temporal, non-linear, participatory, crowdsourced, flexible, networked, nodal, virtual, active, performative, and conceived as co-experiences, in addition to their interactive and immersive properties. The visitors in IIVE are actively performing, changing, contributing and communicating with the content as co-participants negotiating the parameters and contingencies of the space (Kenderdine *et al.*, 2009; Kenderdine 2010a; Kenderdine 2010b; Kocsis *et al.*, 2012). Recognizing the qualities that IIVE provide for visitors has yet to be critically analyzed and requires new methods and modes of visitor engagement. I Sho U is a method that provides museums and researchers with an understanding of the difference between "quality provided" and the "quality experienced" (Black, 2005). The quality experienced in the IIVE discussed in this chapter requires understanding the embodied experience of the visitor and ultimately intends to provide a museum with a vehicle for best practice in design.

I Sho U: Designing a New Paradigm for Participatory Evaluation

Museum visitors today expect learning that stands up as "an experience" (Macdonald, 2007) and expect a physical experience requiring all the senses (Hooper-Greenhill, 2006). Interactive immersive visualization environments are made up of unique display environments, production systems and computer graphics techniques that leverage technological advances in cinema, games, mobile and networked media. These new modes of experience provide galleries, museums and other public institutions innovative ways to present virtual heritage, historic, scientific and artistic digital content. The dynamics provided by the physical and digital parameters of these IIVE present new ways of being and performing in the space. Findings of earlier visitor studies by the authors on *PLACE-Hampi* (Kenderdine, 2013) revealed distinct themes pointing to embodied experience as shown in Figure 1 (Kenderdine *et al.*, 2009; Kenderdine 2010a; Kocsis, 2010; Kenderdine and Schettino, 2011). Social research methods (Hanington and Martin, 2012; Williams and Vogt, 2011) have identified that IIVE facilitate the phenomena

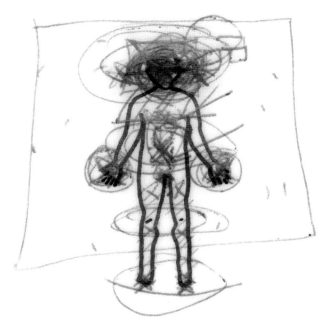

Figure 1.   Aggregated data for 284 visitors to PLACE-Hampi (2006) at the Martin
Gropius Bau, Berlin 2007 © Kocsis 2010.

of modularity, co-experience, time, sequence and nodal interactive
navigation in the exhibition space. However, the subjective, affective
and embodied causality of visitors' experiences are difficult to
record, requiring visual, interactive, and engaging communication
(Martinec and van Leeuwen, 2009). What is required is an interface
between the technology of the space and the visitor.

The authors identified a twofold problem requiring the analysis
of the embodied experience in IIVE and, appropriate methods to
visualize the qualitative, abstract and subjective 'states of being'
experienced by visitors. A conceptual framework based on hybrid,
co-creative, design-led methodology was developed. User-centered
design, visitor research, design thinking, psychology and human
computer interaction (HCI) were all charters used to inform the
design decisions for I Sho U (intended to gauge direct qualitative
participation of visitors). I Sho U, deployed on mini tablet interfaces,
also engages with new qualitative research methods (Blythe *et al.*,

Figure 2. I Sho U in Pacifying the South China Sea 360 scroll experience (2013), Hong Kong Maritime Museum, © iGLAM UNSW and Swinburne University. Photo: Kocsis, 2013.

2003; Hanington, 2003; Hannington and Martin, 2012; Williams and Vogt, 2011) seeking to foster personalization and uncover aspects of visitor diversity and different modes of learning (Hein, 2000; Hooper-Greenhill, 1992; Henning, 2006).

The mobile tablet based application I Sho U enables visitors to share and show their experiences through a "smart" interface (see Figure 2). Given the challenge of retelling experience (Dewey, 2009) and the difficulty in describing subjective experience (following Dourish, 2004; Sanders, 2002; Parry, 2010; Hannington and Martin, 2012) I Sho U employs a strategy of co-creative methods and user-centered design. I Sho U is designed around interaction, introspection and engagement, recruited in the application to determine visitor feelings and response (Schifferstein and Hekkert, 2007) and is based upon the assumptions designers make in developing behavioral and at times emotional affordances (Norman, 2007; Wright and McCarthy, 2010). These properties inform the design, interaction and visualization scheme of the visitor experience.

I Sho U can be deployed on multiple tablets through the museum galleries, for individuals and groups to use in situ (or specifically for the purposes of the study described in this chapter, inside two IIVEs). I Sho U facilitates visitor authorship, participation, action and insight, becoming a conduit between the visitor and the expression of their experience. The interactive visualization, framing experience, represents the "pulse" of the visitor in situ providing direct quantitative data on qualitative subjective experiences.

New exhibition strategies found in museums such as IIVEs demand considerable cognitive load from the visitor and include such factors as embodied cognition, proprioception and co-experience. Cognition is embodied when it is dependent upon features of the physical body, that is, when aspects of the person's body beyond the brain play a significant causal or physically constitutive role in processing (Shapiro, 2011; Johnson, 2007; Prinz, 2009). However, attempts to derive emotional state by gauging bodily responses (heartbeat and facial recognition) have proved unreliable (Kaliouby and Robinson, 2005). Through the cognitive scaffolding of I Sho U the visitor participates in instantaneous, collective and participatory methods focused on their emotional and embodied states.

I Sho U employs narrative, metaphor, game, interactive, and participatory technologies to organize abstract understandings of our physical experience by using patterns, images, drawing and other user-led actions (Hannington and Martin, 2012). Visual metaphor and sophisticated computational aesthetics (Ferster, 2013) are used in I Sho U to describe the visitor's experiential and imaginative immersion in the IIVE, in real-time. The interface displays the visitor's qualitative response data as graphic and aural quanta on the tablet. Visitors can simultaneously record, display and access momentary thoughts, feelings, and actions of being in the exhibition and by doing so reveal their own responses in relation to others.

Data from the application is uploaded in real-time from the tablet over a local network, to a website. Here stakeholders are able to view both individual entries and cumulative data that describe, in a visual form, the experiences of visitors at their galleries. The Data visualization tools enable simultaneous understanding of the overall exhibition and that of individual response enabling stakeholders to gauge the visitor experience in the exhibition. This form of creative, ubiquitous data visualization forms new ground for creative quantification of qualitative data and new ways of seeing and thinking about the visitor in interactive immersion environments. Over time, museum staff and visitors co-create new interface semantics and, visitor responses provide a semiotics for the iterative visual iconography of the visualization system.

I Sho U at the Hong Kong Maritime Museum

Two projects based on the 19th century handscroll *Pacifying the South China Sea Pirates* at the newly opened Hong Kong Maritime Museum, were analyzed over a month long period in May 2013 using I Sho U. The exhibition components are: the 360° 3D animated version of the scroll and, the annotated scroll navigator (see Chapter 13). Docents were deployed at the Museum with five mini iPads offering English, Traditional and Simplified Chinese interface options. The interfaces provided graphic and visually dominant information with text-based information was used only as a support, either as headings or instruction for visitors to participate in a specific activity. Familiar interface navigations strategies were employed: forward, back, pinch, scroll, slide, drag and drop — so as to not add to the cognitive load of undertaking the survey.

The questions asked in I Sho U were structured as themes based on earlier data from visitor studies by the authors (e.g., Kenderdine *et al.,* 2009; Kocsis, 2010) and relevant questions identified by the stakeholders. The themes were sectioned by titles such as "You, Me, Us"; "I think, I feel"; "I think, I like"; "Thank You"; and, "Want to Know More?" In the section "You, Me, Us", visitors were asked to identify (by drag and drop actions of icons of people) if they spoke to someone new or if they attended with others. In "I think, I feel," encouraged visitors to play and engage with visual metaphors related to comfort (see Figure 3), and asked where the exhibition images, audio and motion may affect the body. The graphics used

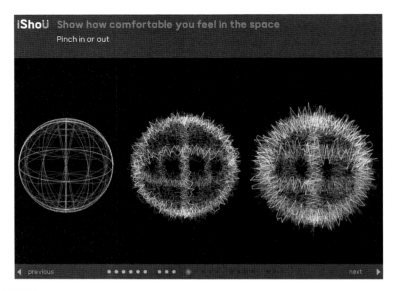

Figure 3.   I Sho U interfaces, I think, I feel, measuring three levels of comfort;
© iGLAM UNSW and Swinburne University. Photo: Kocsis, 2013.

semantic differential and psychometrically controlled scales to measure opinions, attitudes and values in order to gather information about the experience. Graphic plus (+) and minus (−) symbols identified the positive to negative range. The screens for preferred personal space can be seen in Figure 4.

Early observations of the deployment by docents and uptake by visitors were observed over four weeks including over 400 responses. A text entry field was used to elicit specific comments on the usability and meaning of the system for each participant. The aggregated data was visualized online. By providing email addresses participants are able to access the data stored online so that at a glance they can identify their own input in relation to others (and can do so without expert data analysis skills). Using the online data museum stakeholders are able to drill into specific details, moving from aggregated data to individual level responses.

Future deployments of I Sho U aim to allow for stakeholder specifications of particular attributes of the system. Museum staff users of the system will be able to download the application for the

Figure 4. I Sho U interface, preferred personal space. © iGLAM UNSW and Swinburne University. Photo: Kocsis, 2013.

tablet and add or subtract specific modules that are of interest, reflecting their specific visitor communities. For the visitors features that will be added to the system include the ability to take photos (which will upload in real-time to the aggregated data) and to leave audio recordings about their experience. Interestingly, one feature, which predominated in earlier research allowed visitors to hand-draw with a pen on an image outline of a body (Figure 1). This aspect of visualizing the embodied experience had been replaced with more basic body-mapping function in I Sho U. Many visitors wanted to see a more sophisticated canvas and a stylus will be used in coming iterations of I Sho U, allowing visitors to free-form draw (again). It is important for visitors also to understand that they are providing real-time data to museum stakeholders and this will be made clearer in future iterations. The refinement of the visualizations for aggregated data is the subject of concurrent research.

Conclusion

Large-scale interactive immersive environments are enabling museums to provide new ways of seeing, being and learning in exhibitions. These new spaces, as with all convergent technologies, require ongoing input or interaction from the visitor, as the space is contingent on participation. These spaces and environments also affect visitors embodied cognition and co-experience. Understanding the phenomenon of visitor engagement in these contexts is paramount for stakeholders who invest in defining these new forms of exhibition making. Visitor studies in such IIVEs demand innovative approaches, and this chapter demonstrates how I Sho U encourages visitor agency through technological interface and creative visualization. I Sho U utilizes design-led integrative thinking, action, and creative data collection that are led by the visitor. Using this method positions the visitor as integral to the evolution of the design and construction of IIVEs and future museum exhibitions. I Sho U encapsulates the fundamental role of visitor evaluation and evolving social research to impact and improve the design, delivery and dissemination of the museum, actual or virtual.

References

Armstrong, H and Z Stojmirovic (2011). *Participate: Designing with User-Generated Content.* Princeton: Princeton Architectural Press.

Black, G (2005). *The Engaging Museum: Developing Museums for Visitor Involvement.* London: Routledge.

Blythe, MA, K Overbeeke, AF Monk and PC Wright (2003). *Funology: From Usability to Enjoyment.* Dordrecht: Kluwer Academic.

Dean, D (1996). *Museum Exhibition: Theory and Practice.* London: Routledge.

Dewey, J (2009). *Art as Experience.* USA: Pedigree Books.

Dourish, P (2004). Where the Action is: The Foundations of Embodied Interaction. Cambridge, MA: MIT Press.

Falk, JH, J Koran Jr., LD Dierking and L Dreblow (1985). Predicting Visitor Behavior, Curator. *The Museum Journal,* 28(4), 249–258.

Falk, J, LD Dierking and M Adams (2006). Living in a Learning Society: Museums and Free-choice Learning. In S Macdonald (ed.) *A Companion to Museum Studies,* 323–339. Oxford: Blackwell Publishing.

Ferster, B (2013). *Interactive Visualization: Insight through Enquiry.* Cambridge, MA: MIT Press.

Frechtling, J (2002). *The 2002 User-Friendly Handbook for Project Evaluation.* The National Science Foundation Directorate for Education and Human Resources, Division of Research, Evaluation, and Communication, Arlington VA. Available online at: http://www.nsf.gov/pubs/2002/nsf02057/.

Friman, H (2006). A Museum without Walls. *Museum International,* 58(3), 55–59.

Hanington, BM (2003). Methods in the Making: A Perspective on the State of Human Research in Design. *Design Issues,* 19(4), 9–18.

Hanington, BM and B Martin (2012). *Universal Methods of Design: 100 Ways to Research Complex Problems, Develop Innovative Ideas, and Design Effective Solutions.* Gloucester, MA: Rockport Publishers.

Hein, HS (2000). *The Museum in Transition: A Philosophical Perspective.* Washington, DC: Smithsonian Institution.

Henning, M (2006). New Media. In S Macdonald (ed.) *A Companion to Museum Studies,* 302–318. Oxford: Blackwell Publishing.

Hooper-Greenhill, E (1992). *Museums and the Shaping of Knowledge.* London: Routledge.

Hooper-Greenhill, E (2006). Studying Visitors. In S Macdonald (ed.) *A Companion to Museum Studies,* 363–376. Oxford: Blackwell Publishing.

Johnson, M (2007). *The Meaning of the Body: Aesthetics of Human Understanding.* Chicago: University of Chicago Press.

Kaliouby, R and P Robinson (2005). *Real-time Inference of Complex Mental States from Facial Expressions and Head Gestures, Real-Time Vision for HCI.* Berlin: Springer-Verlag.

Kelly, L (2004). Evaluation, Research and Communities of Practice: Program Evaluation in Museums, *Archival Science* 4(1–2), 45–69.

Kenderdine, S (2010a). *INSITU: Immersive Architectures for the Embodiment of Culture and Heritage.* PhD Thesis, RMIT University, Melbourne, Australia.

Kenderdine, S (2010b). Immersive Visualization Architectures and Situated Embodiments of Culture and Heritage. *Information Visualization (IV), 14th International Conference,* July 26–29, 2010, 408–414. IEEE.

Kenderdine, S (2013). *PLACE-Hampi: Inhabiting the Panoramic Imaginary of Vijayanagara.* Heidelberg: Kehrer Verlag.

Kenderdine, S and P Schettino (2011). PLACE-Hampi: Interactive Cinema and New Narratives of Inclusive Cultural Experience. *Inclusive Museums Journal*, 3(3), 141–156.

Kenderdine, S, J Shaw and A Kocsis (2009). Dramaturgies of PLACE: Evaluation, Embodiment and Performance in PLACE-Hampi. *ACE '09 Proceedings of the International Conference on Advances in Computer Entertainment Technology*. New York: ACM.

Klingmann, A (2007). *Brandscapes: Architecture in the Experience Economy.* Cambridge, MA: MIT Press.

Kocsis, A (2010). *Co-Desiging New Media Spaces.* PhD Thesis. University of New South Wales, NSW, Australia.

Kocsis, A, C Barnes and S Huxley (2010). Framing the Phenomenon of Visitor Experience in Interactive Exhibitions. In G Rouette (ed.) *Exhibition Design for Galleries & Museums: An Insider's View*, 10–18. Victoria: Museums Australia.

Kocsis, A, C Barnes and S Kenderdine (2012). Digital Mediation and the Museum Space. *Interiors*, 3(2), 107–126.

Kotler, N and P Kotler (2001). Can Museums be All Things to All People? Missions, Goals, and Marketing's Role. *Museum Management and Curatorship*, 18(3), 271–287.

Macdonald, S (2007). Interconnecting: Museum Visiting and Exhibition Design. *CoDesign: International Journal of CoCreation in Design and the Arts*, 3(1), 149–162.

Macdonald, S and P Basu (2007). *Exhibition Experiments.* Malden, USA: Blackwell Publishing.

MacLeod, S (2005). Reshaping Museum Space: Museum Meanings. London: Routledge.

MacLeod, S, L Hanks and J Hale (eds.) (2012). Museum Making: Narratives, Architectures, Exhibitions. London: Routledge.

Marstine, J (2006). New Museum Theory and Practice: An Introduction. Hoboken, NJ: Blackwell Publishing.

Martinec, R and T van Leeuwen (2009). *The Language of New Media Design: Theory and Practice.* London: Routledge.

Mastai, J (2007). There is No Such Thing as a Visitor. In G Pollock and J Zemans (eds.) *Museums after Modernism: Strategies of Engagement*, 173–177. Oxford: Blackwell Publishing.

Norman, D (2007). *Emotional Design: Why We Love (or Hate) Everyday Things.* New York: Basic Books.

Parry, R (ed.) (2010). *Museums in the Digital Age: Leicester Readers in Museum Studies.* London: Routledge.

Pine, J and JH Gilmore (1999). *The Experience Economy: Work Is Theatre & Every Business a Stage.* Boston: Harvard Business School Publishing.

Prinz, JJ (2009). Is Consciousness Embodied? In P Robbins and M Aydede (eds.) *The Cambridge Handbook of Situated Cognition.* Cambridge: Cambridge University Press.

Sanders, E (2002). From User-centered to Participatory Design Approaches. In J Frascara (ed.) *Design and the Social Sciences: Making Connections.* London: Taylor and Francis.

Sanders, EBN and PJ Stappers (2008). Co-creation and the New Landscape of Design, *CoDesign: International Journal of CoCreation in Design and the Arts,* 4(1), 5–18.

Schifferstein, H and P Hekkert (2007). Product Experience. Oxford: Elsevier.

Screven, C (1990). Uses of Evaluation Before, During and After Exhibit Design. *The International Laboratory for Visitor Studies Review (ILVS) Review,* 1(2), 37–38.

Shapiro, L (2011). *Embodied Cognition.* New York: Routledge.

Simon, N (2010). *The Participatory Museum.* USA: Museum 2.0.

Trevelyan, V (1991*). Dingy Place with Different Kinds of Bits: An Attitudes Survey of London Museums amongst Non-Visitors.* London: London Museums Service.

vom Lehn, D, C Heath and J Hindmarsh (2001). *Exhibiting Interaction: Conduct and Collaboration in Museums and Galleries. Symbolic Interaction,* 24(2), 189–216.

Weil, SE (2002). *Making Museums Matter.* Washington: Smithsonian Institution Scholarly Press.

Williams, M and PW Vogt (2011). *The SAGE Handbook of Innovation in Social Research Methods.* London: Sage Publications.

Wright, P and J McCarthy (2010). *Experience-Centered Design: Designers, Users, and Communities in Dialogue.* San Rafael, CA: Morgan and Claypool Publishers.

16

DIGITAL CULTURAL HERITAGE IS GETTING CROWDED: CROWDSOURCED, CROWD-FUNDED, AND CROWD-ENGAGED

Leonard Steinbach

Here Comes the Crowd

February 8th, 2011 — The National Library of Finland and its corporate partner, Microtask, launched Digitalkoot *(digital community), an online game-based program for correcting/validating the OCR scanning of the Library's immense newspaper archive. Both the language and the scanned media are problematic for OCRs, so words are validated or corrected by two separate volunteers. The goal is "to index the library's enormous archives so that they are searchable on the Internet for easier access to the Finnish cultural heritage." By the time phase one ended in November, nearly 110,000 participants from many nations had participated in this* **crowdsourced** *project, completing more than 8 million word-fixing tasks (Digitalkoot, 2012). "Everyone is welcome and everyone's contribution helps, whether they work five minutes or five hours," said Kai Ekholm, Director of the National Library of Finland. "Our archives are national cultural heritage. I am proud that even such a small nation as we are able to launch something like this" (National Library of Finland, 2011). A next phase was scheduled to begin late 2013 (Digitalkoot, 2012).*

May 29th, 2013 — The Smithsonian Institution's Freer-Sackler Gallery approached the public to raise US$125,000 in support for components of Yoga: The Art of Transformation, *billed as "the world's first exhibition on the visual history of yoga." The campaign, delivered through the cause-based crowdfunding website Razoo.com, ended July 1st exceeding its goal through the generosity of more than 600 personal plus corporate contributors. "So many people have a deep connection with yoga," noted Katie Ziglar, Director of External Affairs at the Freer-Sackler Gallery. "We chose* **crowdfunding** *for this exhibit because of the subject matter's universal appeal" (Business Wire, 2013).*

The examples above demonstrate how these institutions looked to "the crowd" for both the skills and funding for these stellar achievements. This chapter is about *crowdsourcing* and *crowdfunding* — how "the crowd" can help cultural heritage institutions and enthusiasts achieve their aspirations or meet critical needs. It is about how the embrace of an interested, motivated and eager public can help realize the funding of projects, acquisitions and even whole new institutions, and how the contribution of time, talent, and knowledge can amplify the efforts of those for whom cultural heritage knowledge creation and sharing is their lives' work. It is also about the cultural heritage community learning to embrace and reward broad, perhaps heretofore untouched, communities in new ways, simpatico with a new age of online social networking, knowledge sharing and civic engagement.

There is a rapidly expanding body of published resources about, and institutional experience with, crowd contributions to the cultural heritage and the Gallery, Library, Archive, and Museum (GLAM) sectors. The goal here is to provide fundamental information and examples about crowdsourcing and crowdfunding in ways that inspires creative and successful approaches to a form of popular engagement with cultural heritage little imagined or feasible just a few years ago.

Crowdsourcing and crowdfunding in cultural heritage are still relatively new, especially outside North America and Europe. However, international adoption is rapidly expanding as technology tools and platforms become increasingly available, success models emerge, traditional funding sources diminish, and socio-cultural impediments are overcome. Examples presented attempt to demonstrate the international diversity and applicability of the concepts and tools described.

Crowd engagement is no fad — it represents a waterfall of opportunities to organizations of all sizes and resource levels. The American Association of Museum's *Trends Watch 2012* (Merritt and Katz, 2012) reports crowdsourcing as one of its seven major trends. In 2013, the Horizon Report — Museum Edition (Johnson *et al.*, 2013) declared crowdsourcing (including crowdfunding) a top "technology" emerging in the museum sector over the next two years. And Tate included crowdsourcing in their 2010–2012 online strategy plan (Stack, 2010). Even governments have begun using crowdfunding tools to decide how government arts funding is distributed (Hansson, 2011).

About This "Crowd"

The term "crowd" can be a bit ambiguous. On the one hand it can be as broad as the undefined masses reached by the Internet and social media as well as by traditional media and personal outreach. On the other hand the "cultural heritage crowd" may be also be considered groups of individuals with common interests, abilities, and reward values — self-aggregating groups who will hive around an attractive opportunity. Beyond just task functionaries, the cultural heritage crowd may also share an intimate relationship with those they serve by virtue of their passion for a particular project, institution or outcome. Therefore, it is important that these relationships be nurtured, rewarded and trust maintained.

Some institutions may react with a certain trepidation to the openness and anonymity the word "crowd" implies. In response, some may reframe *crowd*sourcing as *community*-sourcing, (Ridge, 2013a) by creating a more circumscribed or familiar crowd. Participants might be restricted to those with existing relationships such as members, correspondents in the institution's database, social network contacts, those geographically nearby, or those who can network further outward to achieve broader but desirable outreach (Ward, 2011). This might prove especially useful when a goal would benefit from participants' prior knowledge of the institution's mission, history or purpose, or their accepted expertise with respect to the task at hand.

Why would crowds emerge around projects? Lawton and Marom (2010) suggest it is because "human nature has always driven people to seek others with common interests and to continue in those interests, the essence of which dates back at least to 'birds of a feather flocking together' attributed to Greek philosopher Democritus (circa 460 BC)." They say that the crowd is "in many ways a revival of our social needs to interact and be part of something larger — our intrinsic hunger for a sense of community." Paul Ford (2011) adds another angle, contending "humans have a fundamental need to be consulted, engaged to exercise their knowledge (and thus power) and no other medium [the web] that has come before has been able to tap into that as effectively." He calls the phenomenon, "Why wasn't I consulted?"

Motivation can also vary by individual and task. Alam and Campbell (2012) bring together, from a GLAM perspective, motivating factors such as fun; challenges; altruism; autonomy and trust; acknowledgment; recognition of achievement — sometimes in competition with others (e.g., through use of online games (Flanagan *et al.*, 2013)); and dedication to principled belief, among others. They note the predominant importance of intrinsic over extrinsic rewards in the GLAM sector, compared with crowdsourcing in the commercial world. For example, titles such as *Citizen Scientists* are sometimes bestowed on "crowds" of science project participants (North Carolina Museum of Sciences, 2013), consistent with science-based institutions' value of the inculcation of scientific practices and values in their fans. The terms "Citizen Archivist" (National Archives, 2013) and "Citizen Historian" (Elissa, 2011) are similarly used. Special mementoes, enduring recognition (e.g., permanent name placement) and special engagement opportunities (e.g., meeting with a curator, celebration events, etc.) seem to have become especially important rewards in crowdfunding campaigns. However, Alam and Campbell also note that more research needs to be done if we are to learn how to design tasks which will assure that a public crowdsource ethos is sustained. Nonetheless, the important point is that careful consideration of crowd-motivators can be critical to the success of any project or campaign.

Finally, Internet access, which is at the core of both crowdsourcing and crowdfunding, can vary greatly among socio-economic and otherwise characterized groups. Brabham advises against undue association of crowdsourcing and crowdfunding with "democratization." He warns that as a result of such disparities some outcomes could suffer from an "aesthetic tyranny" or be biased toward the views and desires of the "homogeneous and elite" (Brabham, 2013).

Some have charged that crowdsourcing can also be crowd exploitation when requesting for free work that should rightfully be, or historically has been, paid for (Ridge, 2013b). However, it is probably also fair to say that our cultural heritage crowd generally feels well compensated in many ways other than by money for the tasks requested. As Owens (2013) puts it, projects which "[provide] meaning to people's lives are projects that — far from exploiting people — can provide a way for them to connect with each other and make meaningful contributions to the public good."

Crowdsourcing

"Crowdsourcing," a derivative of "outsourcing," is attributed to Jeff Howe (2006), in Wired Magazine, where, describing it as an emerging *business model*, he defined it as "...the act of taking a job traditionally performed by a designated agent (usually an employee) and outsourcing it to an undefined, generally large group of people in the form of an open call." In doing so he focused on businesses using "everyday people using their spare cycles to create content, solve problems, even do corporate R&D." Saxton *et al.* (2010) suggest refining this to "a sourcing model in which organizations predominantly use advanced Internet technologies to harness the efforts of a virtual crowd to perform specific organizational tasks."

Perhaps the most popular example of crowdsourcing is Wikipedia, even though it transcends the traditional notion of crowds focusing on a single task. Its more than 77,000 active volunteers have worked on more than 22,000,000 articles in 285 languages (Wikipedia, 2013). However, the act of crowdsourcing well predates the term's invention. For example, in the 1850s a network of 600 volunteer observers in the US, Canada, Mexico, Latin America and the Caribbean used the telegraph to send monthly reports of local weather data to a research scientist under the auspice of the Smithsonian Institution (Bruno, 2011). Today, the Internet, the platforms we can build, and an expanding social networking and participatory culture vastly expand the possibilities. Cultural heritage institutions are quickly learning they can better benefit from a universe of external, interested, talented, and "connected" amateur-enthusiasts rather than maintaining a firewall against them.

Although the concept of crowdsourcing could be characterized as engaging vast masses at a sweep, Owens (2012) suggests that for libraries and museums the "most successful crowdsourcing projects are not about large anonymous masses of people. They are not about crowds. They are about inviting participation from interested and engaged members of the public" — many with special skills, knowledge, interests and opinions ready to share. Overall, these "crowds" may comprise rather small but effective groups, buoyed by a bit of institutional structure, oversight and effective rewards.

Purposes of Crowdsourcing

There have been a many attempts at categorizing the roles of crowdsourcing in cultural heritage, including Ridge (2012),

Bonney *et al.* (2009), as cited by Oomen and Aroyo (2011) and, Brabham (2013). The list below attempts to concisely synthesize some key categories and provide examples with relatively close fit. However, readers are urged to look at the source material for greater delineation, elaboration, and additional examples.

- Tagging (labeling): Described as "allowing members of the public to tag digital objects in their collections with descriptive keywords ... (which) is useful because it can make items in collection records more findable by machines, and therefore by people" (Cairns, 2013). This collection of keywords and other metadata is also related to "folksonomies" — "the result of personal free tagging of information and objects for one's own retrieval" (Vander Wal, 2007) which allows for use of common terms apart from formal taxonomies. Tagging has been shown to be most successful in a gaming context (Von Ahn, 2004) where players are motivated "to win by being the best, the fastest, and most accurate" (Flanagan *et al.*, 2013).
  - o Example: The Museum of Ethnology in Berlin[1] uses a game called *Tag.Check.Score.*, to tag its photographic collection (Tag. Check.Score., 2013).
- Recording personal stories: Such as oral histories or eyewitness accounts.
  - o Example: *Storycorps*[2]

    Storycorps, a non-profit organization, provides "people of all backgrounds and beliefs with the opportunity to record, share, and preserve the stories of our lives." Recordings are archived and accessible from the American Folklife Center at the Library of Congress in Washington, DC. Select stories are available online and via podcasts and CDs are provided to participants.

---

[1] Official website: http://www.smb.museum/smb/home/index.php?lang=en for the museum, and http://cityapps.fokus.fraunhofer.de/tcs for the app.
[2] Official website: http://storycorps.org/

- Stating preferences: Such as what should be in an exhibition.
  - Example: *Split Second*[3]
    The Brooklyn Museum provided a three-stage approach for choosing paintings for a small exhibition. Participants rapidly chose one from a pair of paintings, then wrote about it and rated it, and then rated it again after reviewing interpretive texts. The cited website provides a rich description of the now-completed project, process, and outcomes.
- Contributory projects: Where members of the public contribute information.
  - Example: *Remember Me: Displaced Children of the Holocaust*[4]
    The U.S. Holocaust Museum presents 1,100 photographs of displaced children who were orphaned, displaced or otherwise separated from their families at the end of WWII. Its purpose is to identify them, learn their stories, and possibly reunite them with family members. Close to 200 have been identified so far (see Figure 1).
- Knowledge discovery and management: Mobilizing a crowd to find and assemble information and/or create collective resources.
  - Example: *Europeana 1914–1918: Your Family History of World War*[5]
    Through both its website and in-person "road shows" the project collected, digitized and aggregated memorabilia and stories from the period of the Great War (1914–1918). The information was expressed in formal exhibitions and online access to the results.
- Distributed Human Intelligence Tasking: Wherein participants process or analyze the information on hand, especially large data sets, that computers cannot easily do.
  - Example: New York Public Library's *Map Warper* project[6]
    The Library engages the public in "digitally aligning" (rectifying) historical maps from the NYPL's collections to match today's precise maps." This application is featured in the video cited in Resources at the end of this chapter.

---

[3] Official website: http://www.brooklynmuseum.org/opencollection/labs/splitsecond/
[4] Official website: http://rememberme.ushmm.org/
[5] Official website: http://www.europeana1914-1918.eu/en
[6] Official website: http://maps.nypl.org/warper

November 6, 2013
Marina Del Monte Identified

As soon as Marina Del Monte's son showed her this picture, she recognized herself. She can't remember when the photograph was taken, but... read more

September 4, 2013
Henri Barik Identified

Information about the late Dr. Henri Barik comes from several telephone conversations with...read more

July 10, 2013
Victor Herzog Identified

Not long ago, Victor Herzog Googled his name and was surprised to find it on the Museum's Remember Me? website. He contacted

LATEST ACTIVITY ON YOUTUBE

Find United States Holocaust Memorial Museum on Youtube

LATEST TWEETS

Figure 1. *Remember Me?* confronts the visitor with faces, almost pleading for information, while at the same time sharing news, success stories, and social media feeds.

- Peer-Vetted Creative Production: Wherein an organization mobilizes a crowd to come up with a solution to a problem that has an answer which is subjective or dependent on public support. This is ideal for design, aesthetic, or policy problems.
  - o Example: Guggenheim Museum's (with BMW) *BMW Guggenheim Lab*[7]
    This special 3-year project addressed issues of contemporary urban life through free programs, projects and public discourse using diverse ways of collecting and integrating information and opinions, including game-like activities online and at on-site pavilions in New York, Berlin, and Mumbai.

Crowdsourcing initiatives can vary in duration as well as in purpose. They can be temporary, by virtue of association with an exhibition, a budgetary constraint, an experiment, or completion of a task, say, transcription of an archive. They can also be permanent or open ended, such as the ongoing sharing of stories or contributions of photos about a time or place (Carletti *et al.*, 2013) or the collection of scientific data.

A collateral benefit of crowdsourced projects may also be civic and social engagement of participants. *Europeana 1914–1918* resulted in family discussions of their close-to-home relationships to World War I. *Go! Brooklyn* (described below) led its community into an art world in their midst many had never experienced. The online-only International Museum of Women (also described below) states that, "70 percent of Museum visitors surveyed report personal changes in attitudes, opinions about global women's issues," based on its content (About IMOW, 2013) — much of which was crowdsourced.

This enduring and profound affect of crowdsourced cultural heritage deserves special appreciation. The following sample of crowdsourced projects span additional modes of participation and outcomes. In reviewing these, consider the intrinsic rewards that the participants and the organizers must feel, and the long-term social and civic impact they portend.

---

[7] Official website: http://www.bmwguggenheimlab.org/

- National Library of Finland launched Digitalkoot, an online game-based program for correcting/validating the OCR scanning of the Library's immense newspaper archive, as described in this chapter's introduction. The first phase is complete with the next expected to have commenced by the end of 2013.
- GO! Brooklyn Exhibition[8] is what the Brooklyn Museum called a "community curated open studio project." Brooklyn, New York artists opened their studios to the public for a weekend, whereupon close to 18,000 people made close to 150,000 studio visits in order to nominate 10 artists, among whom five were chosen by curators for a formal exhibition.
- *1001 Stories of Denmark,*[9] a website from the Danish Agency for Culture, encourages the public to contribute "the sights ... their own story or experience from a place, [to] listen to stories from all over Denmark, [and to create or take] their own travel routes and be inspired by others." Android and iPhone apps are also available (see Figure 2).
- International Museum of Women,[10] an online-only museum, "showcases art, stories and ideas to celebrate, inspire and advance the lives of women around the world." Its international thematic exhibitions often include broad public participation through stories, videos and surveys, "giv[ing] voice to women who often go unheard."
- *Life in a Day*[11] is a feature film produced by Ridley Scott (Scott Free Productions), LG Electronics and YouTube comprised of videos selected from more than 80,000 open-call onlne submissions from around the world. Each short video depicted some aspect of life on July 10th, 2010. Ostensibly celebrating YouTube's fifth anniversary, it premiered at the Sundance Film Festival and is now distributed by the National Geographic Society.

---

[8] Official website: http://www.gobrooklynart.org/

[9] Official website: http://www.kulturarv.dk/1001fortaellinger/en_GB

[10] Official website: www.imow.org

[11] Official YouTube website: http://www.youtube.com/user/lifeinaday and http://en.wikipedia.org/wiki/Life_in_a_Day for synopses of reviews and other details.

1001 Stories of Denmark simultaneously beckons the visitor to explore what has been provided and to share their own stories and images, using videos, mapping, a timeline and information about what is currently popular on the site.

- *The Wall*[12] from the Museum of Copenhagen comprises a traveling 12-meter touch screen video wall as well as a complementary web site. It provides "access to a voyage of discovery within the past, present and future of Copenhagen" to which the public is encouraged to contribute images and stories.
- 3Bute.com[13] (pronounced "tribute") "draws attention to Africa-related journalism" by bringing together artists and writers to create 3-page illustrated stories, which are then tagged with crowdsourced context and content. Led by illustrator Bunmi Oloruntoba and literary editor and writer Emmanuel Iduma, it has been described as "3Bute Turns African Lit Into Crowdsourced Comics" (Kennedy, 2012).
- *Transcribe Bushman*[14] from the University of Capetown serves to transcribe the 19th century archive of the Bushman people's "languages, stories, and way of life," thus also preserving the endangered "click" languages of Southern Africa.
- *Zooniverse*[15] is a collection of extraordinary citizen-science projects, in space, climate, humanities, biology, and nature which helps scientists collect and analyze data. Perhaps most noteworthy is its wildly successful progenitor, *Galaxy Zoo*[16] which has its Citizen Scientists help classify galaxies by image characteristics, for later study.
- *The Singapore Memory Project*[17] calls itself "a whole-of-nation movement that aims to capture and document precious moments and memories related to Singapore; recollections not merely from individual Singaporeans, but also organizations, associations, companies and groups." As of 2013, more than 250,000 "memories" have been added.

---

[12] Official website: http://www.copenhagen.dk/en/whats_on/the_wall

[13] Official website: http://3bute.com/

[14] Official website: http://www.mysciencework.com/news/9106/crowdsourcing-to-preserve-bushman-heritage

[15] Official website: https://www.zooniverse.org/

[16] Official website: http://www.galaxyzoo.org/

[17] Official website: http://www.singaporememory.sg/campaigns

Crowdsourcing and Technology Requirements

The extent of oversight and validation of crowdsourced contributions and projects can vary. For example, there may be the need for transcribers' work to be validated by each other or staff, contributed facts may need to be validated or, specific technical tasks may need to be performed. Specialized software applications may be needed to enable online participation, demanding technical resources beyond many organizations' capabilities, or Internet access may not be widespread enough to enable broad participation. Although this whole concept is fundamentally internet-based, it is also valid that volunteers without Internet access may come on site to provide information or take on tasks at local workstations or on paper.

Institutions, lacking technical resources or not, may find that shared application software, open-source modules and even free, hosted, solutions, which are becoming increasingly available, may help meet crowdsourcing needs.

Examples of such available crowdsourcing resources include:

- Metadata Games (www.metadatagames.org) from the Tiltfactor Project (www.tiltfactor.org) at Dartmouth University offers free and open-source software single and multi-player games "for gathering data on photo, audio, and moving image artifacts" and analyzing the data "in novel and exciting ways." Some games are available as iOS or Android apps [Flanagan (2013) offers research findings on this project].
- *From the Page*[18] is a free software that allows volunteers to transcribe handwritten documents on-line. It allows users "to eas[ily] index and annotate subjects within a text. Users can discuss difficult writing or obscure words within a page to refine their transcription." The provider, software engineer Ben Brumfield who has taken a special interest in transcription for the cultural heritage sector, will consider hosting projects or provide software for local installation(Brumfeld is featured in the video cited in Resources at the end of this chapter) (see Figure 3).

---

[18] Official website: http://beta.fromthepage.com/

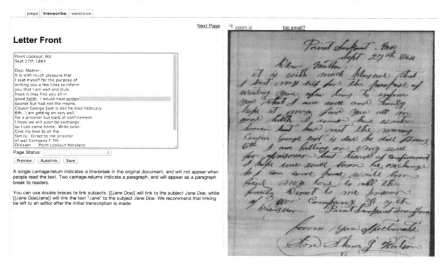

FromThePage

East Civil War Letters — Shemi Watson to Mary Farthing Shackleford Watson

Figure 3. Example of use of FromThePage software to transcribe U.S. Civil War letters. Box on left is where transcriber types what is seen on right. Tabs allow switch to place for notes or to see other version.

- *Scripto*[19] is "a free, open source tool for enabling community transcriptions of document and multimedia files. It is designed for institutions … such as libraries and museums engaging in collaborative transcription projects." It works as an extension to WordPress (publishing platform), Omeka (digital collection content manager), and Drupal (content management framework). It was developed by the Roy Rosenzweig Center for History and New Media, (George Mason University) and funded by the National Endowment for the Humanities (US) and the National Archives and Records Administration's National Historical Publications and Records Commission (US).

---

[19] Official website: http://scripto.org/

- *Map-vectorizer*[20] is open-source code from the New York Public Library's NYPL-lab that is useful in scanning maps to extract polygons and some data for further indexing and manipulation, thereby dramatically reducing the time it would take to do by hand. Described as "OCR for maps," it was created in conjunction with the *Map Warper* project, described earlier.
- *Tag.Check.Score*[21] is open source code from Code for Europe for a game-style tagging application for images. It is currently used by the Museum of Ethnology in Berlin, described earlier.
- *Historypin*[22] is a hosted free map-tagging application developed by private non-profit *We Are What We Do* in association with Google. It uses map-based tours as "a way for millions of people to come together, from across different generations, cultures and places, to share small glimpses of the past and to build up the huge story of human history." Institutions and projects maintain their own identity within the *Historypin* environment. "Tours" can be private or public and more than 50,000 individuals and more than 1,400 institutions have participated.

In Summary

The crowdsourcing examples above may be helpful in exploring its scope, but hardly define its potential — a potential which has already been broadly endorsed. Better understandings and best practices are emerging as tools are developed to meet demands. There is an immense, talented, interested crowd out there and plenty of room for their engagement. Beyond the surface achievements of specific projects may lay enduring relationships between cultural institutions and their communities whose impact we can only begin to fathom.

Crowdfunding — The Basics

Crowdfunding, in essence, is "the raising of funds through the collection of small contributions from the general public using the

---

[20] Official website: https://github.com/NYPL/map-vectorizer
[21] Offical website: https://github.com/codeforeroupe/tagcheckscore
[22] Official website: http://www.historypin.com/

Internet and social media" (Canada Media Fund, 2012). Although in a broader context, crowdfunding includes financial lending or investment models, the cultural heritage sector embraces the "donations, philanthropy and sponsorship [model] where there is no expected financial return."[23] "The primary driver behind individual contributions in this model is a personal desire to support the development and realization of a project that in someway is meaningful to the contributor ... [however, these] typically also use a reward or incentive system to help stimulate contributions" (Canada Media Fund, 2012). While these are excellent crowd-centric definitions, I like Matthew Hollow's take best: "Another potentially liberating aspect of online crowdfunding is the fact that (internet availability permitting) it makes it possible for anyone to promote any project or idea, regardless of size or ambition" (Hollow, 2013).

In this section, we consider crowdfunding efforts for cultural heritage which are (1) focused on single discrete purposes; and, (2) facilitated by a crowdfunding platform (website). However, it is worth noting that the ecosystem of platforms, tools, rules, regulations, legislation, players, competition, and community attitudes, experience and acceptance is extremely dynamic and rapidly evolving.

Modern crowdfunding is generally traced back to the impromptu raising of funds by fans to send British band Marillion on a US tour in 1997. 2003 saw Artistshare[24] launched, "a platform that connects creative artists with fans in order to share the creative process and fund the creation of new artistic works." Industry-leading, U.S.-based crowdfunding websites Indiegogo and Kickstarter emerged in 2008 and 2009 and many others have followed. Yet, broad public crowdfunding can be traced farther back. For example, when funding for the base of the Statue of Liberty ran short in 1885, New York newspaper publisher Joseph Pulitzer, declaring the Statue "the People's statue," promised name recognition in his newspaper to everyone who would send in money. With over 120,000 contributors and associated fundraising events, construction was soon able to resume (Kahn, 2010).

---

[23] For definition of crowdfunding, see http://www.crowdsourcing.org/community/crowdfunding/7.

[24] Official website: http://www.artistshare.com/v4/

North America and Europe are predominant homes of crowdfunding platforms (86 percent of approximately 600 platforms in 2013) with "social causes" within the "donation" model the predominant activity at close to 30 percent, and the sum of creative categories such as "film and performance art," "art (in general)," and "music and recording arts" rivaling that proportion. Of the US$2.7 billion raised in 2012, more than 94 percent was generated in these regions. More than US$5.1 billion was expected in 2013 (Clifford, 2013). However, many of these platforms focus purely on areas such as publishing, business and entrepreneurship, technology development and, most recently, with changing government security regulations, equity financing (Clifford, 2013). Cultural heritage projects will most likely find platforms which focus on "creative" and "cause" projects their best homes.

Crowdfunded Cultural Heritage Projects

From creating a new museum to restoration of a medieval cathedral to supporting an archaeological dig, crowdfunded projects are as diverse as can be imagined, planned, marketed, and find its interested community of benefactors. Here is just a small sample of successful crowdfunding efforts representing diverse project types and geographic regions.

- *Yoga: The Art of Transformation*[25] was billed as "the world's first exhibition on the visual history of yoga" as The Smithsonian Institution, with assistance from businesses, easily surpassed its US$125,000 crowdfunding goal.
- *Let's Build a Goddamn Tesla Museum*[26] is among the most famous museum start-up crowdfunding efforts, having raised more than US$1.3 million from more than 33,000 funders, far surpassing a US$850,000 goal. Much of its success in saving a historic facility

---

[25] Official website: http://www.razoo.com/story/smithsonians/Freer/Sackler

[26] Official website: http://www.indiegogo.com/projects/let-s-build-a-goddamn-tesla-museum–5 and The Oatmeal for more information: http://theoatmeal.com/blog/tesla_museum

and initiating a museum in honor of electricity pioneer Nikola Tesla lies in the sponsor's audacious marketing, the publicity he generated, and a very large personal fanbase for his humor web site, which he used to promote the campaign.

- *Hamish Henderson Archive*[27] exceeded its goal of funding an inventory of this important archive of the Scottish scholar and musicologist's recordings and papers. Surplus funds went toward document preservation and the establishment of an Archive Trust website. This effort led to the acquisition of the Archive by the University of Edinburgh.
- *Saints and Secrets: The Lost History of Leiston Abbey*.[28] Funding through this archaeology-focused platform proved successful for the excavation of the 14th century ruins of Leiston Abbey in the UK, "one of the most completely preserved examples of a Premonstratensian monastery in the United Kingdom … and build[ing] knowledge gained into a five-year Strategic Heritage Plan." Those at a high funding level could even participate in the dig.
- *Restoration of the Cathedral at Chartre* (France)[29] focused on restoring the stained glass windows of this important thirteenth Gothic Cathedral and UNESCO World Heritage Site as part of a larger conversation project. Having quickly reached an initial goal, they used the "momentum" toward expanded restoration funding.
- *More Than a Number @ The Lynn Museum*[30] is a museum exhibition which "tells the story of the survivors of the mass genocide of the 'killing fields' of Cambodia expressed through the powerful and inspirational images and oral histories of its people." Source material was collected from the residents of Lynn, Massachusetts, a small town with among the highest population of Cambodians in the U.S.

---

[27] Official website: http://www.sponsume.com/project/hamish-henderson-archive and see http://www.hendersontrust.org/index.php/en for more information.

[28] Official website: http://digventures.com/projects/saints-secrets-leiston-abbey

[29] Official website: http://www.mymajorcompany.es/projects/chartres-cathedrale?

[30] Official website: http://www.kickstarter.com/projects/mtan/more-than-a-number-the-lynn-museum?

- *The New Museum and the IDEAS CITY Festival.*[31] The New
  Museum in New York City does not crowdfund — not for itself,
  that is. But when they founded the IDEAS CITY Festival, "a
  collaborative initiative between hundreds of organizations and
  artists working together to effect change," they established a
  Kickstarter page to consolidate and endorse what became more
  than 40 successfully funded exhibitions, artworks, films and
  other festival entries.
- *Break Stereotypes about Muslim Women*[32] from the International
  Museum of Women (IMOW), an online-only museum, sought
  funding for an online gallery as follow-on to its *Muslima:
  Muslim Women's Art and Voices* exhibition. Images would be
  selected from those submitted worldwide. A blend of crowdfunding and crowdsourcing.
- *Timbuktu Libraries in Exile*[33] raised two-thirds toward its US$100,000
  goal, of an estimated US$7 million, needed, to store and preserve
  "an irreplaceable trove of (more than 300,000) manuscripts from
  Timbuktu" which was rapidly evacuated during threat of
  destruction by Mali rebels (Morgan, 2013) (see Figure 4).

Crowdfunding Platforms

For most crowdfunding efforts, a sufficient platform (website) is key.
The platform enables projects to be identified, marketed, progress
reported on, and include a secure mechanism for collecting and
distributing funds. The number of appropriate platforms available
may be limited but should prove ample and effective. Additional
sites are emerging with some focusing on local needs and special
interests while others are striving for increased global reach. Here is
a sample of what's out there:

---

[31] Official website: http://www.kickstarter.com/pages/newmuseum

[32] Official website: http://www.indiegogo.com/projects/break-stereotypes-about-muslim-women

[33] Official website: http://www.indiegogo.com/projects/timbuktu-libraries-in-exile and http://t160k.org for more information.

Figure 4. This crowdfunding page for *Timbuktu Libraries in Exile* shows the partial funding of their US$100,000 goal toward preserving more than 300,000 documents hidden from destruction, but extols visitors to continue on to their website.

- *Fringebacker* (http://www.fringebacker.com/en/) in Hong Kong offers a high level of consultation and evaluation before a project is posted on its English/Chinese bilingual platform.
- *Thundafund* (www.thundafund.com) is exploring crowdfunding possibilities in South Africa.
- *Zeczec* (http://www.zeczec.com/) bills itself as the "first crowdsourcing platform for creatives in Taiwan" and
- Flying V (http://www.flyingv.cc/) is also exploring the entrepreneurial spirit in Singapore.
- Argentina-based *Ideame* (http://idea.me/) considers itself "Latin America's Crowdfunding Platform," claiming to "drive educational, social & economic impact" as it rapidly expands in the region.
- *Crowdculture* in Sweden (http://crowdculture.se/en) is an interesting "hybrid" model bringing a "democratizing" influence on public cultural funding. Supported by the Stockholm government, it is "a twist on crowdfunding, [as] the participating individuals' support for different projects will have a leveraging effect, diverting a potentially much larger sum from public funding or other contributing organizations, such as corporations and foundations, to the supported projects." (Hansson, 2011).
- Filling a specialized niche, a group of UK-based archaeologists formed *DigVentures Ltd.* (http://digventures.com/) which "is committed to providing seed capital and building audiences for archaeology projects worldwide."
- Australia based *Pozible* (www.pozible.com), which calls itself a "community-building tool for creative projects and ideas," has recently started serving Singapore and Malaysia. They have recently opened a "research" funding category and accept pledges in Bitcoin. They are also testing a subcription support model (pledged periodic contributions for periodic rewards — think publications, services) and are providing hosting and local hosting services and software.
- *Boosted* (www.boosted.org.nz), from the Arts Foundation in New Zealand, says it is "designed to encourage new streams of private sector support and to grow cultural philanthropy … the culture of giving — and asking — in New Zealand."

- *Zoomaal* (https://www.zoomaal.com/) based in Beirut focuses on projects in the Arab World.
- In France, *My Major Company* (http://www.mymajorcompany.com/) felt so flush in their initial success supporting public arts projects that "it sent letters to more than 300 French mayors, promoting online fund-raising for local civic projects" (Carvajal, 2012).

For those looking to develop their own personal or institutional crowdfunding sites various alternatives are available, including:

- *Fundify* (http://astoundify.com/fundify.html) and *Ignitiondesk* (http://ignitiondeck.com/id/) are offering themes, plug-ins and extensions to create Wordpress-based crowdfunding platforms.
- *Crowdhoster* (http://www.crowdhoster.com/) is a free, hosted, open-source site for a broad range of campaigns.
- *DigVentures* (http://digventures.com/) is offering use of their platform to other archaeological groups.

Meanwhile, Kickstarter, and Indiegogo (among others) are rapidly expanding their global reach as they add new features such as additional currencies and payment methods, more language support, and localized home pages (Wagner, 2013a). Indiegogo announced near end of 2013 that 30 percent of its funding is outside the U.S. and that its European business expanded 300 percent over 2012 (Etherington, 2013). Encouragingly, Kickstarter felt compelled to add "#Museums" to their list of tagged categories and pages, recognizing the growing number of museums using their platform (Alois, 2013).

Success Factors and Challenges

Many success factors and challenges have been identified for cultural heritage crowdfunding. Typical success factors (drawn in great part from Harris *et al.*, (2011), Canada Media Fund (2012) and Ferriss (2012)) include:

- An emotionally and intellectually compelling story which clearly explains what you are trying to do; why; its value for the community; and, its shared purpose with those who choose to give;

- A funding goal that is not so big as to seem unachievable or overreaching nor so small that it seems insignificant;
- Attractively tiered giving levels tied to desirable incentives such as acknowledgement or title (e.g., "producer," "Citizen Archivist"), commemorative products, special events, "insider" views, and unique experiences;
- High quality, confidence building, promotional material including well made videos, enthusiastic, informative text and other images, plans and information;
- Communication and promotion to interested "crowds" through strong existing networks, pertinent blogs, social media, online and traditional news media, personal networks and endorsements, and, word of mouth;
- A precise description of how funds will be used;
- An appropriate funding model, such as in Indiegogo's terms, "fixed"(all or nothing — AoN) or "flexible" (keep it all — KiA). With "fixed," if a predefined target is not met, then money is refunded to contributors. This is most appropriate for projects that are only achievable with full funding. Flexible means that you keep whatever is collected even if a target is not met. This is best suited when partial project goals are achievable at lower funding levels (say, only part of an archive can be documented with the rest deferred), or complementary funding sources are also being pursued;
- A feasible completion schedule;
- Pursuit of only one project at a time so as to not fragment community support;
- Ongoing project progress feedback and participation encouragement;
- A well-chosen crowdfunding platform (more on this later).

Even meeting the right "success factors" cannot assure success. First, it is easy to underestimate "crowd" interest. Additionally, although crowdfunding may be readily accepted in the U.S. where a blend of creative entrepreneurial spirit and private funding of the arts and cultural heritage has been the norm, acculturation of crowdfunding in other regions can have its own special challenges and may take time and adaptation. These challenges include: fear that a project is a scam; feeling that such funding is a government or foundation responsibility (Carvajal, 2012); inappropriateness of "begging" or being seen as a beggar (El Shimi, 2013); and, cultural variation in the perception and ramification of failure (Wagner, 2013b). Inability of a platform to accommodate local payment customs (e.g., predominance of cash vs. credit card), insufficient language support, and not broad enough access to the internet can also be impediments. Yet, initial failures need not douse enthusiasm and optimism … they can be learning experiences. As Philippe Bélaval, president of the French landmarks agency, noted, having experienced mixed results in crowdfunding restoration of statues in France, "to scale a mountain you have to start with a little mountain" (Carvajal, 2012).

Selecting a Crowdfunding Platform

The following is a short list of criteria to consider when choosing a crowdfunding platform (in no specific order):

- Demonstrated success with similar projects; its funders are more likely to discover and support your project;
- Permits posting of just any project or requires a vetting or qualification process, such as the submission of a budget, project and marketing plan. The provision of mentoring or consulting assistance may help assure successful outcome.
- Easily enables sharing the "story" and updates through its text/ blog, images and video support;
- Provides mobile apps for contribution, communications, and project monitoring;
- Easily links to social media for purposes of promotion, soliciting funds and sending project updates;
- Accommodates the desired funding mechanism (fixed vs. flexible, as described earlier) and funding period (e.g., 30, 60, 90 days);
- Accommodates the types of payment most appropriate to targeted audience, such as cash, electronic fund transfer, and various currencies vs. only credit cards;
- Supports benefit of contributing to non-profit organizations, such as appropriate receipts, and contribution administration by authorized organizations;

- Competitive structure including charges for fixed vs. flexible program disbursement (this can differ significantly), and credit card, wire transfer, and currency conversion fees.
- Facilitates contribution matching by other benefactors or associated campaigns;
- Has a strong reputation for preventing fraudulent or apt-to-fail projects from being posted and is considered a "trusted" platform;
- Supports multiple languages both in its interface and project description;
- Has a geographic reach appropriate to the proposed project and sponsor;
- Provides sufficient user resources and guidance online to help assure creation of a successful project.

In Summary

Generally, funding for cultural heritage research, education, preservation, projects, and programs seems more challenging than ever. As a result, the general public, whether or not accustomed to a culture of personal philanthropy, seems called upon by competing interests to fill the need. Crowdfunding is not only a viable means of enticing and aggregating contributions; its platforms have also become tools for gauging and guiding public interest, sentiment and priorities. Meanwhile, the global competition to provide crowdfunding platforms useful to the cultural heritage field is intense, even if riding the coattails of a much broader crowdfunding phenomenon. If you think of crowdfunding as election campaigns and the platforms voting machines, then the public is simply voting for cultural and creative projects with its dollars, kronas, or yen. Cultural heritage institutions and practitioners just have to decide whether they want to be on the ballot.

Conclusion — Just the Beginning

The potential for crowdsourcing and crowdfunding in the cultural heritage sector seems limitless as methods mature, experience is shared, success is demonstrated, antithetical cultural dispositions dissolve and the crowds feel justly rewarded for their contributions. At the core are great ideas, compelling stories, and those who share the passion. At the same time, institutions are challenged to feel comfortable with new levels of transparency as they enlist and empower many of those who have traditionally been considered "outsiders."

Earlier, I suggested that crowd engagement "represents a waterfall of opportunities." But I did not say it was a panacea. The phenomenon is young and still benefits from the scent of the new. A measured, long-term approach to sustainable models may be the most interesting journey ahead. Yet, it is undeniable that we have already entered an era of participatory culture, with new levels of social and civic engagement, just when both the needs and opportunities of the cultural heritage sector seem to be reaching new heights. Therefore I hope that many readers will share my optimism, seriously consider the possibilities, take some risks, and start that journey on the bridge to the crowds. The crowd happily awaits.

Recommended Reading and Resources

The following readings and resources provide good additional background and tools for those considering pursuing crowdfunding and crowdsourcing projects.

- Crowdsourcing.org (http://www.crowdsourcing.org/): This organization is dedicated to news, commentary and resource links relevant to anyone engaged in both crowdfunding and crowdsourcing.
- Museum and the Web (http://www.museumsandtheweb.com/): Website for international conference which often covers crowd-sourcing, crowdfunding, participatory culture and other related topics. Free access is provided to its archive of presented papers.
- *Crowdsourcing*, by Daren Brabham (2013). Cambridge: MIT Press.
- *Crowdsourcing our Cultural Heritage*, edited by Mia Ridge (forthcoming, 2014). London: Ashgate.

- "Crowdsourcing: How and Why Should Libraries Do It?" by Rose Holley (2010). *D-Lib Magazine* 16(3/4). Available online at: http://www.dlib.org/dlib/march10/holley/03holley.html.
- "Digital Humanities and Crowdsourcing: An Exploration" by Laura Carletti, Gabriella Giannachi, Dominic Price, and Derek McAuley. *Proceedings of Museum and the Web Conference April 17–20, 2013 Porltand, OR, USA.* Available online at: http://mw2013.museumsandtheweb.com/paper/digital-humanities-and-crowdsourcing-an-exploration-4/
- *Sharing Public History Work: Crowdsourcing Data and Sources.* Institute of Museum and Library Services' WebWise Conference 2012 sponsored by the U.S. Institute of Library Services (IMLS) (Session 2, June 14th, 2012)
  Chair:
  Sharon M. Leon (Director of Public Projects and Associate Professor, Roy Rosenzweig Center for History and New Media, George Mason University)
  Panelists:
  Ben Brumfield (Independent software developer, FromThePage Open-Source Transcription Software)
  David Klevan (Education Manager, United States Holocaust Memorial Museum)
  Ben Vershbow (Manager, New York Public Library Labs)
  Video available online at: http://www.tvworldwide.com/events/webwise/120229/globe_show/default_go_archive.cfm?gsid=1971&type=flv&test=0&live=0
- *Crowdfunding Nation: The Rise and Evolution of Collaborative Funding,* by Malcolm Harris, Suresh Fernando, Joe Brewer, Beth Buczynski, Kelly McCartney, and Paul M. Davis (2011). San Francisco, CA, USA: Shareable.
- *The Crowdfunding Revolution: How to Raise Venture Capital Using Social Media,* by Kevin Lawton, and Dan Marom (2010). New York, USA: McGraw-Hill Professional Publishing.
- *Your Guide to DIY Crowdfunding Tools (to Avoid Kickstarter Fees),* by P Spinrad. PBS Mediashift. September 16th, 2013. Retrieved from http://www.pbs.org/mediashift/2013/09/your-guide-to-diy-crowdfunding-tools-to-avoid-kickstarter-fees/

Crowdfunding platform sites often present excellent guidance both on the use of their platforms and generally how to achieve a successful campaign. For example:

- *The Handbook* from Pozible. Available online at: www.pozible. com/help/handbook;
- *Indiegogo Field Guide for Campaign Owners.* Available online at: http://landing.indiegogo.com/iggfieldguide/;
- *Kickstarter Creator Handbook.* Available online at http://www. kickstarter.com/help/handbook.

References

About IMOW (2013). Welcome to the International Museum of Women (IMOW). *International Museum of Women.* Avaialble online at: http://imow.org/about/index.

Alam, SL and J Campbell (2012). Crowdsourcing Motivations in a Not-for-Profit GLAM Context: The Australian Newspapers Digitization *Program. Proceedings of the 23rd Australasian Conference on Information Systems (ACIS) 2012,* Geelong, Victoria. Available online at: http://dro.deakin. edu.au/eserv/DU30049107/alam-crowdsourcingmotivations-2012.pdf [Last accessed on February 27th, 2014].

Alois, JD (2013). Kickstarter Now Has #Museums Page. *Crowdfund Insider,* [online] September 25, 2013. Available online at: http://www. crowdfundinsider.com/2013/09/23343-kickstarter-now-has-museums-page/ [Last accessed on February 27th, 2014].

Bonney, R, H Ballard, R Jordan, E McCallie, T Phillips, J Shirk and C Wilderman (2009). Public Participation in Scientific Research: Defining the Field and Assessing Its Potential for Informal Science Education. *A Center for Advancement of Informal Science Education (CAISE) Inquiry Group Report.* Washington, DC: CAISE.

Brabham, D (2013). *Crowdsourcing.* Cambridge, MA: MIT Press.

Bruno, E (2011). Smithsonian Crowdsourcing Since 1849! *The Bigger Picture: Exploring Archives and Smithsonian History,* [online] April 14, 2011. Available online at: http://siarchives.si.edu/blog/smithsonian-crowdsourcing-1849 [Last accessed on February 27th, 2014].

Business Wire (2013). Razoo hosts first major crowdsourcing campaign for the Smithsonian. *BusinessWire* [online] May 29, 2013. Available online at: http://www.businesswire.com/news/home/20130529005932/en/Razoo-Hosts-Major-Crowdfunding-Campaign-Smithsonian [Last accessed on February 27th, 2014].

Cairns, S (2013). Mutualizing Museum Knowledge: Folksonomies and the Changing Shape of Expertise. *Curator: The Museum Journal,* 56(1), 107–109.

Canada Media Fund (2012). Crowdfunding in a Canadian context: Exploring the Potential of Crowdfunding in the Creative Content Industries. Toronto, Canada: Canada Media Fund. Available online at: http://www.cmf-fmc.ca/documents/files/about/publications/CMF-Crowdfunding-Study.pdf [Last accessed on February 27th, 2014].

Carletti, L, G Giannachi, D Price and D McAuley (2013). Digital Humanities and Crowdsourcing: An Exploration. *Proceedings of Museum and the Web Conference,* April 17–20, 2013, Porltand, OR, USA. Available online at: http://mw2013.museumsandtheweb.com/paper/digital-humanities-and-crowdsourcing-an-exploration-4/ [Last accessed on February 27th, 2014].

Carvajal, D (2012). In Need, French Museums Turn to Masses, Chapeaux in Hand. New York Times, [online] December 22nd, 2012. Available online at: http://www.nytimes.com/2012/12/24/arts/design/french-arts-institutions-turn-to-crowdfunding.html [Last accessed on February 27th, 2014].

Clifford, C (2013). Crowdfunding's Growth Spurt Going Strong. *Entrepreneur,* [online] June 26, 2013. Available online at: http://www.entrepreneur.com/article/227212 [Last accessed on February 27th, 2014].

Digitalkoot (2012). Digitalkoot ended November 29th, 2012. *DigiTalkoot,* [online] n.d.. Available online at: http://www.digitalkoot.fi/index_en.html [Last accessed on February 27th, 2014].

El Shimi, R (2013). Egypt's Artists and Activists Crowdfund to Support Projects. *Ahram Online,* [online] September 3rd, 2013. Available online at: http://english.ahram.org.eg/NewsContent/5/35/80688/Arts–Culture/Stage--Street/Egypt%E2%80%99s-artists-and-activists-crowdfund-to-support.aspx [Last accessed on February 27th, 2014].

Elissa, F (2011). More Crowdsourced Scholarship: Citizen History. *Center for the Future of Museums,* [blog] July 28th, 2011. Available online at: http://

futureofmuseums.blogspot.com/2011/07/more-crowdsourced-scholarship-citizen.html [Last accessed on February 27th, 2014].

Etherington, D (2013). Indiegogo's European Presence Grew 300% In The Last Year, 30% Of Funding Now Outside US. *Techcrunch*, [online] October 29th, 2013. Available online at: http://techcrunch.com/2013/10/29/indiegogo-grows-300-percent-europe/[Last accessed on February 27th, 2014].

Ferriss, T (2012). Hacking Kickstarter: How to Raise $100,000 in 10 Days (Includes Successful Templates, E-mails, etc.) *The Blog of Tim Ferriss: Experiments in Lifestyle Design*, [online] December 18th, 2012. Available online at: http://www.fourhourworkweek.com/blog/2012/12/18/hacking-kickstarter-how-to-raise-100000-in-10-days-includes-successful-templates-e-mails-etc/ [Last accessed on February 27th, 2014].

Flanagan, M, S Punjasthitkul, M Seidman, G Kaufman and P Carini (2013). Citizen Archivists at Play: Game Design for Gathering Metadata for Cultural Heritage Institutions. Proceedings of DiGRA 2013, Atlanta, Georgia, August 2013. Available online at http://www.tiltfactor.org/wp-content/uploads2/tiltfactor_citizenArchivistsAtPlay_digra2013.pdf [Last accessed on February 14th, 2014].

Ford, P (2011). The Web is a Customer Service Medium. *Ftrain.com*, [blog] January 6th, 2011. Available online at: http://www.ftrain.com/wwic.html [Last accessed on February 27th, 2014].

Hansson, P (2011). Crowdsourcing Culture with a Twist. *European Research Consortium for Informatics and Mathematics (ERCIM) News — Special Theme: ICT for Cultural Heritage*, 86, 57. Available online at: http://ercim-news.ercim.eu/images/stories/EN86/EN86-web.pdf [Last accessed on February 27th, 2014].

Harris, M, F Suresh, J Brewer, B Buczynski and K McCartney (2011). *Crowdfunding Nation: The Rise and Evolution of Collaborative Funding*. San Francisco, CA: Shareable.

Hollow, M (2013). Crowdfunding and Civic Society in Europe: A Profitable Partnership? *Open Citizenship*, 4(1), 68–73.

Howe, J (2006). The Rise of Crowdsourcing. *Wired Magazine*, 14(6), 1–4. Available online at: http://www.wired.com/wired/archive/14.06/crowds.html [Last accessed on February 27th, 2014].

Johnson, L, S Adams Becker and A Freeman (2013). *The NMC Horizon Report: 2013 Museum Edition.* Austin, Texas: The New Media Consortium. Available online at: http://www.nmc.org/publications/2013-horizon-report-museum [Last accessed on February 27th, 2014].

Kahn, YS (2010). *Enlightening the World: The Creation of the Statue of Liberty.* Ithaca, NY: Cornell University Press.

Kennedy, C (2012). Beyond the Single Story: 3Bute Turns African Lit Into Crowdsourced Comics. *ColorLines: News for Action,* [online] July 6th, 2012. Available online at: http://colorlines.com/archives/2012/07/3bute_solves_africas_single_story_problem_with_collaborative_comics.html [Last accessed on February 27th, 2014].

Lawton, K and D Marom (2010). *The Crowdfunding Revolution: How to Raise Venture Capital Using Social Media.* New York: McGraw-Hill Professional Publishing.

Merritt, E, E Katz and M Philip (2012). *Trends Watch 2012: Museums and the Pulse of the Future.* Washington, DC: American Association of Museums. Available online at: http://www.aam-us.org/docs/center-for-the-future-of-museums/2012_trends_watch_final.pdf [Last accessed on February 27th, 2014].

Morgan, K (2013). Saved from Islamists, Timbuktu's Manuscripts Face New Threat. *CNN Inside Africa,* [online] May 28th, 2013. Available online at: http://www.cnn.com/2013/05/28/world/africa/timbuktu-manuscripts/ [Last accessed on February 27th, 2014].

National Archives (2013). Citizen Archivist Dashboard. *The U.S. National Archives and Records Administration.* Available online at: http://www.archives.gov/citizen-archivist/ [Last accessed on February 27th, 2014].

National Library of Finland (2011). National Library of Finland launched the e-programme Digitalkoot with Microtask. *National Library of Finland,* [online] February 9th, 2011. Available online at: http://www.nationallibrary.fi/infoe/uutiset/1297236955390.html [Last accessed on February 27th, 2014].

North Carolina Museum of Natural Sciences (2013). Citizen Science. *North Carolina Museum of Natural Science: Research and Collections,* [online] n.d. Available online at: http://naturalsciences.org/research-collections/citizen-science [Last accessed on February 27th, 2014].

Oomen, J and L Aroyo (2011). Crowdsourcing in the Cultural Heritage Domain: Opportunities and Challenges. *Proceedings of the 5th International Conference on Communities and Technologies (ICPS)*, June 19–July 2, 2011, Brisbane, Australia. New York: ACM.

Owens, T (2013). Digital Cultural Heritage and the Crowd. *Curator: The Museum Journal*, 56(1), 121–130.

Owens, T (2012). The Crowd and the Library. [blog post] May 20th, 2012. Available online at: http://www.trevorowens.org/2012/05/the-crowd-and-the-library/ [Last accessed on February 27th, 2014].

Ridge, M (2012). Frequently Asked Questions about crowdsourcing in cultural heritage. Open Objects [blog]. June 12, 2012. http://openobjects. blogspot.com/2012/06/frequently-asked-questions-about.html [Last accessed on February 27th, 2014].

Ridge, M (2013a). From Tagging to Theorizing: Deepening Engagement with Culture Heritage Through Crowdsourcing. *Curator: The Museum Journal*, 56(4), 435–450.

Ridge, M (2013b). On the Trickiness of Crowdsourcing Competitions: Some Lessons from Sydney Design. *Open Objects* [blog]. May 27th, 2013. Available online at: http://openobjects.blogspot.com/2013/05/ on-trickiness-of-crowdsourcing.html [Last accessed on February 27th, 2014].

Saxton, D, O Oh and R Kishore (2011). Rules of Crowdsourcing: Models, Issues, and Systems of Control. Available online at: http://papers.ssrn. com/sol3/papers.cfm?abstract_id=2187999. An updated 2013 version is available at *Information Systems Management*, 30(1), 2–20.

Stack, J (2010). Tate Online Strategy 2010–2012. *Tate Papers, Spring 2010, Issue #13*, [online] April 1, 2010. Available online at: http://www.tate. org.uk/research/publications/tate-papers/tate-online-strategy-2010–12 [Last accessed on February 27th, 2014].

Tag.Check.Score. (2013). Tag.Check.Score. — Berlin's Ethnological Museum Crowdsources Information via "Digital Volunteerism." *Code for Europe*, [blog] September 12th, 2013. Available online at: http://codeforeurope. net/2013/09/tag-check-score-berlins-ethnological-museum-crowdsources- information-via-digital-volunteerism/ [Last accessed on February 27th, 2014].

Vander Wal, T (2007). Folksonomy: Coinage and Definition. *Vanderwal.net* [blog] February 2nd, 2007. Available online at: http://vanderwal.net/folksonomy.html [Last accessed on February 27th, 2014].

Von Ahn, L and L Dabbish (2004). Labeling Images with a Computer Game. In Proceedings of the Conference on Human Factors in Computing Systems (CHI '04), April 24–29, 2004, Vienna, Austria. New York: ACM Press.

Wagner, K (2013a). Indiegogo, Kickstarter's Rival is Expanding. *CNN Money*, [online] March 6th, 2013. Available online at: http://tech. fortune. cnn.com/2013/03/06/indiegogo-kickstarters-rival-is-expanding/ [Last accessed on February 27th, 2014].

Wagner, K (2013b). Why crowdfunding hasn't caught on in Asia. CNN Money, [online] July 8th, 2013. Available online at: http://tech.fortune. cnn.com/2013/07/08/why-crowdfunding-hasnt-caught-on-in-asia/ [Last accessed on February 27th, 2014]

Ward, AS (2011). Crowdsourcing vs. Community-sourcing: What's the Difference and the Opportunity? *Amy Sample Ward's Version of NPTECH*, [blog] May 18th, 2011. Available online at: http://amysampleward. org/2011/05/18/crowdsourcing-vs-community-sourcing-whats-the-difference-and-the-opportunity/ [Last accessed on February 27th, 2014].

Wikipedia (2013). Statistics from Wikipedia: About. *Wikipedia*, [online] December 17th, 2013 (modified). Available online at: http://en.wikipedia. org/wiki/Wikipedia:About [Last accessed on February 27th, 2014].

INDEX

Selected Figures in Color

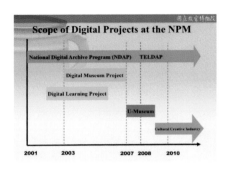

Chapter 1 Figure 1.

Chapter 1 Figure 2.

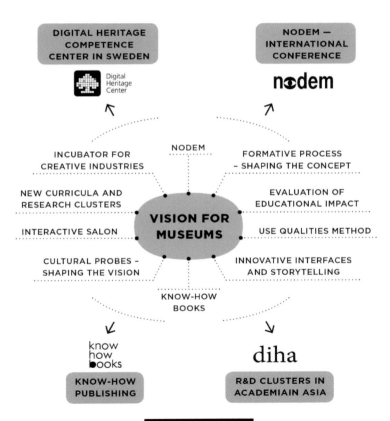

Chapter 2 Figure 1.

Chapter 4 Figure 1.

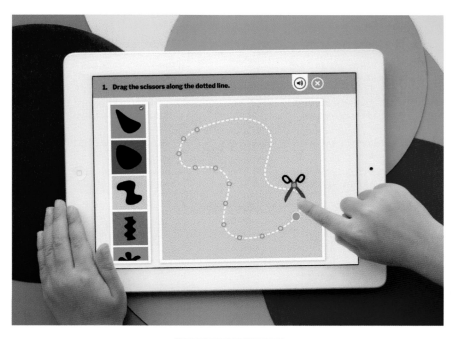

Chapter 4 Figure 2.

Chapter 6 Figure 1.

Chapter 6 Figure 2.

Chapter 7 Figure 2.

Chapter 7 Figure 3.

Chapter 9 Figure 2.

Chapter 9 Figure 4.

Chapter 12 Figure 1.

Chapter 12 Figure 2.

Chapter 13 Figure 2.

Chapter 13 Figure 3.

Chapter 14 Figure 1.

Chapter 14 Figure 4.

Chapter 14 Figure 6.

Chapter 14 Figure 5.

Chapter 15 Figure 2.

Chapter 15 Figure 4.

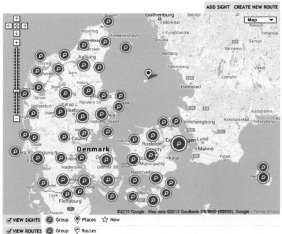

Chapter 16 Figure 2.